Surf and Rescue

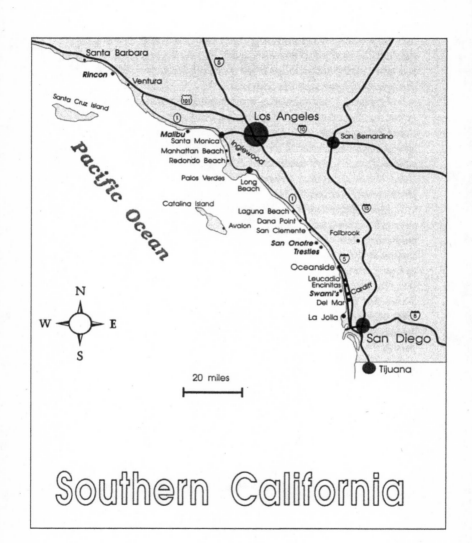

Southern California

SPORT AND SOCIETY

Series Editors
Aram Goudsouzian
Jaime Schultz

Founding Editors
Benjamin G. Rader
Randy Roberts

*A list of books in the series appears
at the end of this book.*

Surf and Rescue

George Freeth and the Birth
of California Beach Culture

PATRICK MOSER

UNIVERSITY OF
ILLINOIS PRESS
Urbana, Chicago, and Springfield

Frontispiece: George Freeth sporting a period bathing
suit that highlights one of his major contributions to
the development of beach culture in early twentieth-
century California: teaching swimming at bathhouses
from Los Angeles to San Diego. Courtesy Los Angeles
County Lifeguard Trust Fund, Witt Family Collection.
Map Courtesy Steven Sorensen.

Library of Congress Cataloging-in-Publication Data
Names: Moser, Patrick (Patrick J.), 1963– author.
Title: Surf and rescue : George Freeth and the birth of
    California beach culture / Patrick Moser.
Description: Urbana : University of Illinois Press,
    [2022] | Series: Sport and society | Includes
    bibliographical references and index.
Identifiers: LCCN 2021056962 (print) | LCCN
    2021056963 (ebook) | ISBN 9780252044441 (Cloth :
    acid-free paper) | ISBN 9780252086526 (Paperback :
    acid-free paper) | ISBN 9780252053443 (eBook)
Subjects: LCSH: Freeth, George, 1883–1919. | Surfers—
    Hawaii—Biography. | Swimming—Coaching. |
    Lifeguards—California—History. | Lifesaving—
    California—History. | Beaches—California. |
    California—Social life and customs. | BISAC:
    SPORTS & RECREATION / Water Sports / Surfing |
    BIOGRAPHY & AUTOBIOGRAPHY / Sports
Classification: LCC GV838.F744 M67 2022 (print) |
    LCC GV838.F744 (ebook) | DDC 797.3/2092 [B]—
    dc23/eng/20220125
LC record available at https://lccn.loc.gov/2021056962
LC ebook record available at https://lccn.loc.gov/2021056963

For Linda, Miles, Julia, and Ryan,
who mean the world to me.

Contents

Acknowledgments

I am grateful to Sandy K. Hall for her friendship and generosity in sharing her research on George Freeth. Arthur C. Verge's work on Freeth has been an inspiration, and he was instrumental in securing photographs from the Los Angeles County Lifeguard Trust Fund. Doug Borthwick was kind enough to provide family information on the Freeths and guide me through Nuʻuanu Cemetery. Stevie Leigh offered thoughtful critiques of the manuscript and helped with the book proposal. My thanks to Jess Ponting and the organizing committee of Impact Zones and Liminal Spaces, a conference at San Diego State University where I presented research on Freeth in April 2019. The librarians at Drury University have been extremely supportive and helpful in processing numerous research materials: William Garvin, Phyllis Holzenberg, Katherine Bohnenkamper, Barbi Dickensheet, Holli Henslee, and Jacqueline Tygart. I am also thankful to work with supportive colleagues in the Department of Languages and Literature at Drury University. Special thanks go to my colleagues Kevin Henderson, Jennifer Silva Brown, and Beth Harville for providing funds to pay for photo permissions. My colleague Rebecca Miller was kind enough to enhance several of the newspaper photographs. Judge Bockman also worked his magic on a number of the photographs for this book.

I appreciate the help of Philip van Bergen and Alfie Windsor for information on Freeth Senior's life aboard the HMS *Conway*. General thanks go to Scott Laderman, Matt Warshaw, Scott Hulet, Geoff Cater, Skipper Funderburg, Charles Kroll, Jerry Person, Wendy Burton, Malcolm Gault-Williams, Gary Lynch, and Gary Kurutz. Dennis L. Noble provided information on the U.S. Life-Saving Service. Peter Meidlinger and Ed Peaco offered helpful suggestions on the manuscript. Many thanks to Tim Cooley, Peter Westwick, and the anonymous reader for the University of Illinois Press for their detailed comments on the manuscript. Their suggestions very much improved the final version. Thanks to Joe Ditler, Carol Clark, and Steven Sorensen for assistance with photo permissions, and to Kathy Moser for her knowledge of medical terminology. I appreciate the help of Daniel Nasset, Mariah Mendes Schaefer, Jennifer Fisher, Tad Ringo, Kevin Cunningham, Michael Roux, Roberta Sparenberg, Heather Gernenz, Jill R. Hughes, and the supportive staff at the University of Illinois Press. Thanks also to Tracy Dalton for her work on the index and to Jack Moser for his photography skills.

Over the years many friends and colleagues have been generous with their time, sharing knowledge of Hawaiian culture, language, history, and surfing: John R. K. Clark, Carlos Andrade, Mark Alapaki Luke, Tino Ramirez, U'ilani Bobbitt, Kaluhialoha Eldridge, Mark Fragale, and Ian Masterson.

I have benefited greatly from the Carol Houck Smith Fellowship awarded by the Bread Loaf Writers' Conference; my two summer workshops with David Shields and Patricia Hampl, along with the many attending writers, have been a true gift.

Numerous librarians and archivists have offered their help and expertise throughout the project: Charles Johnson (Museum of Ventura County); Ed Martinez and Douglas Thompson (Redondo Beach Public Library); Jane Schmauss (California Surf Museum); Tike Karavas (Redondo Beach Historical Museum); Renato Rodriguez and Natalie Fiocrel (San Diego History Center); Alberto Perez and Samantha Ely (San Diego City Clerk Archives); Susan D. Mazza (State Library of Pennsylvania); Tom McAnear, Sarah Waitz, Adebo Adetona, Kim Y. McKeithan, Stanley Coln, and Connie F. Beach-Sims (National Archives and Records Administration); Cara Dellatte (New York Public Library); Michael Holland (Los Angeles City Archives); Janine J. Henri (University of California at Los Angeles); Yuriy Shcherbina (University of Southern Calfifornia); Candice Hooper (Coronado Public Library); Frances Kaplan (California Historical Society); Lorna Hyland (Maritime Archives, National Museums Liverpool); Christina Rice (Los Angeles Public Library); Alison Harding (Natural History Museum at Tring); Susanne Spiessberger and Wendy Johnson (Hawaiian Audubon Society); Tommy Giaquintl (San Diego Police Museum); Suzanne Harrison and Robert Gordon (General Register Office, U.K.); Aaron Seltzer (National Archives at San Francisco); Dore Minatodani (University of Hawai'i at Mānoa); Michael Herlihy (National Library of Australia); Krystal Kakimoto (Bishop Museum Archives); Clara Hur (Hawai'i State Archives); Lisa Caprino, Brian Moeller, and Manuel Flores (Huntington Library); and David Gallagher (Western Neighborhood

Project). I am also indebted to the friendly and knowlegeable staff at the Hawai'i State Library, the Honolulu Bureau of Conveyances, the First Circuit Court in Honolulu, the San Francisco History Center, and the San Diego Central Library.

Family and friends generously provided lodging and good company in Los Angeles, San Diego, and Sonoma County as I conducted research: Chris and Pati Moser; Steven and Jackie Moser and Carie Monseratte; Greg Schneider; Theresa Moser; Pam and Pat Pesetti; Tam Gonsalves; and Miles and Julia Butler. I am thankful for Ryan Moser and for Linda Trinh Moser for their love, thoughtful feedback, and unwavering support.

A Note on Hawaiian Language

I have followed contemporary usage in writing Hawaiian words and names by including diacritical marks (the ʻokina and kahakō) that guide standard pronunciation. However, when referring to or quoting primary historical sources that do not use these marks (e.g., "Hawaii Promotion Committee"), I have preserved the original.

Surf and Rescue

Introduction

California made surfing its official sport in 2018, an acknowledgment that this pastime, born in Oceania and raised in Hawai'i, has had a profound impact on the state's history and popularity as a destination. Assembly Bill 1782 not only recognized surfing as "an iconic California sport" but also noted that the state's coastal areas generate over a trillion dollars annually in economic activity.[1] The bill also listed the many ways that California has had a profound impact on surfing, from innovations in surfboard and wetsuit technology to pioneering surf forecasting and environmental protections. Californians certainly didn't invent surfing. But their beach culture has been promoted so well over the past century that many people think they did.

The Hollywood premiere of *Gidget*, for example—the story of a teenage girl who learns to surf at Malibu—triggered a national fad for the sport in 1959. The film was quickly followed by the hard-driving music of Dick Dale, "King of the Surf Guitar," along with the smooth harmonies of the Beach Boys, as well as Jan and Dean, who broadcast the youthful ideals of beach culture—fun, sun, and romance—to millions of people in the early 1960s. All of the action took place in Southern California, a regional "Surf City," to quote Jan and Dean's most famous song, whose lush beaches millions more could see in the two dozen "beach party" films that drove the fad throughout the 1960s. The television series *Bay Watch*, which reached an estimated one billion viewers every week around the globe during the 1990s, showcased the lives and loves of beautiful, deeply tanned Los Angeles County lifeguards. By that same decade, the surf industry had become a billion-dollar marketing machine itself, with names like Quiksilver, Roxy, Ocean Pacific, Billabong, Rip Curl, O'Neill, Hurley, and Volcom hanging the beach-culture ideal on the shoulders and hips of untold millions who wanted to look as cool and beautiful as the surfers gliding across blue water on silver screens. So inland masses bought the shirts and shorts and surf trunks that emanated life by the beach—a desire for the "endless summer," following Bruce Brown's iconic surf film of the same name, which captured the very American dream of ultimate freedom. Though Southern California remains the epicenter of the beach-culture image largely because of Hollywood's influence, the phenomenon is so vast and pervasive these days that almost any beach conveys the ideals that make that image so appealing.

The beach as a place of health, leisure, and excitement first took hold in California as surfing developed along its shores. When George Freeth arrived in Los Angeles from Honolulu in the summer of 1907, he brought a Native Hawaiian perspective that celebrated all things aquatic. His surfing exhibitions not only showed how much fun one could have in the ocean, but they also helped convince local developers that riding waves could be used to fill their cash registers. The birth of California beach culture as we know it today began in earnest with the idea of profiting from California's most abundant of natural resources, its coastal waves.[2]

Abbot Kinney, the founder of "Venice of America," hired Freeth and fellow Hawaiian Kenneth Winter to draw crowds out to his resort on the west side of Los Angeles. Kinney had a vision of educating Southern Californians in European artistic traditions and exposing them to world cultures. But he quickly discovered that his customers preferred carnival acts to lectures, circus performers to symphonies. To keep visitors arriving on trains and electric trolley cars, he had to constantly introduce new acts. And that's how Freeth and Winter ended up in Venice surfing for twenty dollars a day (over five hundred dollars today), a veritable windfall for the two young Hawaiians.[3]

Surfing had appeared in California as early as 1885 when three teenage Hawaiian princes, attending military school in San Mateo, surfed the mouth of the San Lorenzo River in Santa Cruz.[4] Additional surf sessions were reported in the late 1880s and 1890s at beaches in Los Angeles, San Diego, and San Francisco.[5] But the sport didn't take hold until Freeth arrived and dedicated himself to teaching a younger generation of Californians to ride waves. Freeth's relatively short tenure in California (he died in 1919 at the age of thirty-five in the global flu pandemic) coincided with the rise of coastal resorts. Bathhouses, piers, and amusement parks throughout the Southland provided entertainment and leisure for a great westward migration in the early twentieth century. Tens of thousands of people streamed into the region every year looking for California's version of the American dream:

health and opportunity. Because many of these new residents were strangers to the ocean, the resorts hired lifeguards to protect their patrons from the pervasive problem of drowning. Freeth came to California as a novelty act to draw visitors out to the coast with his surfboard; he stayed to create the foundation of a modern lifeguard service that ensured the safety of those same visitors. Freeth, in fact, used surfing to build the endurance of his lifeguards and to teach them how to negotiate ocean waves and currents in their rescues. Surfing and lifeguarding grew together in early twentieth-century California, and their combination was key to the rise of a beach culture that is now famous around the world. George Freeth, a mixed-race Hawaiian who arrived in California to surf and stayed to save lives, sits at the headwaters of both those traditions.

Many people discovered in those early days that the beach rejuvenated life. The sun, the salt air, the tumble of waves—all of it worked to soothe the cares of living in the fastest-growing region in the country. They also knew, from firsthand experience or newspaper reports, that the beach stole life away from time to time. People drowned, many of them quite young, and relatives went to the beach in the hours and days afterward to wait for the waves to give up their dead. That was usually their only recourse. The undertows and riptides blamed for many of the disappearances were as mysterious as they were deadly.

Freeth became a catalyst for transforming the popular imagination about the beach. He showed Southern Californians that surfing was not just "a royal sport," as Jack London wrote in the summer of 1907—practiced by Native Hawaiians on distant shores—but something their children could do at the local beach, in their own waves.[6] He gave thousands of lessons from Los Angeles to San Diego in swimming, diving, surfing, and ocean rescue. In nearly a dozen years of residence in the Golden State, he normalized the idea of seeing surfers at the beach. And he taught a generation of Southern Californians that they too could have fun and confidence in the ocean.

Freeth succeeded so well because people immediately warmed to him. He had a generous nature, and his confidence in and around the water rubbed off on them. His light skin (inherited from an English father) undoubtedly eased his ability to maneuver through racial hierarchies in California that relegated darker-skinned residents to the social and economic periphery. Nevertheless, Freeth often struggled to make ends meet. He was a superb athlete—strong, fast, fearless—and his willingness to put his life in danger to save complete strangers ingratiated him to every community he lived in. On one mid-December day in the year following his arrival, Freeth saved the lives of seven Japanese fishermen over the course of two hours—leaping into storm surf again and again—a feat for which he would later be awarded a Gold Life-Saving Medal from the U.S. Life-Saving Service under the Department of the Treasury.

Because Freeth chose to dedicate his life to saving the lives of others, he endured much financial hardship. Even in sunny California, where the warm climate became synonymous with health and opportunity, lifeguarding offered only seasonal work. He was restless by nature, but he was also forced to move around to earn a living. He quit jobs over wage complaints. And although beach communities welcomed and admired him, they were not yet ready to pay for year-round lifeguard service. Freeth's hard luck turned out to be a boon for California beach culture. His life as a *keiki auwana* (literally, "wandering child") turned him into a Johnny Appleseed of sorts, spreading surfing and lifeguarding from Los Angeles to San Diego. Part of the reason why Freeth's name and accomplishments are not more broadly known is because he never stayed in one place for very long. He also died young at a time when tens of millions died around him in the influenza pandemic, along with tens of millions more—soldiers and civilians—during World War I. One Hawaiian lifeguard, penniless and itinerant, hardly caused a stir.

Like countless others, Freeth came to California with dreams. He had been a top high diver and swimmer in the Hawaiian Islands, and soon after arriving he registered to compete for a spot in the 1908 Olympics. He tried again in 1912. He was blocked on both occasions by local representatives of the Amateur Athletic Union (AAU) because he had worked as a professional lifeguard. This was the era of Jim Thorpe, when being paid nominal sums of money for playing sports or working in particular vocations—even those unrelated to Olympic events—resulted in lost honors and permanent bans. Freeth battled as hard in the hearing rooms as he did saving lives in the ocean. And though he ultimately lost his case, his charges against dozens of local athletes who'd earned money at various sporting activities forced the nascent AAU in Los Angeles to codify its rules surrounding amateurism.

Beyond his accomplishments in diving, surfing, and lifeguarding, Freeth captained championship water polo teams in California and Hawai'i. He earned a national reputation as an expert on swimming, and his protégés—including Duke Kahanamoku and Ludy Langer—went on to win gold and silver medals in the Olympic Games. His Native Hawaiian heritage and upbringing made him more progressive than most in the Progressive Era. At a time when women were not encouraged to compete seriously in sporting events, Freeth taught them how to swim, row, dive, and surf. He entered them in state and regional tournaments even though their accomplishments were not officially recognized because the AAU didn't sanction women's events. Freeth's sense of beach culture always included women. He trained them hard and promoted their achievements. Although Freeth taught Jack London how to surf at Waikīkī, his work with women in many ways represents a counternarrative to London's hypermasculine stories of mastery and dominance in the surf. With some exceptions, Freeth's egalitarian sense of wave riding—traditionally practiced by both sexes in Hawai'i—was not the path that California surfers chose to follow in the decades after Freeth's death. But it could have been.

Freeth's story also offers a corrective to persistent beliefs that Caucasians newly arrived in the Hawaiian Islands—principally Alexander Hume Ford and Jack London—"saved" surfing from extinction in the early twentieth century through their promotional efforts. Although the two mainlanders were enthusiastic boosters of the sport, Freeth represented the cultural continuity of Native Hawaiians practicing this centuries-old tradition even as he adapted it to new needs and novel shores.

Duke Kahanamoku looms large in the history of surfing in Hawai'i, California, and around the world—and deservedly so. Freeth himself was a strong supporter of Duke, and the two remained close throughout Freeth's life. A look into Freeth's background and his contributions to California beach culture does not diminish Duke's important role in that history. It simply extends the history further back in time. It strengthens the connections between Native Hawaiian traditions and a region of coast dwellers in the process of building their cities, their identities, and their freedoms. California beach culture was born when a bicultural Hawaiian came into contact with a region and a population ripe for new ideas. The result of their union sparked a novel way of seeing the beach that would grow to inspire the imaginations of millions of people around the world.

A Pacific Ocean Childhood

George Douglas Freeth Jr. was born into an Anglo-Hawaiian family at Waikīkī during the last decade of the Hawaiian monarchy. King David Kalākaua (ruled 1874–1891) championed traditional Hawaiian cultural activities like hula and *he'e nalu* (surfing) despite condemnation from a powerful Caucasian elite that within a decade of Freeth's birth would overthrow the monarchy altogether. Freeth's family would not be present for these events. Freeth's father—George Douglas Freeth Sr. (1854–1914)—operated a guano mining business on Laysan, part of the distant chain of Hawaiian islands some nine hundred miles northwest of Honolulu. The whole family had sailed to Laysan in the summer of 1892. By the time they returned to Honolulu in September 1893, the monarchy had become a republic with the support of the U.S. Marines. Many of the businessmen behind the coup were descendants of American missionaries who not only had strong financial connections to the mainland but also actively sought annexation by the United States.

The Freeths likely would not have sided with the republicans. They had close ties to the monarchy, and their general sensibilities were influenced by an English heritage that governed both sides of the family. Freeth's mother, Elizabeth "Lizzie" Kaili Green (1853–1941), was the daughter of a mixed-race Hawaiian woman, Elizabeth Lepeka Kahalaikulani Grimes (c. 1832–1889), and the Englishman William Lowthian Green (1819–1890). Green held numerous high offices in the Kalākaua government. His most important accomplishment was serving as minister of foreign affairs when Kalākaua signed the all-important Reciprocity Treaty with the United States in 1875, ensuring that sugar remained Hawai'i's most profitable industry through the end of the nineteenth century.[1]

George Freeth's mixed-race maternal grandmother, Elizabeth Lepeka Kahalaikulani Grimes. J. Williams & Co., Bishop Museum Archives.

Freeth Senior descended from a distinguished line of English military men, including his father, James Holt Freeth (1817–1904), and his grandfather Sir James Freeth (1786–1867), both of whom ended their careers as generals. Stories have risen about an Irish heritage in the Freeth family. One often reads that Freeth Junior was "half Irish" and that his father was "an Irish sea captain." Although Freeth Senior spent at least four years in Ireland as a child while James Holt Freeth was stationed in the Royal Engineers, his birth registration lists Hythe, Kent, as his birthplace.[2] There is some evidence that Freeth Junior may have believed he came from Irish stock—perhaps stories told to him by his father—but his paternal line descends directly from England.[3]

So Freeth Junior grew up in a household filled with English influences and traditions, perhaps with stories of the great accomplishments of his forebears. His parents and his younger sister were both married in Saint Andrew's Cathedral, the seat of the Anglican Church of Hawai'i. Freeth Junior himself attended 'Iolani College as a young man, a private boys school run by the

George Freeth's maternal grandfather, Englishman William Lowthian Green. Courtesy Mary E. Williams.

Anglican bishop Alfred E. Willis. The origins of the school dated back to the Anglican missionaries requested by King Kamehameha IV (ruled 1855–1863), and the school was named in his honor (born Alexander Liholiho 'Iolani).

But young Freeth also grew up in Waikīkī and Honolulu surrounded by Native Hawaiian traditions that he learned from his mother's side of the family and their extended social circle. The Pacific Ocean became his backyard playground, where he developed a love of the ocean and honed all the aquatic skills that later formed the heart of California beach culture. "I can not remember the day when I couldn't swim," Freeth later recounted. "The first days I can remember were those spent at Waikiki Beach, four miles distant from Honolulu, Hawaii, where, with hundreds of native boys, I swam and dove a greater part of the time."[4]

The regatta held in honor of Kalākaua's forty-seventh birthday—celebrated a week after Freeth's birth (November 8, 1883)—gives a good indication of the environment in which Freeth grew up.[5] The day began with a yacht race from Honolulu Harbor to Waikīkī and back. Old and young competed in all manner of boat races: four-oared gig, five-oared whaleboat, six-paddle canoes, and a six-oared gig race for amateurs and professionals. There were competitions for single sculls, Chinese boats, barges and tubs, and catamarans. A Hawaiian named Poepoe won the swimming contest that day; another Hawaiian, Pelehu, who was over seventy years old, won the diving contest by staying underwater for more than three minutes. In traditional Hawaiian style, much betting took place on individual events and competitors. Earlier in the week the king had also received traditional offerings of pigs, chickens, and taro from the Native Hawaiian community. Kalākaua rounded out the festivities that evening by hosting an expansive luau for nearly a hundred of the regatta's contestants.[6]

Freeth had entered an island world where ocean knowledge and skills were valued and celebrated at the highest levels. He was born into Polynesian and British family traditions of those who ventured across oceans, who strived to excel, and who dedicated themselves to duty and service. Freeth would adopt many of these qualities in his career as a lifeguard. Because his father started numerous business ventures during Freeth's childhood, many of them unsuccessful, young George had to learn his lessons on the move. It was a habit that would stay with him throughout his life.

The same newspaper that recorded Freeth's birth also displayed an ad for "Lawrence & Freeth, Contractors," a short-lived business that Freeth Senior started after leaving his job as superintendent of Honolulu Water Works and clerk of the market. He'd been appointed to the position in April 1880, no doubt a result of his marriage to Lizzie the year before. The *Pacific Commercial Advertiser* reported at the time: "Mr. Freeth is comparatively a stranger in the community, but is a young man of energy and ability, has recently married in the country, and we anticipate he will prove an efficient superintendent."[7] The marriage cemented his connection to the local elite of Honolulu. Lizzie's father became Kalākaua's minister of foreign affairs the year after their marriage.

Because James Holt Freeth had spent his career in the British military, Freeth Senior was well traveled by the time he arrived in the islands. He'd grown up in outposts of the British Empire—Ireland, Nova Scotia, and possibly Ceylon. James Holt Freeth's last posting was on Guernsey Island in the English Channel. The family arrived in 1867, when Freeth Senior was twelve; he attended Elizabeth College on Guernsey until 1870 and then joined a crew of young men aboard the HMS *Conway* training to become officers in the merchant navy.[8] He remained for two years on the *Conway* and then served his apprenticeship in the merchant navy for the Liverpool shipping firm Williamson Milligan & Company. His first assignment was aboard the *Talisman* headed for Calcutta, India. He was also appointed midshipman in the Royal Naval Reserve, a position he held until 1880.[9] Freeth eventually landed in Honolulu after working for three years as a clerk and commission agent in San Francisco for Forbes Brothers, an importing firm.[10]

After resigning his position at the waterworks, Freeth Senior shuffled among various business ventures throughout the 1880s, most of which required sea travel. He was hired to explore and measure the depth of the channels before the placement of submarine cables that established the new technology of telephone communication between the islands.[11] He ran a wholesale liquor business out of Honolulu for three years—Freeth & Peacock—that involved regular crossings to Maui, Kauaʻi, and the Big Island. The partners built a saloon downtown, the Cosmopolitan, and expanded into the import business, beginning with California wines and Budweiser beer. They also invested in the brig *Allie Rowe* to import merchandise from Hong Kong, but the venture failed miserably and the vessel had to be auctioned for a loss.[12]

In April 1887 Freeth & Peacock dissolved their partnership. Three months later the Freeths defaulted on a $5,500 loan taken out three years before, presumably to fund the expanding liquor and import business. As collateral they'd used land deeded to Lizzie by her father: two lots in Kālia, Waikīkī, where the family had been living, and one lot on Fort Street in downtown Honolulu that William Lowthian Green had purchased from King Kamehameha IV and Queen Emma.[13] The interest rate on the loan was high—10 percent per year—so the Freeths actually owed $7,150 (almost $200,000 today). Freeth Senior must have believed profits from the liquor business would cover the debt, but the family lost all of their property in the transaction.

Bankruptcy followed in 1888 with debts totaling over $4,000.[14] Freeth Senior found work as a bookkeeper for general commission agents Macfarlane and Company, a position similar to the one he'd held in San Francisco a decade earlier.[15] Casting about for another line of work, Freeth sailed for Laysan in early 1890 and managed to secure a lease to mine guano for the newly formed North Pacific Phosphate and Fertilizer Company.

During this time the Freeths expanded their family. In addition to the three boys—Willie (b. 1880), Charlie (b. 1882), and George—they had another son, Alexander, who died at three years old in 1888.[16] Marjorie, or "Maggie," was born in 1889, and Dorothy arrived in 1891. Though the Freeths endured financial hardship, they maintained their social connections with Hawaiian royalty.[17] When King Kalākaua staged grand balls at 'Iolani Palace for visiting dignitaries—the sugar baron Claus Spreckels and his wife in 1885, the Prince and Princess Henry de Bourbon in 1889—the Freeths attended.[18] George Junior maintained this tradition with the younger generation of royals: when Prince Jonah Kūhiō, the nephew of Kalākaua, visited Los Angeles in 1909, Freeth played host for a week and gave him a tour of the area.[19] Though Freeth, much like his parents, always seemed to be just scraping by, he had inherited their same ability to draw from privileged bloodlines and mix easily with the highest levels of society. It was a quality that undoubtedly served Freeth Junior well as he interacted with the royal rich of California—Adolph Sutro, Abbot Kinney, Henry Huntington—all of whom prized culture and refinement.

Freeth Senior spent the better part of four years, from 1890 to 1894, as superintendent of the guano operations on Laysan. The small coral island was (and is) a haven for millions of migrant seabirds whose excretions are rich in nitrogen and phosphate, the ingredients for good fertilizer. Once Freeth Senior landed on Laysan and confirmed its potential resources, he quickly built a house, hoisted the Hawaiian flag, and left two men on the island to secure it. He returned to Honolulu in March 1890. By the end of the month, he and Charles N. Spencer (a member of Kalākaua's House of Nobles) incorporated the company and were awarded a lease by Lorrin A. Thurston, minister of the interior, to mine guano from Laysan for twenty years. Freeth and Spencer persuaded others to invest: George N. Wilcox (also a member of the House of Nobles); his younger brother Albert Wilcox (an elected member of the House of Representatives); and J. F. Hackfeld, representing Hackfeld and Company, which provided shipping and financial services to Hawaiian sugar plantation owners.[20] The passage of the McKinley Act in 1890, which removed tariffs from global sugar imports into the United States, all but nullified the benefits of Kalākaua's Reciprocity Treaty and triggered an economic recession in Hawai'i. Freeth's discovery came at an opportune time for those in the sugar industry who may have wanted to diversify their business interests after sugar profits tumbled.

Freeth owned a fifth of the company at the beginning and received an initial salary of two hundred dollars a month (about fifty-five hundred dollars today) to be the superintendent. He was given the grand title "Governor of

Laysan" and was expected to live on the island and oversee day-to-day operations. This included the initial construction of living quarters for himself and the workers and then the mining, storage, and subsequent transport of the guano to Honolulu and European ports. The young Freeth boys, and eventually the whole family, spent extended periods of time on Laysan. In calm weather the trip could be made from Honolulu in five days. If the seas were rough, the passage could take a month. The island is small and largely unprotected from winter storms that march down from the Aleutian Islands near the Arctic Circle. When the *Liholiho* sailed to Laysan in late December 1892, for example, heavy squalls stripped the schooner's sails and rigging, and waves hit the rudder and carried off the steering gear. Heavy seas prevented the ship from landing for three days. Reports filtered back to Honolulu that the weather was so rough on the island at one point that the ship's passengers had to dig a hole on the beach and shelter themselves by climbing under a boat turned upside down.[21]

But the island had its "hard beauty" too, in the words of Hugo Schauinsland, a German zoologist who spent three months on Laysan in the late 1890s collecting bird specimens. He wrote: "The night sky was also especially clear and beautiful, perhaps because the white sand reflected and magnified the moonshine, making it seem almost like daylight, or perhaps the stars shone against the dark ground. Even the Milky Way here looked like a fully lit-up cloud: its mild glow brightening the sky, and even the famous Southern Cross faded before its beauty."[22]

What did young George do during his time on this remote island? He spent about fifteen months on Laysan altogether: three months during the summer of 1891 with his two older brothers, and one year with the entire family—summer of 1892 to summer of 1893.[23] He would have been between seven and nine years old. Laysan is a mile wide by a mile and a half long. A large saltwater lagoon fills the center, ringed by sand dunes that rise to forty feet. A few clumps of coconut trees dot the island, which features scrub grass, mud flats around the lagoon, and wide sandy beaches on the eastern side. During Freeth's time, the lagoon—nearly a mile long, a third of a mile at its widest point—was between twelve and thirty feet deep.[24] One can imagine the lagoon being a placid version of Waikīkī for the Freeth children, a good place for young George to hone his competitive drive against his two older brothers in swimming and underwater diving contests. We can't forget that Freeth Senior hailed from a culture with its own island tradition of "aquatic prowess," which the English considered "a matter of national pride."[25] The long-distance swimming feats of Romantic poet Lord Byron are perhaps the best-known example of this tradition.

Laysan was an island playground for the children. Upon arriving back in Honolulu after spending the summer of 1894 on Laysan, Willie Freeth and his cousin Archie Robertson were reported to be looking "as healthy as their mammas could desire. They will at present go to school but both intend to return to the island where they found the everlasting 'fun.'"[26] Beyond the lagoon and sand dunes, there were white sandy beaches and coral reefs to explore, fish and turtles to be had, and of course millions of seabirds to hunt or harass: ducks, finches, frigate birds, and albatross.

The children encountered the occasional scientist or bird collector during their stays. In June 1891, Henry Palmer, collecting bird specimens for Walter Rothschild in the Hawaiian archipelago, recorded that "Mr. Freeth has just told me his little boy caught one of the finches this morning and then got an egg and offered it to it; the bird broke and ate the egg while being held in the boy's hand. This would give you an idea how tame all the birds are here."[27] Seven-year-old George had recently arrived on the island for the summer. Palmer also noted that Freeth Senior protected the birds on the island "most vigorously"; he would send "a boy" (perhaps one of his sons) ahead of the mule-drawn tram to clear young albatross off the rails so that they didn't get run over. Palmer mentioned that others who came after Freeth were not so conscientious.[28] Rothschild eventually named one of the new species Palmer had collected in Freeth's honor.[29]

George and his siblings probably would have been interested in the guano mining operation itself, mostly done by Japanese laborers contracted by their father. There were about twenty workers on the island when the family lived there from 1892 to 1893. The men worked primarily on the southern end of the island, mining the hardened guano by hand for a dollar a day with picks, crowbars, shovels, and sledges.[30] They'd load the raw material onto cars pulled by mules along railroad tracks that ran to the storage shed on the west end of the island. When ships arrived, the guano would then be hauled down to the wharf and loaded onto small boats or "lighters" for transport. Guano was only shipped from April through September to avoid the winter storms that pounded the region. Over twenty-one million pounds of raw guano were mined from the island in the first five years, the resource all but depleted by 1904 when Hackfeld and Company finally relinquished their right to operations there.[31]

A few pictures were taken of the Freeth children by James J. Williams, a well-known Honolulu photographer who was aboard the *Liholiho* during its rough passage to Laysan in December 1892. Williams was one of the men who'd sheltered under the overturned boat on the beach to ride out a storm. One of his photographs shows four of the Freeth children (minus George)

George Freeth's oldest brother, Willie (*second from left*), helping Japanese workers gather guano on Laysan Island, c. 1893. James J. Williams, Hawai'i State Archives.

sitting on wheelbarrows laden with hundreds of enormous albatross eggs. Large wooden crates stacked on tram cars behind them are loaded with hundreds more. The children had probably been at work collecting them for shipment. Another picture shows the oldest boy, Willie, working alongside the Japanese laborers, doing his part gathering guano to load into wheelbarrows. So perhaps life wasn't all play and no work for the children.

Williams also took a family portrait of the Freeths (minus Maggie and including what appears to be an Asian servant). We see them gathered in the sand before the family residence along with a dozen albatross scattered about; a lighthouse flying the Hawaiian flag centers the shot. Willie (twelve), Charlie (ten), and Dorothy (nearly two) inherited the dark complexion of their mother; nine-year-old George—seemingly small for his age—leans against his father perched on a stool, both of them fair-skinned. George Senior wears a striped outfit that makes him look like a jailbird, though the style apparently came from the Gilbert Islands in Micronesia.

One wonders if George Junior picked up Japanese phrases living in close quarters with the workers for such an extended time. This would have been

The Freeths in front of the family home and lighthouse on Laysan Island, c. 1893. *From left to right:* unidentified woman, Dorothy, George Senior, George Junior, Lizzie, Willie, and Charlie. James J. Williams, Hawai'i State Archives.

his closest contact with the fast-growing population immigrating to Hawai'i, most of whom arrived to work on sugar plantations. There were some hundred Japanese living in Hawai'i at the time of George's birth; this number climbed to nearly seventy thousand by the time he left for California in 1907. In less than two decades the Japanese had become the largest ethnic group in the islands, almost equaling the population of Native Hawaiians and Caucasians combined.[32] Some residents of Honolulu, in fact, supported Freeth's trip to Los Angeles as a strategy to recruit more Caucasians to live in the islands in order to counteract the growing political clout of the Japanese. Freeth's time on Laysan gave him early contact with an ethnic group that would play a significant part in his later heroics. It's probable that he would have already been accustomed to living with Chinese, since his father housed a Chinese cook (Pio Ah) and a Chinese gardener (Sing Tam) after the family left Waikīkī and was living on School Street near downtown Honolulu in the late 1880s.[33]

With hindsight we can imagine the experiences on Laysan that would have been formative for young George: the pull of adventure and travel, the education of enduring storms at sea and landing boats in heavy surf. Life on the island would have been spare: one can spot, in the background of the family portrait, the large tank beside their house where freshwater was stored after running off the galvanized iron roof. Natural springs existed on the island, but the water was too brackish to drink. Young George would have experienced the ocean as both playground and workplace. He would have seen his father organizing people and directing their labors, the kind of skills he demonstrated himself on sports teams throughout his life. And when young George wasn't on Laysan, he would have had to get used to an absent father for long stretches of time.

~

The guano operation on Laysan was labor-intensive but not very profitable. The company was forced to issue additional shares several times to maintain financial solvency. Freeth Senior's number of shares fell as they devalued and he sold them off, and his monthly salary declined. He had spent nearly three years total on Laysan from 1890 through 1894, starting up and maintaining operations. But in the spring of 1895 the company decided to change directions—and superintendents. When the schooner *Ka Moi* left for Laysan in the first week of April that year, the *Evening Bulletin* reported that "Governor Freeth will not go down on her."[34] The company had changed its name to Pacific Guano and Fertilizer Company and built a new plant at Kalihi in Honolulu to manufacture fertilizer.

Beyond legal disputes with his Japanese workers over money owed them, the most sensational event during Freeth's tenure on Laysan was the death of German caretaker Hans Holstein. Holstein had arrived after the Freeths left in September 1893 and spent the next six months on the island by himself. He died of unknown causes two weeks before Captain F. P. Jameson anchored off the island to reprovision. Jameson found Holstein sitting at a desk in Freeth's house, one hand on a book; he'd been writing in his journal every day and had penned a letter to Freeth. As Freeth later told the story, "When I got to Laysan Island I was shocked to find inscribed on the headboard of my caretaker's grave the inscription: 'Sacred to the Memory of G. D. Freeth, Esq., Died, etc.' Jameson had found some of my papers and thought he was burying me."[35]

By July 1895 Freeth Senior had bought into another Honolulu liquor business, the California Wine Company. "Captain Freeth is one of the most popular men in Honolulu," reported one paper, "and his friends hail him back in business with a hearty aloha."[36] Freeth's new partner, Harry Congdon, was described as "the most popular wine seller in Honolulu." The paper added that he and Freeth made "a strong team." Three months later, however, George Lycurgus, whom Freeth had bought out, was petitioning the court to declare

Freeth and Congdon bankrupt. The two hadn't paid on seven hundred dollars' worth of notes they'd used to take over his business. The total amount they owed him seemed to be two thousand dollars.[37] "The partners are well known and popular men here," explained the *Honolulu Advertiser*, "and it is probable they will soon get out of their difficulties. The general tightness in the money market, together with the dull business during the past two months is said to be the cause of the trouble."[38]

The partners did not get out of their difficulties, and the California Wine Company closed its doors. The Freeths—minus Willie, who had sailed for Liverpool the year before to train aboard the HMS *Conway* like his father—were leasing a house on Emma Street by Saint Andrew's Cathedral when Freeth Senior sailed for San Francisco in February 1896 looking for a new business opportunity. That summer he led an expedition to Clipperton Island, about seven hundred miles off the coast of southern Mexico, and started working another guano mining business.

George was fourteen when his father suddenly arrived in the spring of 1898 to take him to Clipperton. Freeth Senior landed on May 26, arranged to have seventy-five Japanese workers transported to Clipperton from Honolulu, and then he and George left for San Francisco on May 31. There are no records of Freeth Senior ever returning to Hawai'i. George and his father would miss another historic date in island history later that summer: on August 12 the United States assumed control of Hawai'i with a transfer-of-sovereignty ceremony at 'Iolani Palace that included lowering the Hawaiian flag and raising the Stars and Stripes. George's youngest sister, Dorothy, later recalled, "I'll never forget annexation day. We all sat around a table in our house and mother was crying. She loved the monarchy and dreaded the change. We heard big guns firing the salute down at Iolani palace and then we knew that Hawaii's flag had come down."[39]

Queen Lili'uokalani had arrived in Honolulu ten days before the ceremony. She had ruled after the death of her brother, Kalākaua, and been illegally deposed in January 1893 by members of the pro-American Hawaiian League (now part of the newly formed Committee of Safety). She had been in Washington, D.C., protesting to President McKinley and the U.S. Senate the annexation of the Hawaiian Islands. But the United States was going to war with Spain, and the annexation of Hawai'i would ensure the nation's dominance in the Pacific. The queen's protests were ignored.

Freeth Senior was working with a British firm, the Pacific Islands Company, to lease Clipperton from Mexico and mine the guano. The Mexican government had even given him an official appointment—temporary inspector of Clipperton—to watch over their interests.[40] He spent most of June in San Francisco organizing supplies. The seventy-five Japanese soon arrived from Honolulu and were quarantined on Angel Island. Once the steam schooner *Alice Blanchard* was loaded and the workers transferred to the ship, Freeth Senior and George climbed aboard. The schooner quietly pulled away from the Vallejo Street wharf, a mere shadow among the large transport ships preparing to deliver more soldiers to the Philippines in the war against Spain.

One observer remarked: "She is not a pretty boat, this Alice Blanchard; her round heavy stern sits low in the water, her white painted spar deck gives her a top-heavy appearance, her battered sides and chafed planking show that she has been nothing but a marine drudge, a humble unobtrusive cargo boat. But probably she is good enough to make Clipperton Island and load guano, as that is all she is required for." The observer continued: "For the task before these men is not a pleasant one to contemplate. Clipperton is merely a desert rock, an annular coral isle, without even a fringing reef to protect its shores from the thundering Pacific breakers." Another reporter at the time described the island as "a lonely, guano-covered, crab-infested reef."[41]

Larger and more isolated than Laysan—its central lagoon plunging to more than two hundred feet in some places—Clipperton would have been more of a workplace for young George. At his age (fourteen), both of his older brothers had left home for vocational training, following in the tradition of their father.[42] One would expect George Senior to put his youngest son to work helping to mine guano on the island and perhaps running one of the heavy, flat-bottomed transport boats out to the *Alice Blanchard* to load the raw material.

George would have watched his father manage the Japanese workers, who went on strike soon after arriving. They were contracted for two years at ten dollars a month, half of what a white man earned at the time. Freeth Senior convinced the Japanese to start mining, but another strike broke out among a smaller group of workers just before the Freeths left the island in mid-September. T. Mutso, who'd been hired to fish for the miners, refused to join the strike and was assaulted by his fellow Japanese. He managed to fight off several of his attackers with a knife and swam out to the *Alice Blanchard*, anchored a mile or two offshore. The ship's crew heard his yells for help; as they were pulling him from the water on the end of a line, a shark jumped up and snapped at Mutso's leg. He later told the mariners that he could feel the sharks "trying to get a hold of his body." He collapsed on the deck once he made it over the rail. Peering down into the phosphorescent light, the crew saw a big school of sharks trolling around the boat.[43]

So George was no stranger to lifesaving at sea. But Clipperton wasn't all work and strife. After spending eight months on the island the following year, a company bookkeeper named Oliver said he rather enjoyed his stay. He'd sailed in the lagoon, swam in the ocean, and hunted some of the migrating birds. After Oliver debarked in San Francisco in late December 1899, he reported that William Freeth, six Japanese, and two Hawaiians had been left on the island "to look after the company's interests."[44] Willie, who had completed his training aboard the HMS *Conway* in 1897, had been working for Hawai'i's Inter Island Steam Navigation Company before taking the job on Clipperton.

Freeth Senior and George arrived in San Diego in late September 1898. They traveled up to San Francisco, where George's father stayed long enough to give an update on Clipperton to a local paper. He then returned to Clipperton via San Diego, leaving George in San Francisco.

A month later Freeth Junior's name started appearing among the young amateurs competing at the Sutro Baths, a public saltwater swimming facility that officially opened to the public in 1896. He won first place in "trick and fancy diving"—that is, performing dives from a springboard rather than from the high dive. Events in which he competed over the next few years at Sutro's included the 50- and 100-yard freestyle, two-man tub race, and various diving competitions. These were the years when Freeth developed his love of competition, traveling back and forth between California and Honolulu—swimming, diving, rowing, playing soccer and football, boxing, pole vaulting—any and all sports, most of which he excelled at.[45] He was a natural athlete, strong and determined, and other players gravitated toward him as a leader. Following in the family tradition, it's likely Freeth attended a vocational school while he lived in San Francisco from October 1898 through October 1899.[46]

The competitions at the Sutro Baths were held every Sunday afternoon as a way to draw San Franciscans out to the beachside resort. The baths were Freeth's introduction to an environment that would shape his life and the life of coastal California. Adolph Sutro's architectural vision was the culmination of a progressive spirit that sought to bring recreation and education to the general public. Sutro had earned his fortune two decades earlier by developing a tunnel nearly four miles long to drain and ventilate flooded shafts in the silver mines of Nevada. Like other visionaries Freeth would encounter the following decade in Southern California—Abbot Kinney in Venice, Henry Huntington in Redondo Beach—Sutro built on a massive scale. Located between Golden Gate Park and the entrance to the San Francisco Bay, the baths covered three acres and could hold ten thousand people in seven dis-

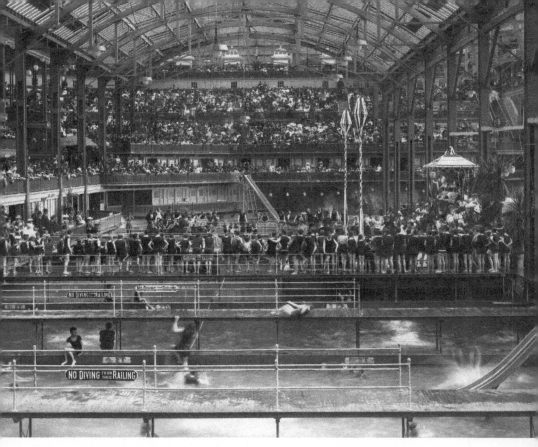

The Sutro Baths in San Francisco (May 1, 1897) as the facility would have looked when Freeth competed there in swimming races. This angle provides an idea of the sprawling size and enormous popularity of bathhouses during the late nineteenth and early twentieth centuries. OpenSFHistory/wnp4/wnp4.0286.jpg.

tinct pools, or "plunges." The main tank of seawater was 275 feet long; five other saltwater tanks, each 28 by 75 feet, increased in depth from 2 to 6 feet, all steam-heated to varying temperatures. There were seven slides, thirty trapeze rings, and a diving board. Galleries rose above the pools on three sides, seating thousands of spectators. The arched roof overhead was made of 100,000 feet of stained glass; the entire west wall, also of glass, provided a breathtaking view of the Pacific Ocean. Altogether the pools held nearly two million gallons of water, filled by either the ocean itself (in one hour) or, at low tide, by a turbine pump (in five hours).[47]

Beyond the healthy recreation of swimming, visitors gained a cultural education thanks to artifacts gathered from Sutro's personal travels. On their way down to the pools, they passed through a world museum of sorts—Egyptian mummies, European paintings and statues, and glass cases filled

The Sutro Baths may have been the first place that Freeth encountered men working officially as lifeguards, or "life savers" as they were often called. OpenSFHistory /wnp4/wnp4.0229.jpg.

with stuffed wild cats from Africa and Asia. Sutro maintained a carnival atmosphere outside his baths with rides, amusements, and food vendors. To ensure the average San Franciscan could afford a ride out to his resort, he built his own electric rail line and charged five cents a person. Like Kinney and Huntington, Sutro used his recreational facilities as a draw to sell real estate around Sutro Heights.

The baths also employed lifeguards, possibly Freeth's first exposure to this vocation. Along with the four "life savers" who protected bathers and put on various swimming and diving exhibitions, Sutro had hired Frederick H. Killick to oversee swim instruction and run an emergency ward on the site in case any bathers required medical help. It's not out of the question that Freeth himself could have worked as one of the lifeguards.

We don't know much about Freeth's year in San Francisco other than brief mentions of his name in the local papers and the Sutro Baths programs. For the festivities on July 4, 1899, he won the 50-yard freestyle and the 120-yard

"Special for a Silver Medal"; he came in second in the 100-yard tub race and the high diving for boys.[48] At the end of the month he won first again in the 50, second in the 100, and first place in "diving for plates."[49] In early November he was aboard the *Moana* headed for Honolulu. He arrived in time to celebrate his sixteenth birthday and to learn that his mother had just begun divorce proceedings against his father.

∽

Lizzie stated in her first divorce petition from October 1899 that Freeth Senior hadn't provided for the family for the past twelve months. She was "without means of her own" and had been forced to provide for herself and the family—Maggie (age ten) and Dorothy (age eight).[50] She listed "lodging housekeeper" as her occupation on the 1900 census. This became her principal employment for most of the next decade while the family rented a house on Emma Street by Saint Andrew's Cathedral. The divorce case had to be postponed due to Freeth Senior's absence (presumably he was on Clipperton). After public notices in the newspapers and an official court letter failed to deliver him, Lizzie's petition was finally granted and the divorce approved in May 1900.

Freeth Junior enrolled in 'Iolani College after returning to Honolulu. He played goalie on the college soccer team and won the pole vault in the field day activities at the end of the school year.[51] He was also listed as a "sub-editor" on the school's newspaper.[52] Outside of school he found work as a painter at the Honolulu Iron Works, a company his grandfather, William Lowthian Green, had been connected with decades earlier. He also played on the company soccer team. When his school entered the championship soccer tournament in January 1901, Freeth played defensive back. He received mention in the papers for his strong play, though his team came in last place. The final game between 'Iolani and England was canceled due to the death of Queen Victoria. By the time the two teams played their make-up game in March, Freeth was back in San Francisco competing at the Sutro Baths.[53]

Very much like his father, Freeth jumped around quite a bit in the early years of the century. He competed at the Sutro Baths on regular Sundays for several months in the spring of 1901, and then we find him back in Honolulu that summer taking part in Regatta Day festivities as part of the Myrtle Rowing Club. In the fall he played end on the Maile Ilima football team. In winter he was back swimming at the Sutro Baths.[54] Perhaps, in the family tradition, he'd found work on a merchant vessel plying between San Francisco and Honolulu. At some point he traveled to Philadelphia to live and work near his brother Charlie, now employed as a draftsman. On July 4, 1903, Freeth entered a tournament in West Chester, Pennsylvania, and took first place in high and fancy diving and the 100-yard freestyle. The local paper mentioned that he was working as a lineman at an area telephone company.[55]

The East Coast couldn't hold Freeth. He later wrote that he returned to Honolulu when he was nineteen years old. After having "bathed at Atlantic City and learned a lot about water feats," he found a new sport to dedicate himself to: he returned to his birthplace, Waikīkī, "determined to learn the lost art of surf-board riding if it was within human possibility."[56]

Renewing a Royal Sport at Waikīkī

Freeth first attempted to ride the waves at Waikīkī on a traditional wooden surfboard given to him by a "native prince," according to one account.[1] This would have been in late 1903, after he had returned from living in Philadelphia. The board was sixteen feet long, four inches thick, and probably weighed two hundred pounds. The shape is what Hawaiians call an *olo*, a craft reserved for royalty.

But Freeth soon realized that the board, however regal, was too cumbersome for his needs. He shaped one that better matched his size and was easier to maneuver. The dimensions followed the basic outline of another traditional Hawaiian shape, the *alaia*: eight feet long, two feet wide, with a large rounded nose, and sides that tapered down to a narrow, squared-off tail. The board weighed about forty pounds. Freeth would rely on this same template wherever he surfed for the rest of his life. He began by catching waves and riding them prone. Since surfboard fins were not introduced until the mid-1930s, he steered the board with his feet. He steadily worked his way up: first on all fours, then to his knees, then one knee and one foot for short distances, and finally standing all the way up and riding into shore. "The native boys had laughed at me when I made my first efforts," Freeth later recounted. "Now they hailed me as the reviver of the lost art. They all took to riding while standing at full height."[2]

Freeth called surfing "a lost art." We know from other sources that the sport, famous as Hawai'i's national pastime and practiced for centuries throughout the island chain, had been in decline for a number of decades. The ravages of Westernization during the nineteenth century included severe depopulation of Native Hawaiians; their numbers had dropped from more than half a million at the time of Captain James Cook's arrival in 1778 to some forty thousand by the turn of the twentieth century. Down but not out, surfing itself continued as a cultural tradition practiced among Native Hawaiians, especially when they could escape the disapproving eyes of white people (or *haole*) in Honolulu.[3] The sport had not yet been extensively tapped as a draw for island tourism, and the influential descendants of Christian missionaries, who had first arrived to convert Native Hawaiians in 1820, still disapproved of surfing as a pagan holdover that only encouraged idleness, gambling, and loose sexuality. Those descendants and their social circle had not only spearheaded the overthrow of the monarchy, but they also controlled the hub of island business—the sugar industry—along with banking, insurance, retail markets, and shipping. They leveraged their influence in Washington, D.C., to have the president of the United States appoint territorial governors who also came from their ranks. Although Caucasians made up less than 20 percent of the population in Hawai'i during this time, their political and economic clout permeated the land.

Surfing went underground, so to speak. Around the time of Freeth's return to Waikīkī, a young Native Hawaiian named Papaheenalu (literally, "surfboard") capped off a luau celebrating Queen Lili'uokalani's sixty-fifth birthday by giving a surfing exhibition. The intimate event took place on September 2, 1903, at her Waikīkī residence, and only close friends and a few retainers had been invited:

> Time and again he went out where the breakers were rolling in high crests, started forward on his board, rose first on his knee, as the board rushed forward, then rising higher and higher, but always carefully until he stood erect, he came like a statue to the shore with his feet in the foam.
> Papaheenalu was cheered to the echo, and many strangers and others besides the guests of the Queen were attracted to the beach by the unusual sight, and enjoyed the rarely seen spectacle.[4]

There couldn't have been too many people on the beach enjoying the exhibition. Waikīkī was a rural haven at this time, several miles distant from the bustling streets of downtown Honolulu. The Moana was the only hotel, flanked by private residences and a local tavern. Most visitors reached the area on a mule-drawn tram car—a forty-five-minute trip—or, by 1903, an electric trolley ride that took half an hour. The inland acreage supported wetland agriculture—bananas, taro, and rice—farmed by the local Asian and Native Hawaiian community.

The year before Papaheenalu's exhibition, state senator D. Kanuha joined over a hundred boys from Kamehameha Schools on a weeklong camping trip to the remote area of Mākua, on the west side of Oʻahu. The group hunted wild goats, fished, cooked pigs in an *imu* (an underground oven), and went surfing. The senator was described as "the acknowledged champion surf-rider."[5]

We can also speculate on the "native prince" who gave Freeth his first surfboard. Two prominent Hawaiian princes were living at this time: David Kawānanakoa and his brother Jonah Kūhiō Kalanianaʻole. Kūhiō—or Prince Cupid, as he was known—was a longtime delegate to the U.S. Congress for the Territory of Hawaiʻi (1903–1922). He and his two older brothers hold the distinction of introducing surfing to California in 1885. The three teenagers were attending Saint Matthew's School, a military academy in San Mateo, when they gave an impromptu surf exhibition in Santa Cruz.[6] Kūhiō's residence at Waikīkī—Pualeilani—would have been a natural place for him to store any sixteen-foot surfboards he might have inherited from past royals. Certainly he could have passed it along to Freeth, whose family he would have known.

Rather than a lost art, then, surfing merely needed the right circumstances, and the right person, to elevate its appeal and potential. That person—drawing on his love of the ocean; his natural athleticism; and, perhaps most importantly, the ability to move easily among Hawaiian and *haole* populations because of his mixed-race background—was George Freeth.

What surfing did lose in its modern incarnation was the collection of religious rites that surrounded the activity in traditional Native Hawaiian culture: from selecting the proper tree from which the board would be crafted to the ceremonies performed at the board's dedication and first use. A red *kūmū*, or goatfish, would have been offered with a prayer as it was placed among the roots of the felled tree. The rarity of the *kūmū* made it an appropriate offering to the gods at canoe launchings, for example, and surfboards would have fallen under a similar protocol.[7] The Hawaiian pantheon is filled with gods and goddesses, *kupua* (part human, part divine figures), and *ʻaumakua* (guardian gods) who surfed and interacted in daily life with the Hawaiian people.[8] But lumber mills would have provided the material for early twentieth-century surfboards rather than *kāhuna* (priests) trekking through sacred forests. More often than not, those mills were located on the Pacific Coast, and they were shipping redwood and pine to the islands. By the time Freeth shaped his first surfboard and landed in California, riding waves would have been considered an entirely secular practice.

Freeth was able to bring attention to surfing because he was such a well-known figure on the Honolulu sports scene. He played third base for the Diamond Head Athletic Club's baseball team and right end on the Maile Ilima football team. This latter won the championship of the Hawaiian Territory in

1904. Freeth and his cousin Archie Robertson were described in the papers as "old Maile players," both of them having first joined the team back in 1901.[9] In the championship photo, Freeth looks to be one of the lighter players in the group; his weight that season was listed as 165 pounds.[10] Though Freeth was naturally fair-skinned, there is a tradition of whitewashing his racial background. He has often been described as having more Nordic features—five foot ten with blue eyes. "He looked about as Hawaiian as Leif Ericson," one article reported.[11] But Freeth described himself as being of medium height (five foot eight or so) with black hair and brown eyes.[12]

Freeth loved team competition, and his skills and determination soon won him leadership roles. During the 1905 season he played quarterback for the Mailes. But he suddenly left for Kaua'i before the championship game in late December. His team ended up playing to a draw against the Punahous of Oahu College and were unable to defend their title. Freeth's departure was work-related but undoubtedly connected to a headline that appeared in the paper ten days later: "Mrs. Freeth Bankrupt."[13] Lizzie had liabilities of over $2,000 (about $60,000 today) and only $6.65 in the bank. The same day that Freeth left for Kaua'i (December 12), announcements started appearing in the local papers for a public auction at the Freeth home on Emma Street, where Lizzie managed boarders for the owner, Mrs. James Campbell (a neighbor and family friend).[14] The details leave little doubt as to the family's financial straits. The list of items to be auctioned included a Westermeyer piano, pictures, rugs, tables, chairs, an oak and walnut bedroom set, mattresses, dining room furniture, a refrigerator, a kitchen stove, and Lizzie's large collection of ferns and palms.[15]

Freeth was working for Mutual Telephone Company as a lineman, the same job he'd held back in Pennsylvania when he was living with (or near) his brother Charlie in Philadelphia.[16] It's possible he requested the job in Nawiliwili on Kaua'i (the company owned a spark-gap station there) because he could not stay at home: most of the family's furniture and appliances were sold at the auction. Freeth's trip to California a year and a half later would follow a similar pattern: Lizzie had to auction all of her furniture the day George left for San Francisco.

Freeth stayed on Kaua'i for six months, returning to O'ahu in May 1906.[17] Later that year he had a chance to finish what he'd started against Oahu College: to beat them in a football game on Christmas Day. This time around he was playing right end for the Diamond Head Athletic Club. Though his team lost—Freeth was captain—he was described as "the bright particular star of the day." Besides playing right end, he also punted on offense, tackled on

The championship football team of the Hawaiian Territory, 1904. Freeth sits in the middle row, fourth from right; his cousin Archie Robinson sits in the same row, second from right. [James J.?] Williams photo, *Pacific Commercial Advertiser*, February 16, 1905.

defense, and scored his team's only touchdown. The reporter indicated that if Freeth had been allowed to play in the second half—a coaches' agreement had benched him—the Diamond Heads would have won.[18]

Another reporter stated that Freeth "plays football just as he goes in for water sports, for the sheer love of the game. It is his speciality among many other specialities."[19] Freeth played multiple sports throughout the year, jumping from one team to the next. Oftentimes his activities overlapped. Within the span of a month he could perform dives at the Healani boathouse in Honolulu Harbor—turning somersaults from trapeze rings and forty-foot platforms—hit a home run for the Diamond Heads, and then run practice drills with the Maile Ilima football team.[20]

Only rarely did one sport disrupt another. At the opening of the Hotel Baths, on Hotel Street in downtown Honolulu, on December 30, 1906—five days after Freeth's hard play in the Christmas Day football game—a reporter wrote, "Many who have had the privilege of seeing Freeth in other exhibitions were a bit disappointed on Saturday night." The reporter went on to explain that both of Freeth's hands were badly swollen from the football game. They pained him so much after his first dive—one of them had actually suffered a broken bone—that he couldn't hit the water hands-first.[21] But the Hawaiian Swimming Club had elected Freeth captain; this was their debut in a brand-new facility, and the house was packed. So he performed.

~

Diving became Freeth's most successful individual sport in island competition. He was a "crack," in the jargon of the times. Like many young Hawaiians, he'd gotten early training by diving for pennies thrown by tourists aboard ships in Honolulu Harbor.[22] In April 1905 the Healani and Myrtle boat clubs decided to hold a water carnival the likes of which the city hadn't seen for nearly a decade.[23] The U.S. Navy cleared two docks in Honolulu Harbor, and two thousand spectators bought tickets to see the young men compete against one another at eight o'clock at night. They decorated the space with strings of electric globes, and the searchlights of the U.S. cruiser *Boston* lit up the surface of the water. Small boats and a tug around the slip were decorated with lanterns. They'd rigged up a diving platform on top of an enormous coal barge for what the papers announced as "the record dive of the Islands." Twenty-one-year-old George Freeth was scheduled to leap eighty feet from the scaffolding.[24] The governor of the territory, George R. Carter, was in attendance along with navy personnel and other local luminaries.

A dozen events were on the program, including the 50-yard freestyle, 100-yard obstacle race, and 300-yard relay race. They also included a "ladies race," where men dressed up as women to swim and dive. Freeth competed in several events as a member of the Healanis. His trapeze flying was reported as "one of the prettiest features of the evening," marked by double somersaults off the rings.[25]

For the eighth event, Freeth made his way up the scaffolding. But when he reached the top and peered down, the searchlights from the *Boston* were so strong that he couldn't see the surface of the water. "I wanted to come down," he later admitted. From that height he had to be able to judge when and where to hit the water or risk serious injury.[26] He almost gave up the dive. But the event had been hyped for weeks in the papers, and two thousand people were expecting him to jump. Instead of climbing down, he got them to throw water onto the surface directly below him so that he could judge the distance. "He flashed through the air from the great height," the *Evening Bulletin* reported, "and went into the water cleanly, making a splendid dive."[27] The feat cemented Freeth's reputation as the top diver in the islands, though he later acknowledged that, under the same circumstances,

Twenty-one-year-old Freeth highlighted in the local press before his championship dive in Honolulu Harbor. *Honolulu Advertiser*, April 9, 1905.

he wouldn't repeat the dive for five hundred dollars.[28] That's quite a statement given his family's financial hardships.

Beyond his sheer nerve and gymnastic talents, Freeth was especially noted for his smooth style as he continued to develop his repertoire—triple somersaults from a flying trapeze, and a corkscrew from beams forty-five feet high in the bathhouse rafters.[29] "The most difficult feats of fancy diving are to him simple," one paper reported, "and he shows an unusual amount of grace in his performances."[30] Freeth would incorporate many of his gymnastics, though in simpler form, in the surf exhibitions he performed at Waikīkī and in Southern California.

～

The center of Hawaiian aquatic sports at this time was Honolulu Harbor. Both the Myrtle and Healani boat clubs were located there, and Freeth's Hawaiian Swimming Club, headquartered at the Hotel Baths in downtown Honolulu, was several blocks away. By November 1905 he was offering swim classes at the Healani Boat Club; the following year he was coaching their swim team. This was quite an honor for Freeth, connecting him to King Kalākaua, who had championed Native Hawaiian sports and competition: the club had been founded in 1890 during the last year of Kalākaua's reign and named after his yacht *Healani* ("heavenly mist"), whose royal berth became the new clubhouse. The Myrtles and Healanis vied against one another for decades, fostering skills in rowing and swimming that Freeth later developed on California's beaches. After the Hotel Baths opened in December 1906, the owners hired Freeth to give swim instruction "at all hours."[31] Presumably he had quit his job at the telephone company to devote himself full-time to his aquatic activities. When the Healanis competed against the Myrtles again in February 1907 at the Hotel Baths, Freeth won the high and fancy diving contest and added water polo to his list of sports: he played center for the Diamond Heads in the inaugural game against the Oahus.[32]

Freeth also spent time during these years at Waikīkī developing his surfing skills. By his own account and by those in the local papers, he had not only succeeded in standing on his board but he also decided to flip upside down and ride waves doing headstands. His diving and trapeze work were good preparation for such balancing maneuvers. By the fall of 1906, Freeth was performing surf exhibitions in front of the Moana Hotel in Waikīkī. Nearly a hundred people reportedly watched him one afternoon at the end of September.[33] Several days beforehand he was cited in the local paper: "George Freeth says surfing is the game."[34]

Local business leaders had picked up on the fad. Several months before Freeth's exhibition, the Hawaii Promotion Committee—a tourist bureau formed in 1903 and partly sponsored by the territorial government—had invited Robert K. Bonine of the Thomas Edison Company to film island scenes to help boost tourism. The result of Bonine's visit included *Surf Board Riders*, the sport's first official film. The one-minute clip would have been bundled with other short scenes from Hawai'i and shown in vaudeville theaters across the United States, Canada, and Europe, where the relatively new medium of "moving pictures" was becoming widely popular. In *Surf Board Riders* one watches native boys standing on their surfboards and riding small breakers toward shore, then executing a dive off the tail as the wave fades. It was the kind of trick Freeth perfected in his own exhibitions, always giving the spectators a show.

The work of the Hawaii Promotion Committee represented a seminal stage in the islands' transformation toward a new economy: members overturned nearly a century-old *haole* tradition of denigrating surfing and began to incorporate the sport as part of a "package" that visitors experienced on their tours of Hawai'i.[35] Although the islands had provided surfing exhibitions, visits to volcanoes, and sumptuous luaus to travelers throughout the nineteenth century, the speed of steamship travel in the early twentieth century—six and a half days from San Francisco to Honolulu—encouraged more mainland travelers to vacation in the new American territory.

～

Many in the Honolulu business community understood that tourism would become critical to Hawai'i's prosperity. Although sugar remained the most powerful and profitable sector in the islands through World War II— the engine behind massive immigration of Asians and other ethnic groups hired to work the plantations—the annexation of Hawai'i opened up new possibilities for diversifying Honolulu's economic base. Freeth, who was well traveled on the mainland and had a flair for showing off, seized on the boosterism of the day to create opportunities for himself with the Hawaii Promotion Committee.

In the spring of 1907, Harry P. Wood, who ran the day-to-day operations of the Hawaii Promotion Committee, invited 250 members of the Los Angeles Chamber of Commerce to tour the islands. His goal was to create business connections between Honolulu and Los Angeles, an area he called "the great tourist gateway and clearing house of the country."[36] Though born on the Big Island, Wood had spent fifteen years working in San Diego. He'd seen the growing population boom in Southern California firsthand; Los Angeles alone tripled its numbers in a decade, from about 100,000 in 1900 to nearly 320,000 in 1910. Wood wanted to encourage Angelenos to spread the word about the many benefits of Hawai'i. He had told the *Hawaiian Star* back in October 1906, "My work on the mainland this year . . . is especially intended to study the conditions existing in Los Angeles, and to plan for the doubling of our efforts in this territory and largely to increase the scope of our work in Southern California. . . . It is here, therefore, that we shall have our recognized center of activity for our tourist propaganda. And it is here that we expect to secure the greatest results this winter."[37]

What would members of the Los Angeles Chamber of Commerce have noticed most when they disembarked in Honolulu? The port town and capital of the islands would have seemed much smaller and quieter than Los Angeles, which had about four times the population. They would have felt the tropical humidity, so different from the dry air that permeated Southern California. A ride in an electric trolley along King Street, a major business thoroughfare, would have taken them past mostly two-story wooden buildings: retail businesses on the bottom and residences above. They'd pass horse-and-buggies along the dirt road as well as numerous bicycles. Men and women of the upper classes would have been garbed in Victorian styles very much like themselves, with white being the color of choice: suits, ties, and hats for the gentlemen; long dresses and decorative hats for the ladies. The islands prided themselves on hospitality, so the visitors would have been escorted and entertained wherever they went during their eight-day visit.

One of the stops for the Angelenos that week was the newly opened Hotel Baths, where Freeth and his Hawaiian Swimming Club put on a show the evening of March 18. Freeth performed a "head-and-tail" dive by having a young protégé, Charles Douglas, lock his feet around Freeth's neck. Douglas then grabbed Freeth's feet, and the two of them tipped off the platform; they separated when they hit the water "amid the deafening applause of the audience."[38]

The visitors also saw a regatta at Waikīkī, which included the first official surfing contest of the twentieth century. A local Waikīkī boy, eleven-year-old Harold Hustace, won the event. Though Freeth himself did not compete, we see his influence in Hustace's style. The boy "stood on his board, head up and head down and as an extra turned a somersault or two."[39] Hustace had also adopted the shorter boards that Freeth had begun performing on several years earlier.[40] Freeth likely did not compete, because the event was for amateurs only.[41] He was a paid swimming instructor at the Hotel Baths, and in the summer of 1907 he was listed as "the professional swimming and surf board expert" giving lessons every day at the Seaside Hotel, which had opened its doors in Waikīkī the year before.[42] Freeth was simply trying to make a living doing what he loved. He probably didn't imagine the consequences of being called a professional.

How and why he ended up at the Seaside leads us into one of the great stories in the sport's history: the beginning of surfing's modern transformation from a local tradition owned mostly by Native Hawaiians to a sport embraced by people around the world.

~

Writer Jack London was at the height of his fame when his picture appeared in the sports section of the *Honolulu Advertiser* on September 9, 1906. He'd sent a letter to Thomas Hobron of the Hawaii Yacht Club thanking him for the navigational charts that Hobron had sent of the islands. Hawai'i would be London's first stop on a planned seven-year voyage around the world. He indicated that the San Francisco earthquake several months before had delayed departure of the *Snark*, a fifty-five-foot ketch that London had designed himself, but he hoped to set off within a few months. "The lure of the voyage has gripped me," London wrote, "and I cannot get away too soon." His short stories and adventure novels—*The Call of the Wild*, *White Fang*, *The Sea-Wolf*—had won him millions of fans. His magazine contracts to publish additional stories from the *Snark*'s travels promised to increase his readership even more.

Freeth's name appeared on the same page as London's picture—one column over, playing centerfield for the Punahous in a losing effort against the Oahus. The two men, with more in common than one might imagine, would meet at Waikīkī the following summer. London's account of their four-hour session in the waves—"Riding the South Seas Surf"—helped introduce surfing across the West as a sport that white people could enjoy too. London had forged out into the wilderness of the waves, so to speak, into a realm where—according to the last famous mainland writer to tackle the sport, Mark Twain—none but natives ever mastered the art.[43]

But London had Freeth, a man whose mixed-race background allowed him to bridge those two worlds and whose transitional place between them was captured in London's colorful prose—"a young god bronzed with sunburn." Unfortunately for London, his own pale skin would get a deep roasting before the day ended.

That day—June 2, 1907—started off harmlessly enough.[44] The Londons had arrived at Pearl Harbor two weeks before and were staying at the Hobron cottage. But they were soon charmed by the atmosphere of Waikīkī—in particular, the opportunity "to enjoy the surf riding."[45] London knew the manager of the Seaside Hotel, Fred Church, from their prospecting days in the Yukon. Church was happy to lodge the couple in a canvas tent by the hotel right on the beach. They all went canoe surfing that morning in rough waves. Afterward, Alexander Hume Ford, a writer and promoter who'd arrived in the islands several weeks before the Londons, lent Jack London a surfboard and guided him to the outside reefs.

Ford himself had recently taken surf lessons from Freeth. The two men had also spent a couple of weeks together in May traveling with a group of U.S. congressmen and their families, who had arrived to survey the new American territory. Freeth had been hired as a lifeguard to help transport the honored guests through any rough surf they encountered on Kaua'i or the Big Island. Freeth was acknowledged as the best all-around swimmer, diver, and surfer in the islands. So, of course, after the Londons arrived and Ford had talked up surfing, the famous adventure writer booked a tent at the Seaside Hotel and paddled out to meet this young marvel.[46]

The description of the surf session that followed—written in bed as London recovered from painful sunburn blisters on the back of his legs—owes much to Freeth. We see Freeth the instructor behind London's newfound knowledge of surfing as he describes for the reader how to slide under breaking waves with a heavy surfboard, where to paddle to catch a wave, and when to relax when one of "the big smokers" rolls you over the reef. We don't need to strain too hard to hear Freeth's advice as an experienced lifeguard when London addresses his readers: "When the undertow catches you and drags you seaward along the bottom, don't struggle against it. If you do you are liable to be drowned, for it is stronger than you. Yield yourself to that undertow. Swim with it, not against it, and you will find the pressure removed. And, swimming with it, fooling it so that it does not hold you, swim upward at the same time. It will be no trouble at all to reach the surface."

Freeth's influence creates a fundamental contradiction in the essay: London wants to champion the idea of mastering the waves—"Get in and wrestle with the sea"—and yet, as all surfers know, the key to success lies in nonresistance: "Yield yourself to that undertow. Swim with it, not against it." London was a game student, tirelessly throwing himself (and his ideals) at the waves until his burning skin finally drove him to the beach. According to his wife Charmian, his face and body were "covered with large swollen blotches, like hives, and his mouth and throat were closing painfully."

The session is deservedly famous. "Riding the South Seas Surf" appeared in October that year in *Woman's Home Companion* and later, with some alterations, in London's book *Cruise of the Snark* (1911). Freeth's fame as a surfer in the islands now spread across the continent and even abroad when the narrative appeared in the city of London's *Pall Mall Magazine* under the title "The Joys of the Surfrider."[47] Freeth's English relatives could have been proud to see the family name associated with such a famous writer. London also used Freeth as the basis for his mixed-race character Stephen Knight in the short story "Aloha Oe," which appeared the following year in *Lady's Realm* magazine. Stephen is described as an "athlete, surf-board rider, a bronzed god of the sea who bitted the crashing breakers, leaped upon their backs, and rode them in to shore."[48]

Stephen is in love with Dorothy Sambrooke, the fifteen-year-old daughter of a U.S. senator. Dorothy shares Stephen's love, but her father's racism quickly scuttles the relationship. "No one had disapproved of his teaching her to ride a surf-board," London writes about Stephen at the end of the story, "nor of his leading her by the hand through the perilous places of the crater of Kilauea. He could have dinner with her and her father, dance with her, and be a member of the entertainment committee; but because there was tropic sunshine in his veins he could not marry her."[49]

The story was evidently the brainchild of Alexander Hume Ford. He'd told London that he had "a lot of whacking good material" for stories and that London was welcome to them.[50] Ford's and Freeth's experience with the U.S. congressmen back in May, several of whom had brought their daughters, had undoubtedly sparked Ford's literary imagination. Dorothy first meets Stephen when he is giving them "their first exhibition of surf riding, out at Waikiki Beach," where, in London's dramatic prose, "he stood poised on the smoking crest of a mighty, mile-long billow, his feet buried in the flying foam, hurling beach-ward with the speed of an express train and stepping calmly ashore at their astounded feet."[51] Though Freeth was a natural model on which to base a love story—known for his quiet strength, athleticism, and humility—his own love life remains a mystery. He was a lifelong bachelor and left no children. There are no direct references to him in any kind of romantic relationship.

Freeth was fair-skinned, as we have mentioned, and race does not appear to have limited his employment opportunities in California. On the contrary, his Native Hawaiian background enhanced his appeal as a draw for tourists. Though cast in the story as one of London's hypermasculine heroes ("in canoe, or on horse or surf-board . . . he had taken charge and she had rendered obedience"), Freeth embodied a more temperate role in his relationship with the ocean. He would not have understood the waves as London had depicted them—something to master or conquer—but rather as a force to respect and enjoy. London had erased women from the sport in his essay "Riding the South Seas Surf"; they are recuperated only when Stephen Knight—as Freeth did in real life—includes them in the form of lessons for young Dorothy. We see competing versions (and visions) of surfing in London's prose at this critical juncture in the sport's history: one that pushes a masculine ideal of power and individuality, another that opens the sport up to pleasure and community.

Though badly sunburned, London did not give up surfing. By the time he recovered enough to venture into the waves again later that month, Freeth was working at the Seaside every day—9:30 A.M. to 6:00 P.M.—giving lessons in surfing, diving, and swimming. In the latter half of June, Charmian wrote that she and Jack had been "swimming and surf-boarding under sun and moon." With reference to Jack's sunburn, she added, "very circumspectly under the sun!"[52] By the end of that month, London was reported as being "quite an expert on the surf board."[53]

Because of their close proximity at the Seaside, London and Freeth at least had the opportunity to continue their lessons and for London to keep the promise he made at the end of "Riding the South Seas Surf": "I shall come in standing up, even as Ford and Freeth. And if I fail to-morrow I shall do it the next day, or the next. Upon one thing I am resolved: the *Snark* shall not sail from Honolulu until I, too, wing my heels with the swiftness of the sea and become a sunburned, skin-peeling Mercury."[54]

Freeth had clearly inspired London. And one can imagine that London inspired Freeth as well: a man not so much older than himself—seven years—who lived a life of travel and adventure, who had overcome poverty to make a name for himself in the world. Back in early May—about six weeks after the visit of the Los Angeles Chamber of Commerce—Freeth approached H. P. Wood and the Hawaii Promotion Committee about traveling to Southern California to give surf exhibitions.[55] He was on the lookout for adventure

The beach behind these two surfers at Waikīkī gives an idea of its largely rural setting in 1907. The Seaside Inn, hidden amid the thick stand of trees (currently the location of the Royal Hawaiian Hotel), is where Jack and Charmian London lived in a beachside tent during their stay. "Hawaii, Surfing," 1907 JPL59. Jack London Collection, Huntington Library, San Marino, California.

and opportunity himself, and that was likely how he ended up working at the Seaside. The Hawaii Promotion Committee connected Freeth to their representative in Los Angeles, Lloyd Childs, but Freeth had to pay his own steamship fare (about sixty dollars one way). Freeth probably leveraged his day with London in the surf for a job at the Seaside, providing the kinds of services that would benefit both himself and the reputation of the hotel.

Alexander Hume Ford took up Freeth's cause by writing an article about him for the *Honolulu Advertiser*, which included a photo of Freeth surfing at Waikīkī.[56] And yet Ford later tried to erase Freeth and Native Hawaiians in general from surfing's timeline by stating, "On the Island of Oahu . . . the sport of surfriding is kept alive, not by natives, but by white men and boys who have learned the sport within recent years."[57] Ford was referring to himself and members of the Outrigger Canoe Club, a largely whites-only organization that he founded in May 1908. Ford often omitted from his articles that he and other *haole* actually learned the sport from Native Hawaiians. Jack London gave Ford a boost as surfing's savior when he wrote in 1916, "Not only did the Hawaii-born not talk about it, but they forgot about it. Just as the sport was at its dying gasp, along came one Alexander Hume Ford from the mainland."[58]

A second photograph that appeared in Ford's article in the *Honolulu Advertiser*—this one of Ford himself—embodies the role that he and other *haole* often play in histories of surfing: Ford is able to stand on the surfboard only because Freeth swam underneath the plank and held it steady while the photographer snapped the picture.[59] In essence we have a Native Hawaiian, rendered invisible, literally holding up a white man so that this latter can claim authority and expertise. The visual was supposed to show how easy it was for a white man to surf, a message Ford would broadcast far and wide to induce more Caucasians to move to Hawai'i and balance out the growing number of Japanese, a population that Ford and Honolulu *haole* considered a threat to their political dominance in the new American territory.[60] One of the unfortunate results of Ford's and London's racial propaganda was the mistaken notion that Native Hawaiians had abandoned their national pastime. But the truth is, Native Hawaiians like Freeth, Duke Kahanamoku, and the beachboys at Waikīkī not only sustained the cultural practice of *he'e nalu*, but they also made it possible for the rest of us to enjoy this exhilarating sport.[61] As Freeth later stated, surfing was "an art that belongs to the natives of the Hawaiian islands."[62]

Given the systemic racism built into island politics and society at the time, we might question whether Freeth's fair skin played a role in Ford's eagerness to promote him and the promotion committee's interest in sending him to the mainland. Did they feel that Freeth, as a *hapa haole*, would be more appealing to the white residents they were hoping to recruit? And how might Freeth have felt about being party to such a program? Freeth left few writings, so we have to draw our conclusions from his actions. He never worked directly for the promotion committee, nor did he sustain a close relationship with Ford. One can imagine him leveraging whatever assets he owned, including his fair skin, to create opportunities for himself. He was light-skinned enough to pass as white in California, though we don't have evidence that he ever actively pursued that goal. His light skin undoubtedly made it easier for him to move into communities and interact with the largely white population who frequented the plunges and the beaches where he worked. Beyond his athletic skills and congenial nature, as a Hawaiian he was perhaps exotic enough to attract attention yet white enough so that Southern Californians felt comfortable around him. As a "bronzed Mercury," in London's words, Freeth embodied a *hapa haole* tradition that extended to female hula dancers touring the United States and later performing in Hollywood films: mixed-raced islanders whose tan skin and Anglo features appealed to the fantasies of white mainlanders.[63]

Freeth never distanced himself from his Native Hawaiian background in the few writings that he did leave. Very much like Duke Kahanamoku, a dark-skinned Native Hawaiian who was also promoted by Ford and the promotion commmittee, Freeth tended toward the humble and laconic. Whatever thoughts he had about race issues he kept to himself.

The society page of that same edition of the *Honolulu Advertiser* that printed Ford's surfing photographs reported that the Freeth women—Lizzie, Marjorie, and Dorothy—had held a dance at their Emma Street house two nights before, receiving their guests on the lanai. One can't help but think it was a farewell party for the Freeths. Ads for the house auction began appearing in the papers the following week—parlor table, chairs, beds, springs, mattresses, dressers, wardrobes, washstands, all of Lizzie's plants. But this time was much worse, because Lizzie and the family had to vacate the premises.

Freeth left for San Francisco aboard the *Alameda* the day of the auction. He was twenty-three years old and had letters of introduction in his pocket from Jack London, Alexander Hume Ford, and the Hawaii Promotion Committee. The local press fêted him ("probably the most expert surf board rider in the world"), and news alerts about his arrival in California soon appeared in papers from San Francisco ("Champion Surf Rider Coming from Honolulu") to San Diego ("George Freeth Responsible for Popularity of an Almost Lost Art—To Teach Californians the Sport").[64] With allowances for the hyperbole of boosterism, Freeth had in fact become the champion diver in the islands and the force behind surfing's renewed popularity at Waikīkī. He'd been hired as a lifeguard—probably the first one to hold that position in the modern history of Hawai'i. He gave surfing, swimming, and diving lessons at the Seaside Hotel, elevating the role of Native Hawaiians, mixed-race Hawaiians, and other locals who instituted the tradition of the Waikīkī beachboy.[65] He was a teacher, a performer, a leader in every sport he played. Now he had the opportunity to bring surfing to California with local high school student Kenneth Winter (also predominantly white), who'd signed on to travel with him.[66]

Those who sent Freeth off with accolades expected him to promote the islands. Freeth had little interest in being a Honolulu booster, but he did love to surf. He was always looking for the next opportunity, and he relished a challenge. He had reached the peak of excellence in so many sports in Hawai'i. Why not see how far he could go in California?

3

A Waterman in Los Angeles

Freeth arrived in Southern California by mid-July. He first tried surfing at Long Beach "but found the rollers there unsatisfactory."[1] So he and Kenneth Winter, who had just finished his junior year in high school at Oahu College, traveled north to meet with Lloyd Childs, the Los Angeles representative of the Hawaii Promotion Committee. Childs had worked with Abbot Kinney before, and he arranged to have Freeth and Winter contracted for the surf exhibitions in Venice.[2] Winter was a member of the Healani Boat Club and had performed with Freeth at the Hotel Baths when the Los Angeles Chamber of Commerce visited Honolulu the previous March. Childs had been on that trip, so perhaps the three men had met during his stay. Winter probably saw the trip as a chance to take a summer vacation in Southern California and earn some easy money. Freeth himself likely had no idea what his plans were that summer other than to give surf exhibitions. His options were open as far as travel goes, and he seemed to be considering working his way east at the end of the summer.[3]

From his time at Atlantic City and San Francisco's Sutro Baths, Freeth would have recognized the carnival-like atmosphere along the boardwalk in Long Beach, a resort area known as "The Pike." The coastal towns to the north—Redondo Beach, Venice, Ocean Park, Santa Monica—had all developed similar beachside attractions to lure Angelenos out on weekends and holidays. Visitors enjoyed bowling alleys, shooting galleries, roller-skating rinks, roller coasters and other rides, along with various food vendors. The centerpiece of all the resorts, however, was usually an elaborate bathhouse, or "plunge." The one in Long Beach had been open since 1902—a two-story, Greek-columned affair that offered heated saltwater pools and baths, bathing

Crowds flocking to Long Beach on opening day of Henry Huntington's trolley service from Los Angeles, July 4, 1902. Dorothy Peyton Gray Transportation Library and Archive.

suit rentals, and private dressing rooms. It had opened on July 4 of that year, the same day Henry Huntington completed laying electric trolley tracks to the city.[4] A one-way trip to Long Beach from downtown Los Angeles took about an hour—twenty-two miles or so, directly south. The week before Freeth and Winter arrived, a heat wave drove an estimated thirty thousand people to the beach cities on the electric trolleys for the July Fourth holiday, most of them going to Long Beach. The local railroads carried another fifteen thousand to the coast.[5]

Long Beach was ahead of its time in placing a lifeguard station on the beach. The service had begun in 1902 with the opening of the Long Beach Bath House. It was reported that in the first five years, only nine lives had been lost in the surf directly in front of the bathhouse, most of them due to "cramps."[6]

But in 1907 the season began in the worst possible way. A railway conductor named Arthur Custer, twenty-two years old, drowned within sight of his wife and others on the beach. The young couple had been married only seven months. The two lifeguards, Carl Witte and F. Moody, along with several volunteers, ran the lifeboat out, but it capsized in the heavy surf. By

The Pike at Long Beach, c. 1907–1915. The small lifeguard station sits on the beach with a crowd of people in front it. The lifeguards worked directly in front of the Long Beach Bath House. The Palos Verdes Peninsula is noticeable in the distance. USC Digital Library. California Historical Society Collection.

the time they righted it and rowed out, Custer had already gone under. One of the witnesses on the beach that day was Thomas Saeger of Los Angeles. His nephew, a young attorney named T. Wright Robinson, had drowned four days earlier. Saeger "has come down to the beach nearly every day," the *Los Angeles Herald* reported, "hoping that the waves may speedily give up their dead."[7] Family members had little recourse at the time other than to wait for the tide or current to beach their loved one.

Venice had similar problems. Four days after Art Custer drowned at Long Beach, two fishermen drowned within sight of two thousand people on the beach. Their launch, *Boston*, had capsized in heavy surf. The two men hung on to the craft for several hours while the crowd grew and rescue attempts were made, but by the time a swimmer finally reached them, the two men had slipped under. The captain, a local man named John Cochran, was later found lashed to his boat with ropes and fishing nets. Apparently he'd tied himself to the craft, unable to swim.[8] The large crowd was indicative of the growing popularity of beaches in Los Angeles and its booming population. Not only had the drownings occurred on a Sunday afternoon in the summer,

Visitors at Long Beach showing off various styles of bathing outfits circa 1910, with two women at far left wringing their hems dry. The added weight of water, especially for women's bathing suits, contributed to the dangers of ocean swimming. Most bathhouses installed a lifeline (stretching behind the visitors in the surf) to try to prevent drownings. USC Digital Library. California Historical Society Collection.

but Venice was the closest beach to downtown Los Angeles. One-way trips on the Venice Short Line cost fifteen cents and took under an hour.

Editorials quickly appeared in the local papers, pleading for more lifeguards. One bystander in Venice, George E. Squires, reported that the "so-called lifesavers stood there doing nothing while the men were drowning. . . . They seemed to have no understanding at all of their duties."[9] In the face of such tragic incidents, the *Los Angeles Times* summed up the area's lifesaving situation: there was no organized lifeguard crew—federal, state, local, or even volunteer—at any point along the Santa Monica Bay; the lifeguards from the bathhouses were not trained to rescue shipwrecked crew in heavy surf and had no lifesaving equipment beyond a boat, lines, and buoys; and a single reel and lifeline had been installed on the beach between Venice and Santa Monica for emergencies but with no crew to practice using it. The paper thus declared that local drownings were "unavoidable."[10]

Abbot Kinney, the founder of Venice, decided that such drownings *were* avoidable. He advertised Venice as the "most desirable beach resort in the world." Men drowning off his pier in front of thousands of spectators—

including members of the city trustee board—was not only a preventable tragedy; it was also bad for business. He enlisted the help of Percy Grant, an experienced captain who ran the boating concession in the resort's canals, to form the Venice Volunteer Life-Saving Corps. They started meeting in late May and placed orders for two new lifeboats and a catamaran with airtight compartments especially designed for rescues. They gathered a list of possible volunteers, many of them employees of Kinney.[11]

At their first tryouts on the evening of June 13, however, one of the aspirants, Charles Watson, drowned in the surf. Watson had come to Venice with the circus as a bareback rider but stayed on to work for Kinney. The *Los Angeles Herald* reported, "Watson's drowning probably constitutes the most heartrending tragedy that was ever enacted within sight of the beach here and took place less than 400 feet from where more than a score of members of the life corps stood absolutely unable to in any way prevent his untimely death."[12]

Watson's dory had capsized as he and another volunteer, Andy Anderson, tried to turn it around in heavy surf. There seemed to be a question of whether Watson even knew how to swim. He slipped under despite Anderson's attempts to reach him. The waves rolled Watson to shore twenty minutes later. They worked over his body for three hours but could not resuscitate him. Civic groups later held a benefit for his wife, left in "straightened circumstances," so that she could travel back to New York with his remains.[13]

Watson's drowning typified the general lifeguarding situation in the Los Angeles area. The bathhouses hired lifeguards for the plunges and beach, but their training, knowledge, and experience were limited. Most of them were not prepared to save swimmers or fishermen who ran into trouble in heavy surf. They simply lacked the basic skills to carry out rescue operations in stormy seas. Even in calmer conditions, their lifesaving and resuscitation techniques were rudimentary at best.

When Freeth and Winter arrived in Venice, people were amazed when they saw them standing on surfboards and riding waves. But Freeth had so much more to offer. His depth of knowledge about the ocean and his broad aquatic skills, developed over two decades of working and playing in the Pacific, made his presence in this small resort town a cultural flashpoint for California beach culture. Over the next three years, Freeth injected Native Hawaiian cultural attitudes about the ocean into the Southern California psyche. He showed Angelenos the many pleasures to be had in the waves and taught them skills of swimming and diving that allowed everyday beachgoers to skirt the ocean's many dangers. They all knew Freeth came from an exotic place—the Hawaiian Islands—but his Anglo features and genuine interest in their well-being made his lessons as enjoyable and accessible as Hawaiian *hapa haole* music, which would become a fad in concert halls across the country the following decade.[14]

Yes, Freeth could certainly surf. As for the rest of his talents, it wouldn't take him long to show people what he was truly capable of.

~

The first advertisement for the "Hawaiian Surf Riders" provides a small clue to the ideal behind the founding of Abbot Kinney's resort: "These skillful gentry will also give lessons in their peculiar art, the most fascinating of aquatic sports."[15] The refined language and focus on instruction highlight the importance of culture and education. When Kinney started building Venice of America in 1904 from a fifteen-acre tract of sand dunes and salt marsh, he envisioned a year-round resort where residents and visitors would benefit from the best of European culture: concerts, dancing, theater—much of it delivered through the era's popular "Chautauqua" assemblies that combined education and entertainment.[16] Kinney made a $2 million investment in Venice: he dredged five miles of canals below sea level and piped in ocean water; he hired real Italians to ply the waterways in gondolas; he divided the land into 592 lots, many of them on the small islands within the canals; and he gave the waterways romantic names, a few inspired by the Italian city of Venice itself—Rialto, Lion, Altair, Aldebaran, Venus, Coral, and Cabrillo.[17]

And that was just the beginning. Kinney built a Grand Canal—seventy feet wide, four feet deep, half a mile long—that flowed into the Grand Basin or lagoon where Freeth performed his swimming and diving exhibitions. Around the lagoon stood the bathhouse where Freeth worked and the Antler Hotel along with the amphitheater that held two thousand spectators. Because visitors were often more interested in carnival than culture, Kinney built the Midway Plaisance alongside the lagoon and filled it with exotic theme-park attractions: Darkness and Dawn, the Temple of Mirth, the Streets of Cairo, Fair Japan. He paired Madame Chiquita—a South American woman thirty inches tall—with a man who stood over eight feet. He hired the Igorots, a tribe of Filipino headhunters, to dress up and take pictures with tourists. Miniature trains with real steam engines pulled visitors around the canals every twenty minutes from 6:00 A.M. to 11:00 P.M., every day of the year. The three-mile circuit was originally installed to show prospective buyers their real estate options. Venice of America had opened on July 4, 1905, to thirty thousand visitors. It was reported that 335 lots sold within two hours.[18]

As part of the entertainment, a visitor could take a camel ride from the lagoon down Windward Avenue to Kinney's Pleasure Pier, a couple of blocks

A swimming race in the Grand Basin at Venice of America on opening day, July 4, 1905. Freeth competed in swimming contests here and gave diving exhibitions. Security Pacific National Banks Collection/Los Angeles Public Library.

away. Thousands of lights strung across the street lit the way in the evenings. Once on the twelve-hundred-foot pier, they could enjoy music and dancing in the pavilion, dinner in the Ship Café—a replica of a three-masted Spanish galleon built on the south side of the pier—or see a play in the auditorium, which sat nearly four thousand people. Kinney's resort competed with others along the Santa Monica Bay for the title "Coney Island of the West." But Coney Island was seasonal. The stellar climate of Los Angeles—one of the driving forces behind its population growth—meant that Venice had to entertain visitors year-round. This required a constant need for new attractions, which is why Freeth and Winter landed there in July 1907.

The extent to which surfing actually helped Kinney is questionable. The novelty of riding waves would have attracted visitors, but the sport has a fickle history with planned exhibitions, because everything depends on the vagaries of swell. If the surf doesn't show, there is no show. And people start to grumble. Even Hawaiian royalty have fallen victim to Mother Nature: to celebrate King Kamehameha Day in 1877, King David Kalākaua arranged for a surf contest at Waikīkī to promote Native Hawaiian traditions. But His

Majesty could not drum up surf that day, and the event flopped.[19] Down the coast from Venice, in Redondo Beach, the Hotel Redondo hired the Royal Hawaiian Band to play for a week in the summer of 1895. The program included ten of "the finest Hawaiian surf riders, high divers and swimmers."[20] The *Los Angeles Herald* reported that "the day was a succession of disappointments. There was not any surf to whirl them ashore. . . . The Hawaiians could do nothing much in the choppy water and their manager called them off the scene. The crowd went home."[21]

Freeth and Winter were first advertised in the papers on July 14 and then every day the following week. Lloyd Childs had also begun showing Edison's *Surf Board Riders*, filmed the previous summer at Waikīkī, in the Chamber of Commerce Building in downtown Los Angeles. Not only could the audience learn about Hawai'i in Childs's daily lectures, but Freeth and Winter offered a live complement to what potential tourists were seeing on the screen.[22] The films had arrived in Los Angeles a few weeks before Freeth and Winter, a circumstance undoubtedly coordinated by H. P. Wood and the Hawaii Promotion Committee to give the islands maximum exposure for the upcoming winter season.[23] Hawai'i was in the early stages of cultivating California tourists, a group that quickly became the islands' most numerous and devoted vacationers for decades to come.[24]

Abbot Kinney soon dropped the tagline "Hawaiian Surf Riders" from the Venice of America ads. Venice is not known for great surf in the summertime. A combination of small waves and inconsistent swell probably forced Kinney to scratch surfing as a main attraction in order to prevent thousands of visitors from going home disappointed.

What would a surf session have looked like in the summer of 1907? Because traditional surfboards were heavy and cumbersome, and their weight increased as water soaked into the wood, Hawaiians before the twentieth century often swam out to the surf and either pushed or pulled their boards with them. Freeth's boards were comparatively shorter and lighter than traditional boards. Given the small summer surf in Venice, with waves breaking fairly close to shore, he and Winter would have paddled out on top of their boards and reached the lineup in short order. In large winter surf breaking farther out, Freeth might have found it more effective to swim his board out and push it through the breakers or else slip underneath the board, as he had recommended to Jack London, grab the sides, and hang on for dear life as the wave exploded over the top of him. California beach waves are shiftier and break faster than the long-rolling surf at Waikīkī, so Freeth's strength, reflexes, and balance would have been tested: a burst of paddling to catch the wave, a sudden jump to his feet, then a wide stance so that he didn't fall in the white water. Unlike surfers today, Freeth didn't have a fin on the tail of his board, so he normally kept his feet pointed toward the nose, more or less parallel, so that he could control the board's direction by dragging a foot off one side or the other. His usual path was not horizontal across the face of the wave, as surfers ride today, but straight into shore. He normally ended his rides with a showy dive off the deck to please the crowds.

It's hard to know what the financial arrangements were if the Hawaiians paddled out but couldn't put on an exciting show due to lack of surf. In any case, Freeth started looking for a more stable source of income soon after arriving in Venice. By early August he and Winter had moved to the lagoon for the "Great Gold Medal Swimming Contest" where the Hawaiians defended "local honors against all comers."[25] Along with his normal advertisement of Venice as "The Finest Beach Resort in the World," Kinney started adding to his tagline "and Safest." This was undoubtedly a bit of public relations to counteract the drowning disasters of the previous months. But with Freeth now working in the bathhouse and helping out the Volunteer Life Savers, for once Kinney's hyperbole was justified.

Despite the drowning of Charles Watson, Kinney and Grant continued to support the Venice Volunteer Life Saving Corps. They modeled the program after the U.S. Volunteer Life Saving Corps, which had started in New York in the early 1890s. Perhaps because the corps promoted popular ideals of civic pride and athleticism, the organization grew rapidly. The *Buffalo Courier* reported that by 1902, 734 crews had been established across the East Coast, with over 6,000 members.[26] This was the era of President Theodore Roosevelt's "The Strenuous Life," where individual effort was considered a prized path to national honor and greatness. Venice was the first community on the West Coast to establish a volunteer corps, though it was not yet affiliated with the national organization. Kinney, an avid outdoorsman himself, located his lifesaving station at the north end of the pier in an old wave motor house that he'd renovated. His wife, Margaret, helped raise money for lifesaving equipment through the local women's clubs, including a brand-new six-man boat that she christened *Venice*.

Kenneth Winter returned to Honolulu at the end of September. In a report that captures Freeth's strong sense of adventure and earlier sea travels with his father—and perhaps the desire to show folks back home that he'd made something of himself—Winter relayed to the local Honolulu press: "After the season was over, Freeth shipped with a wrecking crew that will go around South America and up the Mexican Coast looking up old wrecks and obtaining from them what things of value they might find. Freeth has gone as a diver and will get big money for his services. This will be a great adventure for George and he will have some great yarns to spin when he again comes home."[27] Winter added that Freeth intended to land in Atlantic City by the following summer. The article ended with this authoritative statement: "Venice was the only place in California where the surf was suitable for board riding."

Freeth had a habit of spinning yarns about his plans, but he didn't ship out to South America or anywhere else. He decided to stay in Venice. He was settling into the community and making new friends. He crewed the lifeboat as first lieutenant and went on fishing trips with local sportsmen up the coast near Malibu.[28] As we might expect, he also threw himself into team competition. After a water basketball match between the Venice Life Savers and the YMCA at Bimini Baths—a hot springs resort on the western edge of downtown Los Angeles—Freeth's teammates surprised him with a gold watch and a card that read:

> Mr. George D. Freeth—King of the Surf Board, Captain of Venice Basketball team, First Lieutenant of Venice Volunteer Life Saving Corps, and leader in Aquatic Sports and General Good Fellowship—is reliable, sober, honest, and industrious (just a man, that's all), and since he has a birthday and 24 years of such a record, we, his comrades and citizens of Venice, extend our best wishes and a watch, that he may continue to keep abreast of the times to the century mark at least.[29]

Beyond his surfboard riding, Freeth had made a strong impression on the small community in a short amount of time. They saw him as a leader and role model. The gold watch was a typical gift of the era, many given away as prizes. But the birthday card seems special: a personal testimony to the positive impact that Freeth was making on the young men around him. They would have admired his tremendous skills in the ocean and were probably eager to learn from him. Their tokens of respect and affection make his abrupt departure the following month all the more puzzling. A report on the game and celebration afterward captured the touching humility that was typical of Freeth in such situations: "Mr. Freeth, though considerably overcome by the surprise, responded happily, saying only, 'Thank you.'"

The Thanksgiving Day program at Venice later that month gives a good idea of how Freeth spent much of his time at Kinney's resort. At 10:00 A.M. he ran a boat drill and mock rescue with the Volunteer Life Savers. At 11:00 A.M. he performed a fancy diving show with the plunge manager, Jake Cox. The boat races began at 11:30 A.M. in single and double skulls, the latter event including women. The 50-yard freestyle swimming competition was held at

2:30 P.M. Freeth ended the day at 8:00 P.M. with a water basketball game in the plunge.[30] In between events he worked as a lifeguard in the bathhouse.

Sometimes Freeth performed late at night with Jake Cox, the two leaping from rafters in the plunge or diving from the tower that Kinney had built in the middle of the lagoon. Cox had devised a special "fire dive" that involved dressing up in a thick cotton suit, dousing himself with kerosene, and then lighting himself on fire with a starter's pistol. He'd plummet through the air and snuff himself out in the water. To keep the show interesting, he later performed the trick by jumping from an airplane into the ocean.[31]

In mid-December the Volunteer Life Savers decided to reorganize: they drew up new by-laws and a constitution and elected Freeth captain. They also intended to become something of a sports center, fielding teams against other local clubs in regional and national competitions.[32]

Everything seemed to be going well for Freeth. He'd been in Venice for five months and had quickly established himself as a leader in the community. He'd been honored and celebrated as an athlete and role model. But right before Christmas he packed his bags, grabbed his surfboard, and moved down the coast to Redondo Beach.[33]

We don't know why Freeth left Venice. Perhaps it was an issue of job security. Winter months were the slow period at California's beach resorts, and Freeth wouldn't have had much seniority. He may have gotten a better offer in Redondo. As he'd done in Venice, Freeth quickly integrated into his new community. He organized a water basketball team to play against Venice on Christmas Day in the Redondo Bath House. But when the Venice team didn't show, he had enough players to hold an inter-squad scrimmage. When Venice finally arrived in early January, Freeth's team beat them ten to two. By then Freeth was giving surfing exhibitions and helping to organize Redondo's first athletic club, with Freeth himself slotted to be head instructor. He also had plans to form a swimming club at the plunge and to start his own Volunteer Life Saving Corps. The Venice Volunteers had voted back in October not to join the national organization. They worried that the move might cost them local support, which they'd relied on for the past year to fund their lifesaving equipment. But Freeth himself was interested in affiliating with the home office in New York. Perhaps the vote—twenty-one volunteers against and three in favor—had played a role in his departure.[34]

As for Venice, a report in the *Los Angeles Times* in late January indicated that Freeth's break with them had caused some hard feelings.

Freeth would have taken one of Huntington's electric trolleys to Redondo, perhaps half an hour ride south along the Santa Monica Bay. The Red Cars, as they were known, provided critical infrastructure not only for the development of Los Angeles but also for the rise of beach culture itself. Easy access to the coast ensured that thousands of people on any given weekend or holiday could witness and participate in the exciting possibilities the beach had to offer. Two sets of parallel tracks ran along the fourteen miles of coastline between Venice and Redondo: the inner pair for cars pulling north, the outer pair for those pushing south. Freeth would have passed outlying communities whose populations measured in the hundreds: Playa Del Rey, Manhattan Beach, and Hermosa Beach. The latter two were built among sand dunes overlooking the tracks. The residents tended fields of wheat and barley or raised flocks of sheep. Though farming remained a mainstay of Southern California's agricultural-based economy for decades to come, especially growing citrus, emerging industries in petroleum, manufacturing, tourism, banking, and motion pictures were right around the corner. All of these would spur tremendous growth and innovation in the region, including the novelty of beach culture. During Freeth's time, life in Manhattan and Hermosa would have been fairly gritty due to the daily onshore breezes that washed over the dunes and blasted the cottages and residents with sand.

Perhaps the sparse population and unpleasant conditions partially explain why Black people would be allowed to bathe in Manhattan Beach, at a spot called Bruce's Beach. Several years after Freeth passed by, an African American couple, Willa and Charles Bruce, opened a bathhouse and dining hall that catered to Black people. The family ran the establishment until 1924, when city officials used eminent domain to condemn their properties and close down the resort. At that time the only other beach along the Santa Monica Bay where Black people could bathe in relative peace was the so-called Ink Well in the Ocean Park area, just north of Venice.[35] Freeth's bicultural background was key to the birth of California beach culture—introducing Native Hawaiian sports and attitudes to a region in the process of developing its identity—but the benefits of sun, sand, and surf would largely be promoted by and for the majority-white population. As Lawrence Culver notes in *The Frontier of Leisure*: "In Los Angeles, recreation became synonymous with whiteness."[36] When darker skin in the form of suntanning became part of California beach culture in later decades, the understood audience for product advertisements was obviously those with light skin. It was partly Freeth's light skin that allowed him to move so easily among white residents in this highly segregated and race-conscious region.

Rufus Marshall (*standing*) with a friend at Santa Monica Beach, c. 1915. African Americans gathered near an area known sometimes as the "Ink Well," one of only two stretches of coast along the Santa Monica Bay where they faced less harassment from white beachgoers. Shades of L.A. Collection/Los Angeles Public Library.

Freeth might have been amused that much of the sand above the tracks in Manhattan Beach would end up carpeting the beach at Waikīkī as Manhattan Beach became a popular destination and cleared land for development.[37] Below the tracks, Freeth would have noticed piles of seaweed and heaps of lumber, the latter floating north in great quantities from Redondo's busy wharves.

Redondo would have had a lot of appeal for Freeth. The small town had more of an industrial hum than Venice, with its three wharves off-loading tons of lumber, oil, and other freight destined for the development of the Los Angeles basin. A deep-water canyon, beginning less than five hundred feet from shore and dropping down more than thirteen hundred feet, allowed bigger ships to approach the wharves, thus giving Redondo a natural advantage over Venice in its development as a commercial hub for the region.[38] Freeth had spent much time around ships and harbors in his youth. One can imagine him feeling right at home in Redondo, a port that cleared four hundred vessels the year before he arrived.[39]

Venice's population was similar to that of Redondo—about three thousand—but it was founded as a resort town; its constant preoccupation was entertaining visitors. And though Redondo was moving in a similar direction, the trains running out to all three wharves—their cars loaded directly with freight from the steam and sailing ships—gave the town more of a workmanlike atmosphere that may have attracted Freeth.

It's worth mentioning that the same deep-water canyon that brought in bigger ships also creates bigger waves in Redondo; that gap in the ocean floor allows swells to push closer to land before rising up and breaking with greater force. From a surfer's perspective, Redondo would have been a better choice for Freeth's exhibitions, especially in winter, when the waves are bigger. Redondo was also well known for its great hauls of fish—bass, mackerel, barracuda, yellowtail, trout, sardines, halibut, and sand dabs—perhaps another benefit of the canyon's presence. Freeth later introduced spear fishing with a glass mask at Redondo. He would reportedly swim around the base of the wharves and spear twelve to fourteen fish at a time.[40] In addition to his lifeguard work, Freeth was able to enjoy great waves and catch his dinner in the surf. He moved around quite a bit in his life, but Redondo held him longer than any other city in California.

Behind Redondo's dynamic growth, of course, was one man: Henry Huntington. Huntington had created a vast network of transportation and utility interests in the Los Angeles area. He controlled twenty-three companies in Southern California alone in 1907, including the electric trolleys that were key to linking people and communities across the basin.[41] Huntington bought the Los Angeles and Redondo Railway in July 1905. At the same time, he purchased the Redondo Improvement Company, which owned 90 percent of the town, including the three wharves and the bathhouse. One week later he acquired over a thousand acres of coastal property—the Downey Ranch—that ran from Redondo Beach, around the Palos Verdes Peninsula, all the way to San Pedro.[42] When word of the deals got out and Huntington announced plans to invest in Redondo, the real estate frenzy began. He made $3 million in land sales.[43] When Huntington opened a two-story, Spanish Mission–style dancing pavilion on July 4, 1907, one of his employees, C. H. Burnett, hailed the attraction as "a powerful example of what could be accomplished by

Freeth surfing near Wharf Number 1, c. 1909. He looks ready to end his ride with his signature backflip into the whitewater.

collective push and hustle."[44] Freeth's drive to organize, and his competitive personality, thrived in this environment.

It's not known if Freeth and Huntington met before Freeth moved to Redondo. A myth persists that Huntington had seen Freeth surfing in Hawai'i and brought him over to Redondo as a tourist draw. But Huntington biographer James Thorpe makes no mention of the industrialist ever visiting the islands. It was Freeth's idea to travel to California, and the Hawaii Promotion Committee arranged for his employment with Abbot Kinney.[45] It's likely that the paths of Freeth and Huntington did cross at least once: during opening-day celebrations for the new bathhouse on July 1, 1909. Freeth had been hired as a lifeguard and Huntington was on site to tour the facility in the afternoon and evening.[46] This probable contact highlights the general roles played by various actors in the rise of surfing and California beach culture in the early twentieth century: Native Hawaiians like Freeth (and later Duke

Kahanamoku), who contributed their cultural knowledge and skills, and the largely Caucasian elites—H. P. Wood, Alexander Hume Ford, Jack London, Abbot Kinney, and Henry Huntington—who financed and marketed activities like surfing to boost development, increase their bottom line, and even maintain powerful political and social ideologies. But such distinctions are always tentative. Freeth marketed himself and his surfing throughout his life. He loved to surf, and surfing provided him with much-needed additional income as he hopped from town to town and job to job.

～

About the same time that Freeth moved to Redondo, the local papers announced the swimming championships of Southern California. The winners would travel north to compete in the Olympic tryouts at Stanford University in May 1908.[47] Recall that Freeth won a contest in the 100-yard freestyle in Pennsylvania in 1903, with a reported time of one minute and six seconds. American Charles Daniels, who had won a silver medal in the 100-yard freestyle at the 1904 Olympics in Saint Louis, qualified for the finals with a time of one minute and seven seconds. Daniels would win gold in the 1908 London Olympics in the 100-meter freestyle with a time of one minute and five seconds. Though Freeth's time was unofficial in Pennsylvania, one can see how he might think he had a good shot of at least qualifying for the Olympics.

Bimini Baths in Los Angeles would host the tryouts over three successive Friday evenings beginning in late January. Freeth had already organized his swimming club at Redondo, so perhaps he had his eye on the dates. He applied for his amateur card, but members of the Venice team had heard about his plans—perhaps from Freeth himself during their water basketball match on January 10—and they submitted a protest on the grounds that he was a professional swimmer and lifeguard.[48] Five days before the tryouts, the registration committee rejected Freeth's application. He was supposed to get a hearing in mid-February, but by then the tryouts were over.[49] Ben Watlington of the Los Angeles Athletic Club and Frank Holborow of Bimini Baths would represent Los Angeles at Stanford. Holborow's winning time in the 100-yard freestyle was one minute and twenty-six seconds.[50]

Freeth landed in Los Angeles just as the Amateur Athletic Union (AAU) was being formed in Southern California. George Braden, who worked at the Pasadena YMCA and chaired the registration committee that rejected Freeth's application, was among the first to champion the idea of a Southern California branch of the AAU.[51] At a meeting in downtown Los Angeles on January 5, 1908, Sidney Peixotto, president of the Pacific branch of the AAU, based in San Francisco (which governed amateur sports in Los Angeles and

Hawai'i), recommended that Braden wait a year before applying as a separate branch. Peixotto had the backing of James E. Sullivan, president of the national organization in New York. Sullivan felt that it was better for the AAU to shore up several regional branches that were struggling before admitting any new ones.[52] He explained several months later exactly what that struggle entailed. With reference to public school athletic instructors and coaches who resisted his updates to the rule book, Sullivan railed:

> As fast as we can make rules they seek means of getting around them. . . . The time has come when it is essential to the good of sport that something drastic should be done. . . . I won't say what the changes will be, but the old rule book will look as though an earthquake had struck it. . . . And these new rules will be enforced if we have to throw out every athlete in the country. . . . When the new rules go into effect the lawless element will have its chance to come out into the open and fight fair. And if amateur athletics thinks it can get along without the A.A.U. let it say so, and I will resign the presidency on the spot.[53]

Braden and other officials in Los Angeles had an incentive to crack down on athletes in the Southland to show their support for the broader movement within the AAU, especially if they wanted their branch application accepted.

The bathhouses that provided so much pleasure for Angelenos, and a necessary income for Freeth, fell under Sullivan's wrath. The AAU decided in 1908 that all lifeguards were essentially professionals and barred them from competition.[54] Sullivan's revisions to the rule book were an attempt to make amateurs across the country answer to a uniform code, but the distinction between professional and amateur remained murky. The AAU provided no universal definition of amateurism that covered all the sports they represented. An athlete could get paid as a professional baseball player, for example, and then turn around and enter a golf tournament as an amateur. Such loopholes forced the AAU to determine infractions on a case-by-case basis, and many decisions were left to the discretion of local registration committees. As a general rule, an athlete was allowed to compete unless someone lodged a protest.[55] The protest by Freeth's former team in Venice had blocked him from the Olympic trials.

Freeth wasn't finished with the registration committee, but he had other interests to pursue. Water polo was a relatively new sport in the Los Angeles area. Various cities had attempted to organize a league as early as 1903, but the idea didn't take hold until the fall of 1907.[56] Leslie Henry, a manager at the Los Angeles Athletic Club, organized water polo games against Bimini Baths in January 1908.[57] Scrimmages continued into February and March, with teams from Redondo and Venice joining play. Once the four teams had a chance to take each other's measure, representatives met in downtown Los Angeles and agreed on by-laws and a schedule of games.[58]

The sport was extremely quick by today's standards: seven-minute halves, with a five-minute break in between (compared to the current rules of four eight-minute quarters).[59] It was also brazenly physical; one newspaper referred to water polo as "submarine football."[60] At that time players had to touch the goal with the ball in their hand to score—they couldn't throw it into the net—which required goalies to physically block opposing players.[61] The result was often a scrum in front of the net—what the rule book permitted as "indiscriminate tackling"—with players piling on top of one another. The *Los Angeles Herald* reported, "It is nothing unusual for eleven players to pile on one, and the entire twelve then to go to the bottom."[62]

What happened under that pile often determined the outcome of a game—holds and body blows that punished players who tried to hang on to the ball. "About half the game is played under the surface," the *Honolulu Advertiser* reported, "and, as the tanks seldom are crystal clear, the referee, unaided by umpires as in other ball games, has small chance to see the tactics used down at the bottom."[63] One tactic was the "hand spread," where a player pushed his thumb and fingers into the mouth, eye, ear, and nostrils of his opponent. The *Advertiser* noted with understatement, "With this hold a quick wrench backwards and sideways usually causes a relaxation of the hold on the ball." Additional tactics included back strangles, digging heels into an opponent's kidneys, and cracking their ear drums. Again the *Advertiser*: "The game is to push the palm of the hand sharply against the victim's ear, breaking the membrane by the force of the water." The paper described an underwater choking contest in a game between teams from New York and Chicago: two players fought over the ball for a minute and six seconds in thirty feet of water; the loser finally had to be hauled out of the tank. The *Advertiser* summed up its report: "Generally the team that most completely drowns its opponents wins the game."

Freeth excelled in such conditions. He'd been a football star in Honolulu, where one reporter waxed, tongue-in-cheek, "Talking about football, George is—oh, well, what is the use? Ask any of the boys who played with him. You needn't look for any who played against him—they are all dead."[64] The same paper had reported a week earlier, "Danger or no danger he goes after a thing to win."[65] Freeth possessed the strength and agility, not to mention endurance and determination, that soon earned him the reputation as the best water polo player on the Pacific Coast.[66] Not only could he easily dive thirty or forty feet into the ocean, but he could also hold his breath for minutes at a time.[67] He would have been a formidable opponent in any aquatic scrap.

The first water polo season attracted much fanfare around Los Angeles. Newspapers reported large groups of "rooters" following their teams to away games on specially ordered trolleys.[68] The matches, held on Friday nights over a six-week period, drew between five hundred and two thousand spectators at each contest. This was a time, of course, before radio and television. Such live sporting events were a welcome diversion for the average citizen, who worked nine hours a day, six days a week.[69] Sports, and "physical culture" in general (the period term that covered exercise, dieting, and competition), also attracted the region's movers and shakers, thus knitting together all levels of society. The Los Angeles Athletic Club, where Freeth himself would later work, was founded in 1880 and patronized over the years by a who's who of industrialists, oil tycoons, politicians, railroad magnates (including Henry Huntington), and Hollywood stars like Charlie Chaplin, who actually lived at the facility. If it was one thing an entire region could get behind during an era of boosterism, it was the local sports team. Admission to the water polo games was ten cents, used to help pay the traveling expenses of the visiting team, which was allowed under amateur rules.[70] Although Freeth had been refused amateur status as a swimmer, he was allowed to play water polo because the games, while being held under amateur rules, were not sanctioned by the AAU.

Freeth was both captain of the team and the goalie. He trained seven young men how to play the sport and guided them to the first championship of the Southern California Water Polo League. They tied each of their opponents in the first three games and then beat them all in the back half of the season. Their championship came down to the final night, where they beat the second-place team, the Los Angeles Athletic Club, two to zero. Freeth scored both goals to ensure the win.[71] One of his signature moves was to leave the goal and swim across the tank to score just before halftime or in the final minute of the game. His team's victory was even more impressive since Redondo hadn't been expected to compete well against the more established clubs.[72]

Another one of Freeth's winning moves had been to recruit Louis Hammel to the Redondo team for the second half of the season. Hammel had worked with Freeth as a Volunteer Life Saver in Venice but wasn't playing on the Venice water polo team. Hammel's presence sparked the offense, and Redondo won the next three games, outscoring their opponents six to zero. Henry Huntington's Los Angeles and Redondo Railway awarded the team the "gold bar trophy" at the end of the season. C. H. Burnett, president of the Redondo Chamber of Commerce, presented individual trophies to the players at a celebration at Huntington's dance pavilion.[73] Freeth had put Redondo on the sporting map, boosting the pride and sense of identity of this new and growing community.

~

Beyond the pleasure of competition, Freeth understood the great benefits of water polo for training lifeguards and keeping them in shape. The same techniques that players used to break holds and evade tackles helped them to fend off the desperate clutches of drowning swimmers. Experts of the time recommended violent measures for lifeguards to protect themselves—"A vicious bite on the arm or a sudden twist of the thumb or wrist may help you."[74] In the most drastic cases, a lifeguard should knock the swimmer out: "Should you have the slightest doubt of your ability to handle a struggling man (or woman, for the matter of that) stop their struggling first by a determined blow of your fist on the jaw, just below the ear . . . and then carry them in."[75]

One of Freeth's great legacies in California was the young generation of lifeguards he trained so that they wouldn't doubt their abilities in the water. Tom Witt, who started competing in diving events when he was seven years old, described his training in Redondo: "I can remember Freeth's instructions and encouraging words. Freeth taught all us kids confidence, style and fearlessness of the water."[76] Not only did Freeth's expertise save many lives, but he also advanced lifeguarding techniques beyond the practice of injuring people in order to save them.

One of Freeth's early rescues in the Redondo plunge came on a Sunday afternoon in late February 1908. Carl Balmer, an inland visitor, decided to slide down the pool's "chute" even though he didn't know how to swim. He sank to the bottom and remained there while a group of spectators looked down at him and discussed how they might save him, though nobody attempted to do so. Somebody alerted Freeth. Freeth was fully dressed—he was just recovering from the mumps. But when he arrived poolside and saw Balmer facedown in the deep end, he dove in and pulled him out. It took ten minutes of "hard work" to resuscitate him.[77] Most methods of reviving an unconscious person during this era involved pressing the abdomen to expel water and then moving various parts of the body—arms, legs, even the tongue—to encourage reanimation.[78] The idea of introducing air into the lungs had not yet become standard, but stories of victims being revived after three or four hours encouraged lifeguards to keep working over a person.[79] In the summer of 1912, Freeth himself revived a drowning victim, A. P. Broadwell, after laboring for nearly three hours.[80]

The next report of Freeth saving a swimmer came in mid-June from Venice. It's the first indication that he'd left Redondo and was now working for Abbot Kinney again. The swimmer, Fred Ravilla, had ignored warnings and swam out beyond the safety line—a fixed rope between the shore and surf that swimmers could hang on to. So Freeth had to go get him. He worked on Ravilla for half an hour before the man regained consciousness.[81]

Lucky for Ravilla that Freeth had decided, within ten days of winning the water polo championship for Redondo, to move back to Venice. Freeth had probably been drawn back by the opening of Abbot Kinney's new one-hundred-thousand-dollar bathhouse, situated on the beach boardwalk. It was a two-story, Spanish Renaissance–style building that fit thousands of people in the pool and balcony. Redondo had Huntington's grand dancing pavilion, but the old bathhouse would have felt shabby compared to Kinney's fancy plunge, with its fifty-foot domed roof, its great windows facing the beach, its grand columns, and electric lightbulbs decorating the structure. It probably gave Kinney some satisfaction too—stealing Freeth from Huntington. Kinney always wanted the best for his resort, and Freeth had proven himself the top lifeguard, surfer, and water polo player in Los Angeles. Twenty thousand people were estimated to have attended opening-day festivities on June 21, and Freeth, who always enjoyed performing, would have relished being a star attraction.[82]

And he was. You couldn't have missed him if you'd tried. Freeth opened the water sports that day with a surfing exhibition. "The tide was running high," the *Los Angeles Times* reported, "and the white-crested waves fairly raced shoreward."[83] He then swam the 50-yard freestyle against Frank Holborow (and lost). He put on a diving exhibition with Jake Cox from the rafters of the new plunge. The program ended with a water polo match between Venice and Frank Holborow's Bimini Baths, with Freeth's team winning two to one. To top off his day, Freeth helped rescue a swimmer in the plunge. Surfing, swimming, diving, water polo, lifesaving—all in one day. Could Freeth have been any more in his element? Venice turned out to be a good move for Freeth, setting him up for the single most heroic day of his life.

The Rescue

Freeth did not make the Olympics in 1908, but he did hold "the championship of the world" in surfing, at least according to newspaper reports that summer, and he offered to go up against anyone.[1] Who could take that offer? Most anybody who surfed in California at that point would have been trained by Freeth. He never entered a surf contest, so his championship was a nominal title, one earned by general consensus rather than any particular performance. The references to being world champion were undoubtedly part of a marketing campaign to attract visitors to Kinney's resort, where Freeth settled in to work the beach and bathhouse during the summer of 1908. Surfing in California has idyllic origins—three royal Hawaiian teenagers riding waves in Santa Cruz simply for the pleasure: no promotions, no prizes, no hope of any gain other than an enjoyable summer afternoon in the ocean and perhaps bragging rights among the brothers for who caught the biggest wave or held the longest ride.

But ever since that day the irresistible excitement and exotic appeal of surfing has attracted promoters who've used the sport to "boom" any number of enterprises. Like Kinney's resort. Or hotels. Fourteen years before Freeth landed in Los Angeles, the La Jolla Park Hotel in San Diego advertised "Native Hawaiian Surf Riders" giving daily exhibitions for the summer.[2] One of the surfers, John Ahia, later wrote a letter to the Hawaiian-language newspaper *Kuokoa* in which he described getting paid ten dollars a day for performing. "It may be true that I'm the most unskilled of surfers there (Hawaii)," Ahia joked, "but I'm the number one surfer here in California." He also praised the lack of discrimination that he found in the Golden State: "This is a fine land, where all are equal. I am just like all the others who are staying in this Hotel."[3] Though California had its own race issues, Ahia's comment offers a glimpse of the second-class status that he felt as a Native Hawaiian after the overthrow of the monarchy.

The following year, in January 1894, a group of Honolulu businessmen sent two Native Hawaiian surfers—James Apu and Kapahee—to perform at the California Midwinter International Exposition in San Francisco. Essentially a world's fair, the event ran from late January to early July. The surfers formed part of a large cultural exhibit meant to drum up tourism for the islands.[4] As mentioned in the previous chapter, the Hotel Redondo joined the surfing act in the summer of 1895, convincing members of the Royal Hawaiian Band to put on a diving and surfing show. Freeth was simply the latest generation of Hawaiians to sell his talents for the sake of boosting local business, just as he'd done for the Moana and Seaside hotels at Waikīkī. The critical difference between Freeth and his predecessors, however, was that he did more than put on exhibitions. He also stayed and taught the locals how to make surfboards and ride the waves themselves. It would take a couple of decades for Californians to truly master the sport and create their own homegrown surf culture. But even then, in the depths of the Great Depression, California surfers on the shores of San Onofre, Palos Verdes, and Malibu would be inspired by another generation of Hawaiians—the Waikīkī beachboys—to pursue romantic ideals of the beach lifestyle: surfing, diving, playing the ukulele, and holding luaus. The young people who inherited those ideals after World War II would drive the greatest marketing boom the sport had ever seen, beginning with the Hollywood hit *Gidget*, a film that branded the beach lifestyle squarely into California's identity.

After Kinney's grand opening of the bathhouse in June 1908, Freeth continued to do what he did best: performing in the plunge and riding his surfboard in front of big crowds on the holidays: Independence Day, Los Angeles Day (August 8)—where officials and residents from downtown were honored and entertained—and Labor Day.[5] He also kept beach visitors safe. In late July, he and fellow lifeguards Louis Hammel and Frank Holborow rescued B. Nolle, who'd capsized his canoe in the surf at Ocean Park. Typical of Freeth, he swam out to the man while Hammel and Holborow launched the lifeboat. The crew landed Nolle on the beach less than eight minutes after the siren had sounded from the top of the lifeguard station, an indication of the lifesaving crew's growing expertise under Freeth's leadership.[6]

Freeth also helped found another swimming organization, the Venice Aquatic Club, which appeared for the first time on July 4, less than a month after his move from Redondo. The group entertained visitors in Kinney's new bathhouse with trapeze diving, relay and obstacle races, and both high and fancy diving.[7]

Freeth's reputation in water polo continued to grow after he moved back to Venice. The Life Savers beat the Bimini Water Rats on opening day of Kinney's bathhouse, and the string of victories they piled up over the next few months demonstrated their complete dominance in the sport. In July they beat Freeth's old team from Redondo, the league champions, five to zero and seven to one in consecutive weeks. In August they beat Bimini again six to zero, and they beat their toughest rival, the Los Angeles Athletic Club, one to zero in front of fifteen hundred spectators. In September they beat Los Angeles again and then trounced Redondo once more, seven to zero.[8] As the team's regular goalie, Freeth essentially shut out his opponents that entire summer. In the game on July 30, where Redondo managed to score a goal, Freeth was noted as "the star of the game" because he scored three goals himself. The *Los Angeles Herald* reported that the two thousand spectators that night were "the largest crowd that ever witnessed a water polo game in Southern California."[9] The Venice Life Savers had come in last place the previous spring, but Freeth transformed them into the top team in the league.

No other club could match their speed and strength. Louis Hammel had followed Freeth from Redondo, and Freeth also recruited Frank Holborow—the short-distance swimming champion of Southern California—from the Bimini Water Rats. Sherwood Kinney (Abbot Kinney's eighteen-year-old son) and local lifeguards Harvey Crum and Harold Marcoux rounded out the starters. As Venice kept winning and more spectators came to the games, the local AAU decided to put its foot down, specifically targeting Freeth:

> The local commission will take immediate steps to seggregate [sic] professional and amateur athletes at Venice, George Freeth, the champion Hawaiian swimmer and surf-board rider, being the particular target for the Investigating Committee. Freeth has been playing regularly with the Venice water polo team, several of his team-mates being recognized athletes in good amateur standing, and who are in danger of suspension if further playing with the alleged professionals is indulged in. Freeth has promised to appear before the local amateur commission several times, but as yet has not conferred with the latter board regarding his pro and non-pro standing.[10]

Despite the public warnings, Freeth forced the issue: he continued to play (and win) with well-known amateurs, so the local commission shut his team down.

The Venice Life Savers water polo team, August 1908. *Back row, left to right*: Harold Marcoux, Fred Fair, Frank Holborow, Sherwood Kinney. *Front row, left to right*: Andrew Scholz, Louis Hammel, Freeth, Harvey Crum. Courtesy Arthur C. Verge/Kinney Family.

On October 1 they suspended Freeth, Hammel, and Holborow indefinitely.[11] At the same meeting, Leslie Henry's Southern California Swimming Association was sanctioned to hold all championship events in swimming, diving, and water polo.[12] It was the commission's strongest move yet to show their intention of both cleaning up amateur aquatic sports in Los Angeles and organizing a water polo league that "played correctly and according to the national rules."[13]

Freeth never played another water polo game for Venice. In a follow-up hearing two weeks later, the commission disqualified him and Hammel from participating in amateur events.[14] Frank Holborow got off more lightly. He returned to the Bimini team and continued to swim competitively and play water polo. He was allowed to remain an amateur as long as he wasn't playing with professional players, Freeth in particular.[15]

The decision galled Freeth. There's no question that he was a professional according to AAU rules, but he and Hammel were being punished for engaging in the same activities that dozens of other athletes in the area had engaged in as well, including fellow Venice lifeguard Frank Holborow.[16] "If our men are professionals," said Venice water polo team manager Fred McCarver, "so are all the bath house employees on this coast. This thing of making fish of one and flesh of another is not going to end here."[17] Never one to dodge a scrap, Freeth promised that "he would take the matter before the national association and compel the same action in regard to all athletes who are in the employ of any bath house on the coast."[18] The hearings continued into the following year with Freeth roiling aquatic sports in Los Angeles by naming thirty-eight men and bringing evidence to back up his accusations.

With his water polo season ended, Freeth turned to other pursuits. In early October he began training a group of young women to row, practicing in the Venice canals and Grand Lagoon.[19] They rowed for pleasure and exercise, but Freeth kept open the possibility of competition against other clubs. Although women competed in the early years of Southern California amateur swimming, the AAU did not sanction their events or admit them to the organization until November 1914.[20] American women were not allowed to compete in Olympic swimming events until 1920. But as Freeth's Hawaiian background had given him a head start in ocean-related skills when he arrived in California, so too when it came to his beliefs about women in sports. Hawaiian women fill the annals of aquatic activities in the islands, so training young women to row and swim in California would have seemed completely natural to him.[21] At the Waikīkī regatta held in honor of the Great White Fleet's arrival in July 1908—President Theodore Roosevelt's flexing of imperial muscle by sending sixteen battleships on a circumnavigation of the globe—one of the events included three teams of Native Hawaiian women competing in a canoe race. The largely *haole* Outrigger Canoe Club did not field—nor would they have approved of—a team of white women taking part in such an event.[22]

On Labor Day 1908, two young women known as the "Seaweed Sisters"—Dorothy Newkirk and Avis Gordon—competed with Freeth in a three-and-a-half-mile swim between the Santa Monica Pier and the Venice Breakwater. Newkirk and Gordon had become notable not only for their swimming exploits but also for wearing men's bathing suits, which helped lower their racing times.[23] Freeth won the competition that day in one hour and thirteen minutes, racing against lifeguard Harvey Crum (a member of Freeth's water

"The Seaweed Sisters"—Dorothy Newkirk and Avis Gordon—competing in men's bathing suits with Freeth in the Labor Day ocean swim between Santa Monica and Venice. *Los Angeles Times*, May 23, 1909.

polo team) and another man named Crawford, who developed cramps during the swim. Despite a heavy swell and crosscurrents, both women finished strongly: Newkirk in an hour and thirty-seven minutes, and Gordon in an hour and forty-one minutes (both were given a ten-minute handicap against the men's times).[24] The event highlights Freeth's great effectiveness as a coach. He typically competed alongside his students, encouraging them to challenge both him and themselves. He followed the same strategy whether it was Olympic gold-medalist Duke Kahanamoku or local high school sensation Dorothy Newkirk.[25] It would not be surprising at all if Freeth had encouraged the women to don male suits, both to improve their times and to increase their safety, since women's suits of this era were more akin to dresses in their length and weight.

An article on Freeth teaching women how to row in Venice described them, probably tongue-in-cheek, as "the auxiliary of the Life Saving Corps."[26] But if that organization *had* accepted women, there is little doubt that Freeth would have encouraged his young protégées to join, and he would have trained them to succeed. A pair of sisters he also coached in Venice, Lyba and Nita Sheffield, later organized a Girls' Life-Saving Corps when they entered the University of California at Berkeley. They eventually wrote a textbook in 1920, called *Swimming Simplified*, which included several chapters on rescue techniques and a picture of Freeth on a three-wheeled motorcycle that he later developed for lifeguarding.

~

The Venice Volunteer Life Saving Corps had finally joined the national organization in July 1908, meriting a profile in the *Los Angeles Herald* two weeks after Freeth was suspended by the AAU.[27] The article offered a brief history of the local organization's founding and a couple of grainy photographs: the men posed in front of their station at the north end of the pier, and a smaller group on the landing inside the breakwater with what looks to be a resuscitation device. Freeth sits front and center in the first photograph. He's wearing a bathing suit, flanked on either side by members of his water polo team, as if they'd just been pulled from practice for the group picture. Behind them stand thirteen men in uniform, most of them in the white sailor outfits inspired by the U.S. Life-Saving Service, a government organization established on the Eastern Seaboard in 1873 to help ships in distress. The service employed "surfmen" and "keepers," who donned heavy oilskin suits and launched large rowboats to perform strenuous, time-consuming rescues.[28] Freeth's bathing suit tells us a lot about the innovative mind-set he brought to lifeguarding. On the afternoon of December 16, when the emergency siren on the station house blew, he was already in his bathing suit, ready to dive into the ocean and swim to the Japanese fishermen rather than launching a lifeboat.

That day, a Wednesday, dawned much like the previous one in Los Angeles: a storm over the Colorado River Valley stalled rather than moving east, which kept the area under cold weather, overcast skies, and light rain. Sunrise was just before 7:00 A.M., with temperatures in the low forties and a sharp frost in the forecast. The mercury climbed to the upper fifties that day, about the same temperature as the ocean in which a number of the Japanese would soon find themselves. Their clutch of boats set out that morning from Maikura, a small fishing village seven miles north of Venice. A light breeze blew out of the northeast, giving the boats a tailwind as they rowed south.

The skies darkened in Santa Monica around 11:00 A.M., and a hard rain fell for ten or fifteen minutes. A strong wind blew in from the sea, clearing out the clouds but bringing high surf. South of Santa Monica in Venice, waves began breaking over the rock breakwater fronting the pier, which ran off Windward Avenue in the shape of a large *T*.

A squall descended on the area in the early afternoon. When the first of five fishing boats appeared in the storm, the siren sounded on top of the lifesaving station at the north end of the Venice Pier. The lifeguards stood watching, wanting to help the Japanese fishermen, but the waves were too big for them to launch their lifeboat. Several boats inside the protection of the breakwater had already been smashed by waves crashing over the pier. "There seemed to be absolutely no means of communicating with the men in the boats," read the affidavits later submitted to Franklin MacVeagh, secretary of the U.S. Treasury, "and from their hopeless and helpless condition, which could be seen from the pier, it was apparent that unless something was done immediately the boats and men would both be destroyed."[29]

Los Angeles newspapers offer varying accounts of what exactly happened that day, an indication of the general chaos the storm caused around the Venice Pier.[30] By general consensus, eleven men were rescued in all: nine Japanese and two Russians. Four boats contained two men each, and one boat held the remaining three.

The first boat of fishermen approached from the south just after 1:30 P.M. The two Japanese—Tom Matsuma and a "helper"—were trying to get behind the shelter of the breakwater, straining against wind and waves blowing from the northwest.[31] The Life Savers tracked them from the pier. They weren't able to launch their boat, because waves were smashing into the rocks of the breakwater, sending spray fifteen to twenty feet into the air. Freeth volunteered to dive into the surf and swim a rescue line out to the fishermen so that they could be hauled in.

He dove over the breakwater and swam to the boat. The Japanese were exhausted from their exertions. Rather than using the lifeline, Freeth climbed into the boat and took hold of the oars. He rowed them through the storm and behind the breakwater, where the Volunteer Life Savers pulled the two fishermen onto the pier.

Then the second boat was spotted containing the two Russians: Nick Agelzoff and William Desotil.[32] Freeth climbed back onto the pier, ran to the end, and dove off a second time. As he was swimming toward the Russians, a third boat overtook him with two more Japanese. They too were exhausted. Freeth climbed aboard, but instead of taking them toward the pier—they were probably already in the surf line—he guided the boat through the waves, making a safe landing on the beach. The affidavits described him steering "with a skill that enables the Hawaiin's [*sic*] to pilot their surf boards over the breakers."[33] The Russians, meanwhile, had been driven close enough to the pier where the Life Savers could throw out ropes and pull them to safety.[34]

Freeth was taken to his quarters in the lifesaving station and given a rubdown to counter the effects of hypothermia. The ocean temperature in mid-December at Venice would have been between fifty and sixty degrees. At that temperature, the normal time before exhaustion or unconsciousness sets in is one to two hours.[35] Freeth had probably spent the better part of an hour swimming and rowing through cold, stormy surf.

As Freeth was being attended to, the siren sounded once again: two more boats were in trouble, this time driven from the north. The fourth boat was in the most desperate straits: the storm had swamped the small craft and thrown all three men into the ocean. One of the occupants was reportedly the leader of the Japanese colony, a man named Yomada.[36] The Volunteers, standing on the pier, heaved life buoys toward the fishermen, but they landed far short.

Freeth got up and dove off the pier for the third time that day. He grabbed the floating life buoys as he swam out and managed to strap one around each of the men as they clung to the side of the boat. He kept them near the overturned craft until three of the Volunteers—Percy Grant, Louis Hammel, and George Fair—finally managed to launch the lifeboat. When the Volunteers arrived, they pulled the three fishermen and an exhausted Freeth into the lifeboat and rowed them back to the pier. The final boat drifted close enough to the pier that ropes could be thrown to the remaining fishermen, who were hauled in.

The rescue played out over nearly two hours, the multiple sirens bringing hundreds of spectators to the shore and pier. Freeth was ultimately given credit for saving seven men by himself. "There is not another man on the beach," concluded the affidavits, "or perhaps in America, that could have accomplished the wonderful feat that FREETH accomplished in this matter." In a moment of humorous bravado, Freeth later explained to a Honolulu reporter that his gold medal specified saving only seven men because "he hauled in the other four so easily that he would not permit the full number to be mentioned."[37]

The same storm that drove the eleven fishermen toward Venice had also forced three more crews of Japanese to abandon their small boats just south of the Long Wharf in Santa Monica. Interestingly, all six men were able to swim through the waves and save themselves on the beach: T. O. Shiro, T. Caneshira, I. Igi, T. Yamauchi, Y. Kato, and T. Tokushima.[38] The incident doesn't discount Freeth's heroism—the Japanese who traveled to Venice the next day to present him with money and a gold watch clearly appreciated his efforts—but it does suggest that the fishermen were probably more capable in the water than some of the newspaper accounts implied. The *Los Angeles Examiner*, for example, reported that the Japanese on one boat "had given up hope and were crying. Grabbing a boat hook and threatening to kill the Japanese unless they obeyed him," Freeth ordered one of them to take the tiller.[39] Melodramatic accounts were the norm in newspapers at the time, but Freeth's actions needed no preposterous heroics or exaggerated victims. As an ethnic group the Japanese were under general duress in California that year: the "Gentleman's Agreement" between the United States and Japan had taken effect, a policy aimed at reducing Japanese immigration and thus calming the fears of Californians over the rising Japanese population. Recall that a similar racism had triggered Honolulu's elite to fund programs to bring more Caucasians to Hawai'i to balance out the growing political clout of the Japanese. Freeth's and Winter's arrivals in Venice the year before had been part of the general effort to recruit more white residents to the islands.

Freeth recovered fairly quickly from his exertions. Several of the local women's clubs held an impromptu benefit that evening in the Ship Café to raise money for the Volunteer Life Savers. The *Los Angeles Herald* reported, "When the boys of the crew appeared they were given a warm round of applause and George Freeth was given an ovation which befitted the hero."[40]

The following morning Freeth was reported walking about the pier "apparently as well as ever. Other members of the life-saving crew were also out, unaffected by their hard experience in the water."[41] Although Freeth's routine quickly returned to normal, those two hours became a defining point in his life. He showed all the qualities that have shored up his legend in the surfing and lifeguarding communities ever since: bravery, endurance, and tenacity; incredible ocean skills in diving, swimming, and rowing; and the successful demonstration of lifesaving techniques far in advance of his era. We can compare the results of December 16 and the eleven men rescued with the numerous lives lost at Los Angeles beaches before Freeth arrived on the scene: the well-meaning but ineffectual rescue attempts that often ended in friends or relatives waiting for the waves to give up their dead. And because area rescuers lacked the basic skills and ocean knowledge that Freeth possessed, public response generally registered the incidents as tragic but unavoidable.

In two brief hours, Freeth proved what could be done with the right knowl-edge and training. He demonstrated in particular how his methods differed from other lifeguards of the period. In calm ocean waters or a swimming pool, most of them could and did save lives. But they didn't have the swim-ming skills or ocean knowledge to be effective in storm conditions. None of the Venice Volunteers had ventured into the heavy surf outside of the boat. Their training was to throw lifelines and to crew the lifeboat, not to swim. The same was true for the surfmen and keepers of the U.S. Life-Saving Service, who drilled weekly with mortar cannons, signal flags, and heavy rowboats. Swimming out to shipwrecked sailors would have seemed ludicrous to them.

Freeth understood that Los Angeles beaches were a much different envi-ronment from the coastlines of the Eastern Seaboard, Alaska, the Great Lakes, or even Northern California, where the surfmen and keepers constantly monitored the horizon. Taking the time to gather a crew and launch a boat would ultimately cost more lives than it would save. Most victims fell into trouble close to shore, and swimming from the beach was the most effective way of helping them. So Freeth started to train lifeguards to swim in all ocean conditions. Teaching the young men to surf was also part of their education in understanding how to move quickly through waves and currents.

But Freeth remained an anomaly. Los Angeles didn't support a regular lifeguard program for another two decades. When Los Angeles County fi-nally did hold tryouts for thirty openings in the summer of 1930, however, all of the requirements derived directly from Freeth's training, including the task of swimming half a mile through the surf from the beach.[42] Other than the U.S. Life-Saving Service, national organizations that initiated rescue programs were still a number of years off: the YMCA in 1912 and the Red Cross in 1914.[43] It would remain for the next generation, some of whom were trained and inspired by Freeth, to apply his techniques across the beaches of Los Angeles County.

5

Amateur Troubles

A delegation of Japanese traveled from the fishing village down to Venice the day after the rescue to show their gratitude to Freeth and the lifesaving crew. In an afternoon ceremony at the Japanese Exposition building on the Venice Pier, H. Sano, the head of the delegation, presented "the hero of the beach" with $50.00 and a gold watch.[1] They also contributed $37.50 to the crew's "sick fund." This was a time before the advent of workers' compensation or personal health insurance, so employees often had to rely on public charity to help them through sickness or injuries. Abbot Kinney made a speech commending Freeth, and the spokesman of the Japanese delegation—apparently speaking in Japanese—"added some very nice sounding words of gratitude for the kindness shown them during their mishaps yesterday."[2] Kinney's openness to cultivating relationships with the Japanese at a time when they were experiencing widespread racism is a testament to the enlightened spirit on which Venice was founded. His progressiveness extended to African Americans as well. He hired Arthur L. Reese to run a janitorial service in Venice and sold him the Venice Boat and Canoe Company, which ran the concession in the canals. Reese later showed a flair for decorating Kinney's buildings, hanging "lights, streamers, flowers, flags, or whatever he could think of" to cover up unsightly rafters and beams.[3] He eventually became a member of the Venice Chamber of Commerce and the official town decorator. Reese's son, Mercier Reese, recalled that "Mr. Kinney always addressed my father as Mr. Reese, which was unusual in those days."[4] Kinney eventually bequeathed his family home on the Grand Canal to Arthur Reese's cousin, Irving Tabor.

In the days after the visit of the Japanese, Freeth's heroics spread up and down the Pacific Coast, reported in newspapers in San Francisco, Oregon,

Washington, and, of course, Hawai'i. Industrialist Andrew Carnegie had established the Carnegie Hero Fund Commission in 1904 to honor those who risked their lives to save others, and early reports mentioned that several local organizations would apply for a Carnegie Medal on Freeth's behalf.[5] One of those reports took the opportunity to use Freeth as a model of Carnegie's pacifist ideology. In an editorial titled "True Bravery," the writer praised Freeth's actions, because they were concerned with "the preservation and not with the destruction of life."[6] The writer went on to mention, as did other reports, that Freeth had been responsible for saving, or helping to save, approximately fifty lives since arriving in Southern California. Individual reports from area newspapers record at least twelve people he'd saved since the summer of 1907 (including the Japanese fishermen), but many of his rescues undoubtedly never made the press.[7]

If applications were made for a Carnegie Medal on Freeth's behalf, they probably would have been rejected, since the honor precluded those who worked in vocations that required them to save lives "unless the rescues are clearly beyond the line of duty."[8] Perhaps feeling that Freeth's actions *were* beyond the line of duty, local members of the Venice Chamber of Commerce began to rally around him the very afternoon of his rescues.[9] The following week they passed a resolution to petition the U.S. Congress for a medal honoring Freeth's achievements. The Ocean Park Chamber of Commerce passed a similar resolution that same week, as did the board of trustees for Ocean Park (Venice fell under their jurisdiction at the time). The trustees encouraged all civic and commercial bodies in Los Angeles to join the resolution, including the Los Angeles Chamber of Commerce, the Santa Monica City Council, the Japanese Chamber of Commerce, and the Los Angeles County Board of Supervisors.[10]

The Venice Life Savers ran drills every Sunday morning, and the drill they conducted four days after their rescue of the Japanese fishermen attracted a large crowd. Descriptions indicate that Freeth's methods of swimming out to a victim were already being practiced, since some of the Volunteers dove off the breakwater with life buoys and lines to reach the swimmer.[11] The members continued their newfound fame by dressing up in fine white uniforms and marching in the Tournament of Roses Parade in Pasadena on New Year's Day, 1909. The *Los Angeles Herald* reported that the group won first prize in the W class (marching clubs) and was awarded a silver cup that they planned to display at the station house.[12]

In an interesting twist to Freeth's heroics, the *Redondo Reflex* later reported that Freeth was not actually working for Kinney when he rescued the Japanese: "At the time of this remarkable rescue Freeth was not, as generally

U.S. Vol. Life Saving Corps of Venice Cal.

The Venice Volunteer Life Saving Corps in dress uniforms at the Tournament of Roses Parade in Pasadena, January 1, 1909. Captain Freeth stands at the far left. Courtesy Los Angeles County Lifeguard Trust Fund, Elayne Alexander Collection.

supposed, a member of the Venice lifeguard, and was under no obligation save that which would prompt any naturally brave man to risk his life for the humble fishermen."[13] Some evidence to support this statement comes from the Ocean Park Board of Trustees meeting on December 21, five days after the rescue. The trustees nominated Freeth to receive a congressional medal and suggested him as a good fit for an opening with the harbor police, an indication that he may have been unemployed.[14] At some point Freeth took this job, because the same board of trustees accepted his resignation little more than two months later, in early March.[15] The only incident reported about Freeth as a police officer involves his kicking three men out of Venice for begging on the main tourist thoroughfare, Windward Avenue.[16]

A couple of possibilities explain Freeth's sudden resignation and his move back to Redondo. A local editorial (likely from the *Venice Vanguard*) provides background information on his employment and points toward economic hardship:

> Some of the people on this beach are harboring an impression that George Freeth, the intrepid savior of those who get beyond their depth in the con-

tiguous briny, is on the city's pay-roll in recognition of services rendered some weeks ago, when he saved the lives of a colony of Jap fishermen.

The truth about George, however, is that he is not now working for the city or anybody else. 'Tis true the city placed George on its pay roll to the extent of $40 a month, with the understanding that he was to act as a night watchman for twelve hours at a stretch, but George didn't feel that he needed a job so badly as that and promptly declined the generous offer of the city dads. He was willing to risk his life to save one or more people from drowning and this without hope of remuneration, but when it came to hurrying himself into an untimely grave through loss of sleep in the interest of 2,700 people at the rate of $40 per month, George bucked.

Today George is doing nothin, that is, he is micawberizing. 'Tis true he is likely to receive a Carnegie medal, but a Carnegie medal isn't worth the material it is made of when it comes to the purchase of a meal ticket. George is also liable to an act of Congress in recognition of his bravery, but a whole carload of acts of Congress would not have half the effect upon a lunch-counter man as would a small piece of silver with the words, "One Dollar" stamped on it.

The other day Abbot Kinney met poor George upon the street and, patting him on the back, said: 'George, you are a brave boy, and I want you to continue to help uphold the flag of Venice, for Venice is your home,' but George couldn't get anything at a grocery store on a ship-load of that kind of heated air. The truth is, George has drawn just $12 from the Abbot Kinney Company since last fall.

As for the city dads, they would like very much to have it appear that they have done a great deal for George, yet the fact is the city dads are a measley [*sic*] pack of grand-stand players, in so far as recognition of the services of George Freeth is concerned.[17]

If we are to believe the editorial, Freeth had been laid off from his lifeguard job at the Venice bathhouse sometime after the summer season. The fifty dollars given to him on December 17 by the Japanese fishermen would have been something of a lifeline itself if Freeth hadn't worked in several months, allowing him perhaps to pay off bills and live a bit more comfortably. He did finally take the job as a harbor police officer but soon resigned. Perhaps, as the editorial explained, the long hours and low pay made him quit. At the very least, the editorial offers a glimpse into the kind of financial struggles that dogged Freeth for much of his life.

But it was also water polo season. Leslie Henry, president of the Southern California Swimming Association, was organizing a new league to be played under AAU rules.[18] Local reports indicated that the winning team would compete for the national championship at the world's fair in Seattle later that year.[19] Freeth was slotted for a hearing on January 13, 1909, in front of the local commission to follow up on their decision to suspend him the previous October, but for uknown reasons he missed that meeting. The following month Freeth was declared a professional, along with a local athlete named Folsom, and barred from amateur competition. The *Los Angeles Herald* reported, "Chairman Braden will send out notices to all members of the A.A.U. notifying them of the action of the committee and warning them against playing or competing against Folsom and Freeth according to the rules of the A.A.U."[20] Any amateur who knowingly competed against a professional would also have been considered a professional.

Commenting on Braden's decision, Freeth declared that "he did not think a man should be placed in the professional class just because he made his bread and butter by swimming."[21] Here we see the clear disadvantage that impoverished athletes like Freeth had when it came to competition: the AAU forced him to choose between using his talents to make a living or using them to compete as an amateur.

Within two weeks of his ban, Freeth had resigned from the harbor police, moved to Redondo, and began playing goalie for his old championship team, which beat the Los Angeles Athletic Club three to zero.[22] Maybe Freeth thought he could circumvent Braden's ruling simply by switching teams.

The Venice Life Savers were understandably upset. They argued that because Freeth had been barred from playing on the Venice team, he shouldn't be allowed to move down the coast and play for Redondo.[23] The mixed signals sent by the commission caused no end of problems that year in the water polo league, which never really launched because of the confusion between amateur and professional status among the players. Freeth himself stood at the center of the controversy. His Redondo team beat Bimini two to one on April 3, but he was not allowed to play in a follow-up game on April 9, because the registration committee had met two nights before and rejected his application for reinstatement. The committee had received evidence from a "Mr. Culver" of Santa Monica, who stated that Freeth had not only received pay for lifeguarding at Venice but had also accepted fifty dollars for saving the lives of Japanese fishermen.[24] One of the AAU's criteria for when an athlete becomes a professional is if he accepts "a purse of money."[25]

Freeth fought back. Four days later, on April 11, he compiled a list of thirty-eight athletes whom he identified as professionals, and their names were published in the Los Angeles newspapers. Many of them were men who had worked and competed alongside Freeth in Venice and Redondo, including Sherwood Kinney, Louis Hammel, Harvey Crum, and Frank Holborow. Freeth accused men of competing against professionals and accepting money for lifeguarding, swimming, diving, playing baseball, and even participating in a marathon dance contest. The *Los Angeles Herald* wrote, "Freeth claims that he has evidence of all those mentioned, and if he makes his proposition stick there will be a thinning of the ranks of coast athletes for some time to come."[26]

The list included a number of men whom Freeth probably considered close friends, who had known him since his arrival in Venice, which brings up the question of how they might have felt about Freeth as a whistle-blower. The *Los Angeles Times* reported, "Freeth did not bring the charges in a spirit of malice, but said that inasmuch as he had been refused amateur standing, the other men whom he had been playing with for several years should take the same medicine."[27] Freeth did not agree with the AAU's definition of amateurism, but if the organization was going to ban him because he'd worked in a bathhouse or accepted money for diving exhibitions, then anybody who earned money the same way should also be banned. When Freeth and twenty of the men he had accused finally squared off at the YMCA in downtown Los Angeles the following month, the *Times* reported that "although there were a good many personal remarks, everybody entered good-naturedly into the investigation and there was no quarreling."[28] Any antipathy seemed to be directed not against Freeth himself but against the registration committee and especially Chairman George Braden, whom Frank Holborow threatened to punch at a meeting the previous week for having canceled his amateur standing.[29]

It took about five weeks for Braden to resolve Freeth's charges, which were decided on a case-by-case basis. We can make a couple of observations about the process. First, we see Braden's committee—and Los Angeles amateur athletics in general—in the early stages of its existence trying to establish and enforce regulations passed down from the national organization in New York. Two weeks before Freeth's ban back in February, Sidney Peixotto, president of the Pacific Athletic Association (PAA), came to Los Angeles to help Southern California form its own separate branch of the AAU.[30] He oversaw the election of Charles Raitt as the president of the Southern California Commission of the PAA and Braden as chairman of the registration committee.

By all accounts Braden had been the most active booster of amateur athletics in Los Angeles since the city's initial interest in joining the AAU in December 1907. Many of those present at the meeting had expected Braden to be elected president. However, because the national body opposed branch presidents who were connected to athletic programs that competed in amateur events (Braden worked at Occidental College), Peixotto had recruited Charles Raitt, superintendent of the Los Angeles public playgrounds, to serve as president.

Many members were unhappy with Peixotto's perceived interference in Los Angeles affairs. Raitt initially accepted the position of president but then resigned in favor of Braden (at the same meeting when Freeth was banned) to prevent hard feelings, asserting that he had enough to do as superintendent of playgrounds without having to oversee the region's amateur athletics. But Braden refused to be considered for the position and supported Raitt's election. At a meeting on March 3, Raitt was pressed to reconsider. He finally acquiesced and offered to stay on as president.[31] Under the combined leadership of Raitt and Braden, Los Angeles was eventually admitted into the AAU as the Southern Pacific Association in November 1908.[32]

It's hard to know if the organizational controversy impacted Freeth's case specifically. But what we see are the growing pains of Los Angeles amateur athletics and the commission's concerted effort—given its trial status as a future member of the AAU—to crack down on anybody associated with professionalism. AAU president James E. Sullivan was cleaning house on the national level, and Los Angeles followed suit in Southern California.

The second observation concerns Freeth's unrelenting competitiveness. He continued to play water polo until early April, forcing the commission to clarify its position on amateur status. In a rather bizarre sequence of events—though what turned out to be fairly standard for Freeth—he left Los Angeles on May 2 to join a group of Hawaiians in San Francisco who were traveling home on the steamship *Mongolia*. His stated intentions were to spend a couple of months in the islands visiting family and recruiting Hawaiian swimmers to return with him and work as beach lifeguards and play in a professional water polo league.[33] Freeth had apparently accepted his fate with the AAU and was already planning new opportunities for himself.

The Hawaiians Freeth met in San Francisco couldn't have been more prestigious. They included Colonel Samuel Parker, a wealthy Hawaiian landowner who had given away George's younger sister Dorothy at her wedding three months before.[34] Parker's stepdaughter by his second marriage, Princess Kawānanakoa, was also there. She was the young widow of Prince David Kawānanakoa, the heir to the throne, who had passed away the year before in San Francisco.[35] Prince Jonah Kūhiō Kalaniana'ole and his wife also formed part of the group; they were traveling back from Washington, D.C., where "Prince Cupid," as he was known, served as the territorial representative.[36] Kūhiō was, of course, the brother of David Kawānanakoa—the two had surfed in California in 1885 while attending school in San Mateo—which made him the brother-in-law of the princess. The group had left Los Angeles in late April after Freeth had shown them around the area. They joined up with Freeth's sister Marjorie, who was returning to Hawai'i after having attended the College of Notre Dame in Belmont, California.[37] Princess Kawānanakoa was a year older than Freeth and had graduated from the same school as Marjorie in 1900.

The high-ranking group was a testament to the Freeths' prestigious social connections, and Freeth had apparently been offered round-trip tickets to Honolulu to travel with them. But after several days in San Francisco—visiting with Marjorie and the royal family—Freeth abruptly decided not to go to Hawai'i. Instead, he returned to Los Angeles and substantiated the charges against the men he'd accused of professionalism.[38] Jack London had described a Hawaiian surfer at Waikīkī as a "Mercury.... His heels are winged, and in them is the swiftness of the sea." We might say that Freeth—himself described by London as "a young god"—was highly mercurial.

What made him do an about-face and dive back into the amateur/professional fray? To Freeth's unrelenting competitiveness we must add an uncompromising sense of fairness. The *Los Angeles Times* reported on May 13 that he decided to return "to make good his charges."[39] The *Los Angeles Herald* reported on the same day that Freeth's charges had been dismissed at the last meeting on May 4 (Freeth had already left for San Francisco) "on the ground that no evidence was brought before the commission against the youngsters."[40] Although this last report was untrue—Holborow would be suspended and the fate of the others would depend on their testimony before the registration committee—Freeth must have felt there was a point of honor at stake. The matter was important enough for him to cancel his travel plans and leave his family and affluent friends at the last minute: the group sailed from San Francisco on May 6, and Freeth arrived back in Los Angeles on May 8. He had accused thirty-eight men of being professionals and then left town. He decided to finish what he'd started and make sure that the rules applied fairly to everyone. He attended the meeting on May 13 to personally voice his charges and present his evidence.

As we know, Freeth's friends and coworkers didn't seem to hold him personally responsible for bringing the charges but rather faulted the AAU for its lack of clarity. A group of swimmers and Life Savers in Venice had even given Freeth "a rousing benefit performance at the plunge" as a bon voyage the night before he left for San Francisco. "His friends followed him in almost every daredevil water stunt that he could devise," reported the *Los Angeles Herald*, "after which they gave three cheers for Freeth and bid him godspeed on his journey."[41] The scene sounds fairly festive, especially given Freeth's recent departure from Venice and his accusations of professionalism against many of the men. In response, they threw him a party. Clearly he was still much admired in the community. The fondness and respect they'd showed him on his twenty-fourth birthday, a few months after he'd arrived in California, were still present.

It's a tribute to Freeth's character that he showed up at that meeting and was willing to shoulder whatever response came his way from the crowd of men. Freeth had been a leader and role model since his arrival in Los Angeles. He had worked alongside so many young men and women, competing with them and training them in the plunges and the ocean. He had also gained much press through his surf exhibitions and heroic rescues. But in between all of these public displays was a man whose day-to-day investment in the younger generation—teaching them how to swim, to surf, and to save lives in the ocean—was creating the foundation of California beach culture.

The *Los Angeles Times* called Freeth's charges "the most sweeping ever made in the west" and predicted that if the charges held, "the local amateur swimming ranks will be almost wiped out." The paper added that nearly all of the players on the four teams in the water polo league were included on Freeth's list along with "nearly all the men who hold the amateur swimming records of the south."[42] Leslie Henry, who organized the swimming and water polo competitions in Los Angeles, had a clear interest in defending the athletes. He planned to hold the Pacific Coast Swimming Championships in July and bring the winners to the national championships held in Seattle during the world's fair. Henry stated that he believed "all of Freeth's charges will be refuted."[43]

Henry began defending the swimmers in the papers several weeks before the registration committee was due to meet. He took the blame for some of the men, claiming that they were ignorant of the rules. In other cases he claimed the men had not acted as lifeguards, as Freeth had asserted, but were either volunteers or "bath house attendants."[44] As far as competing against professionals, Henry argued that the races Freeth mentioned were only "practice games" in which the professionals were acting as instructors. Frank Holborow's case was of special interest to Henry, since Holborow was the Southern Californian champion in the 50- and 100-meter freestyle. Holborow had already been suspended once by the registration committee for working as a lifeguard, but they'd reinstated him "on the condition that he would not again violate the amateur rules."[45] But when the committee was presented with evidence of a recent letter Holborow had written applying for a lifeguard job, they expelled him.

Holborow later explained to the committee that he'd written the letter on behalf of F. K. McCarver, president of the Venice Chamber of Commerce, "who was desirous of getting particulars regarding the life guard positions at the various beaches."[46] The explanation seems concocted. Holborow's father had also appeared before the registration committee to explain that his son "was well fixed financially and did not need to enter the service for a livelihood."[47] Holborow seems to have been given special consideration because of his standing in the community. Although the registration committee admitted that he had violated the rules, "owing to lack of evidence they decided to allow him a card."[48] Holborow went on to win gold medals at the Pacific Coast Swimming Championships in July and traveled north to represent Southern California in the national championships.[49]

Holborow told the papers that if hadn't been reinstated by the registration committee, he was making plans to turn professional and tour the country competing against Freeth, which sounds like an idea that Freeth himself might have suggested. The *Los Angeles Times* stated, "Holborow is the only swimmer in the South who has beaten Freeth in the short distances, and Freeth is Holborow's superior in the middle and long distances."[50]

In the final decision concerning Freeth's charges, the committee "was disposed to [be] lenient toward the men."[51] Although the numbers reported by the papers don't strictly coincide, most of the athletes were acquitted due to lack of evidence. Up to nine were declared professionals—most of them had worked as lifeguards in Venice or Redondo—and a handful were temporarily suspended pending further investigation. Freeth withdrew his charges against two brothers who hadn't been paid as lifeguards. A number of the men didn't seem to care whether they were classed as amateurs or professionals. The highest-profile swimmers had gotten off cleanly—Frank Holborow and Marcus Lee, both of whom won the Pacific Coast Swimming Championships two months later. With some exceptions, the principal rule that seems to have been enforced from Freeth's charges was the 1908 AAU decision that banned all lifeguards from competing in amateur events.

The ruling stuck in Freeth's craw. The following summer, in an article titled "Freeth Throws Bomb into Amateur Ranks," he accused Marcus Lee of being paid for swimming exhibitions, and he accused several amateur water polo players of working as lifeguards.[52] In another article that summer—"Hot Charges from Freeth"—he challenged Braden's committee to revoke the amateur status of athletes who played for money on the side. He'd been banned from amateur sports for similar offenses, he argued, "and justice ought to prevail."[53]

One can imagine several possible contributing factors to Freeth's ban. Native Hawaiians had been described since the time of Captain James Cook as "almost amphibious." Several of Cook's mariners would write that water appeared to be the islanders' "natural element."[54] Freeth's friend and protégé, Ludy Langer, used similar language when he recalled that water was Freeth's "natural place."[55] Perhaps Freeth had been the victim of cultural bias: the sense that his race gave him a natural advantage over his Caucasian counterparts. His ban also could have been informed by economic discrimination: whereas Freeth absolutely depended on his lifeguard salary for his "bread and butter," Frank Holborow's father could argue that his son was "well fixed financially." Perhaps the registration committee was disposed to be lenient toward those who didn't need to work for a living. Freeth was also a newcomer to the community; he could not depend on the same support system as Holborow and Langer. It's true as well that Freeth pushed hard at whatever he did, and he made impulsive decisions. It may be that he simply rubbed certain people the wrong way.

Amid the confusion of the committee's rulings on professionals and amateurs, Freeth's water polo team in Redondo decided to disband. The team manager told the *Los Angeles Herald*, "Our players have lost all interest in the game on account of the uncertainty as to their amateur standing before the members of the A.A.U. If the cases could have been heard at once I am under the strong impression that the boys would put their shoulder to the wheel and stay with the plunge they are representing. The board has delayed its decision so many times the members have become impatient on the subject and the action at tonight's meeting was the result."[56] Because the AAU eventually declared that most of the players for Venice and Redondo were professionals, the two clubs decided to form the first professional water polo league in Southern California. Their inaugural game was set for July 1 in Redondo, at the grand opening of Henry Huntington's new bathhouse.

6

A Gold Life-Saving Medal

Embracing the civic boosterism of the times, the *Redondo Reflex* described Huntington's new four-story, $150,000 bathhouse as "the largest hot salt plunge in the world."[1] The three pools stretched 218 feet altogether. They consisted of a main tank, a baby pool, and a pool 9 feet deep for high diving and water polo games. Huntington hired the most experienced bathhouse manager in the area, Fred Killick, to be his superintendent. Killick had managed the Sutro Baths in San Francisco for ten years—Freeth would have seen him there—and had left his job as manager of Bimini Baths to work in Redondo Beach.

The pools were lined with pale green tiles, and electric fountains glowed with colored lights on either end of the main tank. There were slides and trapeze rings for the more adventurous patrons, and Jake Cox performed his fire dive on opening night from a platform built into the rafters under the skylights. The pools were advertised as holding up to two thousand people, but on one hot August day that year, twenty-six hundred bathers were recorded in the plunge.[2] Thousands of spectators could watch from the upper galleries in opera chairs or enjoy the sun parlor room, the smoking room, or the hairdressing and massage parlors. The Schoneman-Blanchard band came over from Huntington's pavilion on opening day and played in the balcony. Because numbers were important to the bathhouse's prestige, there were 62 tub baths, 1,350 dressing rooms, 10,000 bathing suits, and 20,000 towels offered to visitors. The bathhouse attendants were dressed in white. Freeth and two of his water polo players, Harvey Crum and Walter Barton, patrolled the tanks in what has become the standard lifeguard uniform: red bathing suits.

Henry Huntington's Redondo Beach Bath House, or "plunge." Courtesy Arthur C. Verge.

Seven thousand "incandescents" illuminated the Spanish Renaissance building inside and out. In honor of the coming Elks convention—such gatherings were the bread and butter of the beach resorts during the summer—all the interior lights glowed purple and white. The Redondo Chamber of Commerce reported in its annual review the following April that a hundred thousand people had visited the new bathhouse in its first nine months of operation.[3] The three buildings stretching south of Wharf Number 1—Huntington's pavilion, the Casino (a bar and dance hall), and the bathhouse— anchored Redondo's growing attractions for visitors along the waterfront.

The three wharves continued to ship industrial products into Los Angeles, as San Pedro was being developed as the area's main harbor, but Redondo followed the lead of other beach communities and invested in the future of tourism. Huntington's bathhouse was the latest addition to the "exotic and fantastical" architecture that decorated boardwalks in Venice, Long Beach, Ocean Park, and Santa Monica, all of them vying to draw "picnics" and conventions to their beaches.[4] C. H. Burnett, president of Redondo's Chamber of Commerce, stated in his year-end review for 1909 that Redondo had succeeded in hosting "more picnics than all of the other resorts put together" the summer before, a number he estimated to be about twenty thousand visitors.[5]

The Ocean Park Bath House north of Venice, part of the whimsical resort architecture that drew thousands of visitors out to the Santa Monica Bay. USC Digital Library. California Historical Society Collection.

Two months after the opening of the bathhouse, for example, Pasadena mayor Thomas Earley and approximately six thousand of his citizens arrived in Redondo by train for their sixth annual picnic day.[6] Beyond swimming, drinking, and dancing at the three waterfront establishments, Redondo offered the visitors turns on a human roulette wheel, tugboat excursions, and public space to compete in various foot races: 50-yard dashes for boys and girls under fourteen, for men over fifty, and for "fat men over 200 pounds." There was a women's egg race, a women's potato race, a pie-eating contest, and swim competitions in the new plunge, including a "novelty umbrella swimming race." To further entertain the visitors, Freeth and his water polo team played a match against the Pasadena YMCA and beat them three to zero.

Ever since Freeth had joined their team in mid-March, Redondo remained undefeated in amateur water polo. The club continued that streak when it turned professional and beat the Venice Life Savers three to one on the opening night of Huntington's bathhouse. Freeth received special mention for making "one of his sensational across-the-tank swims, partly under water, in order to get through the line" and score one of the goals.[7]

The defeat soured the Venice club on its decision to turn professional. The club rejoined the amateur ranks for a series of water polo games that Leslie Henry organized that summer to raise money to send Frank Holborow and Marcus Lee to Seattle for the national swimming championships. Sherwood Kinney had been declared an amateur in May, but he played on the professional team against Redondo on July 1. However, he was back in the pool as an amateur when Venice played Redondo again on July 31, so declarations of amateur and professional status were still a bit arbitrary. Redondo, now the sole professional team in the area, had been permitted to play the amateur teams of Venice and Los Angeles through "a special order" from the local commission of the AAU.[8] Freeth's team beat Venice three to zero at the end of July and raised $25 of the estimated $250 needed to send Holborow and Lee north.[9]

Given Redondo's dominance, the Los Angeles water polo clubs decided to create an all-star amateur team to challenge Freeth and his teammates in a follow-up game the first week of August. Freeth scored the only goal toward the end of the first half on what was described as a "rough and tumble play." "The fact that Freeth was goal keeper for the winning team," the reporter added, "and had to cross the plunge to score the point testifies to the bitterness of the contest. Freeth afterward stated that it was the toughest game he ever played in."[10]

Redondo played Venice again in September (Venice had decided once more to become professional) and beat them four to zero. Frank Holborow had finally given up his amateur status and declared himself a professional for the Venice team; he earned $2.60 from the gate receipts that night.[11] Holborow offered to race Freeth "for a purse and side bet of any amount up to $1000." Freeth responded gamely that he was willing to put up the money for any race over half a mile and added, "I don't get my feet wet until I have gone a mile."[12] One can hardly imagine Freeth scraping together $100 let alone $1,000. But competition and the possibility of a payday enticed him the following summer. He agreed to a professional bout against Holborow at Bimini Baths. Their race was the feature event of the evening, Holborow beating Freeth in the 75-yard freestyle by "a scant two feet."[13]

By early September 1909, Freeth's organized water polo days in Southern California effectively came to an end. As with his surfing, he simply had no competition. He had captained the Redondo team to the first league championship in June 1908. When he moved to Venice that same summer, he transformed the Life Savers from the worst team in the league to the most dominant. They won five straight games by a combined score of twenty-two to one. When Freeth moved back to Redondo in 1909, his team won six straight games by a combined score of eighteen to two. In the twenty-some games that Freeth played during those two years, his teams lost only one match. He managed eight shutouts in his last eleven games. And he could have counted on one hand the times an opposing team had scored against him during his career as a goalie.

Freeth continued to try to arrange games for Redondo. In December 1909 he sent out a "defy" through the papers, asking if any team in Southern California—amateur or professional—wanted to play in an exhibition.[14] It wasn't until the following May that Venice accepted the challenge, with foreseeable results: Redondo won two to zero. Not only did Freeth play goalie and manage another shutout, but he also scored both points for his team.[15]

Freeth would have to travel all the way to Waikīkī and recruit Duke Kahanamoku as a teammate to get his next water polo match.

∾

As interest waned in water polo circles outside of Redondo in the fall of 1909, Freeth found other outlets for his competitive drive. He and lifeguard Walter Barton won a two-man surfboat race that was part of the celebration to dedicate the new municipal pier in Santa Monica.[16] Several of Freeth's protégées—Seaweed Sister Dorothy Newkirk and the Sheffield sisters—also competed in swimming races that day. Freeth played quarterback on the newly established Redondo football team and was credited with helping them overcome the superior size of their opponent, the Asuza Athletic Club, with his "brilliant punt work" during their first game, which ended in a scoreless tie.[17] The Redondo players were game enough, but many of the men were inexperienced: the team held its daily drills on the beach with a water polo ball; for practice jerseys they wore bathing suits.[18] Freeth and two of his lifeguards also served as replacements on the local rugby team that winter, the Los Angeles Castaways, in games against Polytechnic High School and Stanford University.[19]

But lifesaving and general rescue work remained Freeth's priority. When he'd arrived in Redondo in March 1909, he wanted to establish a lifesaving station along the lines of the volunteer corps at Venice.[20] In October of that year, just before Freeth started practicing football on the beach, Venice withdrew from the U.S. Volunteer Life-Saving Corps and reverted to a purely local organization. They applied for a charter from the State of California and started raising funds to acquire new equipment, including a self-bailing surfboat. Venice also installed lifesaving gear—a red flag, a signal gong, a buoy, and six hundred feet of rope—along streets that fronted the beach so that anybody might initiate a rescue. Venice seemed to be interested in raising their standards to the level of the government-funded U.S. Life-Saving Service.[21]

When Freeth got wind of these changes, he was reported to have contacted the U.S. Volunteer Life-Saving Corps headquarters in New York to request an official transfer of the lifesaving station from Venice. Both his stature as captain in the Venice corps and the need for additional safety in Redondo due to the large shipping industry gave the local paper enough confidence to print the headline "Transfer of Volunteer U.S. Life Saving Station from Venice to this Port Almost Assured."[22]

It doesn't appear as if that transfer ever succeeded. But Redondo didn't seem to mind. They believed they had the best lifesaving crew on the coast. Ten days after the paper's announcement, the lifeguards saved the lives of two local fishermen whose boat had gotten caught in a riptide and overturned. The method of the rescue tells us a good deal about how Freeth was steadily transforming lifesaving techniques in Los Angeles.

The two fishermen, Joe Bisbee and Ralph Redeker, were trying to land their boat late one afternoon in a heavy sea north of Wharf Number 1. Lifeguard Walter Barton, although off duty, heard about the emergency and ran down to the shore from nearby Pacific Avenue. Apparently Barton wore his bathing suit under his street clothes when he wasn't working at the bathhouse. Like Superman, he stripped off his clothes as he ran and leaped into the surf. He knew that Redeker couldn't swim (both Redeker and Bisbee played on Redondo's football team), so Barton grabbed Redeker first and pulled him into shore. He dove back into the surf for Bisbee, who'd gotten carried out beyond the breakers and was yelling for help. By the time Barton reached him, Bisbee was unconscious. Barton managed to swim him back through the surf and land him on the beach.

Freeth and Harvey Crum, working at the bathhouse, had been alerted by telephone. They covered the four blocks in a minute and started working on Bisbee as Barton jumped back into the surf for a third time to recover the fishermen's boat.[23]

Bisbee and Redeker both survived due to the quick work of all three lifeguards. During Freeth's rescue of the Japanese fishermen the year before, he'd been the only one to swim through heavy surf to reach the men in trouble. Barton had immediately jumped into the surf to save the two fishermen. It's true that the Redondo lifeguards didn't own a rescue boat, but that circumstance suggests that Freeth's novel rescue technique back in 1908 had become the standard in Redondo by 1909. The lifeguards didn't need a boat to rescue fishermen or anybody else in trouble. Freeth had trained, encouraged, or shown them by example that swimming out through the surf, even in stormy conditions, was the most effective way to conduct rescues along the beaches of the Santa Monica Bay. Though Freeth had built up an impressive record in water polo, his record in lifeguarding was even better. In the eleven years he lived and worked in California, there are no records of anyone ever drowning on his watch.

$\sim$

Freeth received surprise visitors in the spring of 1910: Harry P. Wood and Lloyd Childs of the Hawaii Promotion Committee. The two had sailed from Honolulu to open a Hawaiian bazaar on the boardwalk at Atlantic City, New Jersey. Wood intended to bring Freeth along with him so that Freeth could give surfing and lifesaving exhibitions at the eastern resort. Along with various Hawaiian decorations and pineapples that would be sliced and served to the easterners, Wood was having surfboards and outrigger canoes shipped for the exhibitions. Wood had been working for several years to establish an office at Atlantic City to boost Hawaiian tourism.[24] He had already started agencies in Los Angeles, San Francisco, Chicago, New York, and Boston. Now he was finally getting his chance to get a foothold in New Jersey, and he wanted Freeth to be his star attraction to promote Hawai'i. It was a testament not only to the national reputation that Freeth had developed but also to the growing mark of the Hawaiian tourist industry.

Alexander Hume Ford had written a fanciful account for the *Honolulu Advertiser* of Freeth stowing away on a steamer and surfing at Atlantic City in his younger years—and being arrested for it—but there's no evidence that Freeth ever surfed there.[25] Freeth's own account mentioned that he "bathed" at Atlantic City but said nothing about surfing. But now Freeth had his chance, and the Hawaii Promotion Committee was going to pay his expenses. Wood arrived in Los Angeles in late March, and the *Los Angeles Herald* picked up the story with the headline "Hawaiian Swimmer May Accept Eastern Offer."[26]

We don't know why Freeth didn't go in the end, but he never did return to the East Coast. Perhaps Wood's offer wasn't generous enough to tempt Freeth to abandon the life he was building in Redondo. Freeth apparently had regular employment during this period: he was listed in the Redondo Beach Register of Voters working as an electrician and living at 109 Commercial Street near the bathhouse and Wharf Number 1. Freeth was a savvy promoter in many ways, but he never seemed that interested in working with the Hawaii Promotion Committee to boost the islands.

Although Wood was primarily interested in Hawaiian tourism, he seems to have had a sense that he was on a historic mission: introducing surfing to the East Coast of the United States. His goal was to have Freeth "show the people how we enjoy surfing sports." "The surf boards which he will use," Wood announced, "are the best that have ever been made here and no doubt some of the many sightseers will order some to use on the curling breakers of the Atlantic, after they have seen Freeth ride them."[27]

Though Wood could not induce Freeth to come along, he and Childs forged ahead. They opened their exhibit on the boardwalk in late May, but Wood later reported that the weather was terrible.[28] By late June the exhibit had attracted the attention of the New York press:

> The latest novelty on the Boardwalk is the Hawaiian exhibit, which makes it possible for Americans to learn something of the territory of which the executive power is vested in a governor appointed by the President of the United States. A huge surf board of heavy wood, on which the Hawaiian boys ride the long, swelling surf of the Hawaiian beach, will soon be tried on the Atlantic City beach, the Hawaiian boys, however, preferring to wait until our cold northern water had acquired Hawaiian temperature.[29]

The "Hawaiian boys" mentioned in the article seem to have been musicians who were part of the promotion committee's entertainment package. Wood had long since left before the surfing exhibition finally took place in early August, a time of year when ocean temperatures are closer to those at Waikīkī. A "wealthy young man from Honolulu," student Alvin D. Keech, ended up amusing the crowd for several hours riding waves on the board, doing "dare-devil stunts," and also giving lessons.[30] The paper reported that his board was made of koa and weighed about fifty pounds. Later reports indicate that Keech was still entertaining visitors at the end of August by surfing at night under a searchlight.[31] The performance of Keech and the Hawaiian musicians—reported to have ridden waves up the coast at Asbury Park—preceded Duke Kahanamoku's debut at Atlantic City by two years.[32]

Summer was Freeth's busiest season on the beaches, and he continued to lifeguard, give surfing and diving exhibitions, and compete in swimming races in front of the large crowds that inundated Redondo during the big holidays. Of note is his race against seventeen-year-old local boy Ludy Langer, who beat Freeth in the 440-yard freestyle on July 4. The races that day were supposed to be held in the ocean, but rough seas forced a change of venue to the Redondo plunge (probably a factor in Freeth's loss).[33] Langer, of course,

At Redondo Beach, c. 1910. Freeth's instruction of surfing to children taught them to understand ocean waves and currents, a foundation of knowledge crucial to the development of California beach culture. Courtesy Los Angeles County Lifeguard Trust Fund, Witt Family Collection.

would later become a multiple national champion in the 220, 440, and the mile. He won a silver medal in the 400-meter freestyle at the 1920 Olympics. Though Langer competed as an amateur throughout his career in the AAU, at the University of California at Berkeley, and as a member of the Hawaiian Hui Nalu, the *Redondo Reflex* reported that he earned five dollars for his win against Freeth. Freeth himself earned three dollars for second place. Langer was in the early stages of his career, but it's interesting that he would compete against a professional like Freeth and take money for the win, however small a purse. Ten days before the match, the *Los Angeles Times* had reported that Freeth was bringing charges against a number of Southern California water polo players and swimmers for being "profesh."[34] We see not only Freeth's ongoing ambivalence toward definitions of amateur and professional status but also his player/manager strategy of competing with those whom he coached and mentored.

Freeth had probably met Langer the year before when the Hawaiian moved back to Redondo in March 1909. Langer, then a sophomore at Redondo

Freeth with young Redondo swimmers, c. 1910. *Standing, left to right*: Ludy Langer, Freeth, unknown. *Seated, left to right*: Ray Kegeris, Cliff Bowes, Tommy Witt. Courtesy Redondo Beach Historical Museum.

Union High School, had competed in various races the same night that Freeth played in his inaugural water polo match as a member of the Redondo club.[35] Langer also competed in a race several months later on the opening day of Huntington's bathhouse.[36] In 1980, at the age of eighty-seven—blind and retired, still living in Los Angeles—Langer described Freeth's impact with dramatic recall: "I remember George. . . . You couldn't forget him. To see him in the water—well, I can't describe it. He had absolutely no fear of it. It was his natural place. There was something else about George—he was generous, generous to a fault. He coached I don't know how many of us—four of us went to the Olympics—and he never charged us a dime."[37]

One of the perks Freeth enjoyed in the bathhouses where he worked was the possibility of earning extra income by giving private swim lessons. He always seemed to be scraping by financially, and he left several jobs in California because of low pay. But when he spotted young talent with potential, his love for water sports and for developing their abilities outweighed all other considerations, even his own well-being.

~

The first indication that Freeth was going to receive a gold medal for his rescue of the Japanese fishermen back in 1908 was a letter written to him in July 1910 from Charles D. Hilles, assistant secretary of the U.S. Treasury.[38] The medal finally arrived in early August along with another letter of congratulations by Oliver M. Maxam, assistant general superintendent of the U.S. Life-Saving Service.[39] Newspapers of the time often mistakenly reported that Freeth had won the Congressional Gold Medal, the first recipient of which was George Washington. It may be that Freeth himself confused the two when he gave interviews. The medal he received was the Gold Life-Saving Medal of the U.S. Life-Saving Service, an agency under the secretary of the treasury. The medal was created to honor employees of the Life-Saving Service, but it was also awarded to civilians like Freeth "who endanger their lives by extreme and heroic daring."[40] Freeth's medal was one of seven gold medals awarded that year along with twenty-eight silver medals.

The medal had followed a rather tortuous path before landing on Freeth's doorstep. Six affidavits had been secured by E. B. Browne, treasurer of the Venice Chamber of Commerce, within a few months of Freeth's rescue. These had been forwarded to Frank P. Flint, U.S. senator from California, who'd passed them on to the secretary of the Treasury along with articles from the local papers that detailed Freeth's rescue. Because Flint hadn't included certificates by a U.S. government official vouching for the credibility of the witnesses—and ignored a letter from the Life-Saving Service agency asking him to provide them—Freeth's application sat in a drawer for the rest of 1909.

The *Redondo Breeze* reported that an anonymous "Redondo Beach party" lobbied local U.S. congressman James McLachlan, who wrote his own letter to the Treasury in January 1910 to inquire about the medal. McLachlan, incidentally, was one of the congressmen who'd visited Hawai'i in the spring of 1907 when Freeth was acting as the official lifeguard.[41] McLachlan secured the correct forms from assistant U.S. attorney Frank Stewart confirming that the six men who signed the affidavits were "reputable and credible citizens."[42] The Treasury Department referred Freeth's case to the Committee on Life-Saving Medals in mid-June, and the medal was finally awarded on June 24.

The medal itself was 99.9 percent pure gold, worth about $150 at the time (gold was approximately $20 an ounce in 1910, so the medal itself weighed between seven and eight ounces). It was round and hung from a pendant below the head of an eagle and a multicolored silk ribbon. Engraved on the front were three men in a boat carrying out a rescue; on the back stood a monument, topped by an eagle, on which was inscribed: "To George Freeth for heroically rescuing seven fishermen, December 16, 1908."[43] Freeth would later make "one of the most remarkable diving feats on the Pacific coast" to recover the medal. One afternoon he was stepping off a Standard Oil barge onto Wharf Number 1 at Redondo. The medal's fob, which he'd also been using to hang his watch on, caught on the gangplank, and his prized possession dropped straight between the wharf and the barge into forty feet of water. Freeth changed into his bathing suit and made two dives through heavy winter surf: the first to locate the medal, half buried in sand on the bottom; the second with the help of an iron weight to recover the medal.[44]

The same *Redondo Reflex* article that reported Freeth receiving his medal also mentioned, almost as an afterthought, "Freeth also pulled out a man and small boy who were overcome in the plunge Sunday [July 17], the latter due to the foolhardiness of the father, who threw the little fellow over the rail into the water beyond his depth."[45] Amazingly enough, the same edition (the *Reflex* was a weekly paper) reported Freeth saving the life of E. C. Butterfield in the plunge on July 18. Butterfield, an employee in the county tax collector's office, had swum across the large middle tank. He then tried swimming across the deepwater tank. He got about halfway across and "felt a conviction that he was not going to be able to make it and suddenly sank to the bottom."

The incident happened in the early afternoon between shifts. Freeth was coming on duty and had stopped to talk with a friend before changing into his bathing suit. A child alerted him to Butterfield, and Freeth dove into the pool fully clothed and found the man in a crouch on the bottom, unconscious. He pulled him up and worked on him, eventually bringing him around.

Newspapers generally credited Freeth with saving some fifty lives by December 1908, a number that grew closer to eighty by late 1910.[46] It's hard to pin down an exact number of people that Freeth saved, or helped to save, in his first three years in Los Angeles. If we count individual newspaper reports that provide concrete numbers and actual names, we arrive at a total of seventeen.[47] But since Freeth managed to rescue three people in two days, it might not be too much of a stretch to raise that number considerably with swimmers Freeth helped to save on the beach or in the plunges and for which a report was never made to the papers. Victims often refused to give their names to the press, perhaps out of embarrassment, so it's easy to imagine Freeth involved in numerous anonymous rescues.[48]

Freeth eventually received a second medal in May 1912. The New York–based U.S. Volunteer Life-Saving Corps awarded him a silver medal, which credited him, according to local newspaper reports, with having saved nine of the Japanese fishermen.[49] The medal was divided into three parts connected by small chain links. The first part was topped by an eagle with an inscription that read: "Presented to G. D. Freeth for Saving from Drowning." The second part held three men in a lifeboat. The third was a medallion surrounded by the insignia of the Volunteer Life-Saving Corps: a life buoy, two oars, and an anchor.

One of the more unusual outcomes of Freeth's famous rescue appeared in a report on the Yamato picnic in the summer of 1910. Several hundred employees and friends of the company, which ran a Japanese bazaar in downtown Los Angeles, traveled out to the beach in mid-August. They arrived at the Japanese fishing village above Port Los Angeles known as Maikura. But the grateful residents had changed its name to "Freeth" in honor of their Hawaiian rescuer.[50]

The *Hawaiian Gazette* picked up the story from the *Los Angeles Examiner* and provided more information the following year:

> Incense is burning in a hundred braziers before the huts of the Japanese fisher folk in Freeth tonight. And, around the grinning Shinto in the palm temple a hundred little Asiatics chant and salaam and place offerings of poi and rice—all for an American youth who risked his life to save eleven of the villagers during a storm at sea at Venice three years ago.
>
> George Freeth, a care-free, adventurous, broad-shouldered young fellow, who served on the Venice life-saving corps several years, is an unconscious recipient of the pagan devotion. Though the queer ceremony is all for him, he knows nothing of it.[51]

It's interesting that Freeth is referred to in the article as "an American youth" rather than the more typical appellation of "Hawaiian." Although he may have been unaware of any Shinto rituals performed in his honor, it seems likely that he would have seen, or at least heard about, the Los Angeles newspaper reports from August 1910 that mention the name change of the village.

Freeth closed out the summer of 1910 in typical fashion: diving, surfing, and entertaining crowds of visitors. In late August he gave a surfing exhibition with an English newspaper correspondent, Lyons Montgomery, who was described as "an expert swimmer and surf-board rider."[52] A few days later, Freeth joined Al Christie and Louis Hammel in a deep-sea diving exhibi-

Freeth proudly displaying his two medals, c. 1912: *left*, the U.S. Volunteer Life-Saving Corps Silver Medal; *right*, the U.S. Life-Saving Service Gold Life-Saving Medal. Courtesy Los Angeles County Lifeguard Trust Fund.

tion south of Wharf Number 1. Christie and Hammel had been working as divers in Redondo the previous week to recover lost anchors. On this day, a Sunday, they moved closer to the wharf and showed off their equipment—260 pounds of gear, including the helmet and lead weights—in about twenty feet of water. When someone on the wharf dared Freeth to dive down and shake Christie's hand, Freeth jumped in easily enough and came back up "holding Christie in both hands. In response to the applause from the crowd Freeth repeated the performance several times."[53]

Since the surf was up that day, Freeth followed the diving exhibition by grabbing his board and catching a few waves to entertain the crowd. It was probably one of his last surf sessions that summer. "The breakers were unusually high," reported the *Reflex*, "and the sight of Freeth meeting the wave,

Freeth and the wide-nose, narrow-tail style of surfboard that he used throughout his life to perform exhibitions. Courtesy Los Angeles County Lifeguard Trust Fund.

climbing to a standing position upon the board and riding the crest of the huge wave in, called forth loud applause from the people."[54] As the main tourist season rolled to a close, Freeth turned his sights toward Hawai'i. He must have missed his family. And with a gold medal awarded by the U.S. Treasury pinned to his chest, he could return home with a lot of pride, certainly in better circumstances than when he'd left. He'd been gone for over three years. In that time he had done what all true pioneers do in their fields: he transformed people's imaginations about what was possible. As a surfer, he'd shown Southern Californians that they could learn to ride waves at their own beaches. Contrary to the promotional writing of Alexander Hume Ford and others, Waikīkī was not the only place where one could stand on a surfboard.

In its annual New Year publication promoting Southern California— "more like a book of six handsome volumes than a newspaper"—the *Los Angeles Times* described one of the color illustrations in its 1911 issue that portrayed the "Sunshine, the Joy, the Business, the Prosperity of 'Happy Land.'" The illustration, etched from a photograph and titled *A Nymph of the Sunset Sea*, presented a "beautiful girl bather breaking through a first page of glittering breakers on a surf-board, with arms outstretched in greeting."[55] Not only had Freeth changed the mind-set of Angelenos when it came to new ways of enjoying the ocean, but his many exhibitions and enthusiasm for surfing had built the foundation for using the sport to market the health and prosperity of the region.

Later that summer the *Times* covered the rise of surfer girls at Venice. "Heretofore only the summer boys have attempted to quell these Neptunian bronks," writer Laurie Johnson waxed, "but now the dauntless young suffragettes of Kinneytown seem bound that no mere man shall best them at anything." The "commodore of the surf-board fleet"—young Frances Guihan—was pictured standing next to a surfboard that followed the exact outline of Freeth's boards. As the article detailed, "The best are made of redwood, they are from eight to ten feet long, two inches thick, and weigh from forty to fifty pounds. The front, or bow, is fully two feet wide, tapering to not more than eighteen inches at the rear—or stern."[56] Guihan, her Venetian surfing friends, and her surfboard were all a direct legacy of Freeth. Illustrations of female surfers also appeared on the cover of *Sunset*, the major promotional magazine of the West, in the summers of 1911 and 1912. The sport, associated with the exoticism of Hawaiians and the Hawaiian Islands since the time of Captain Cook, was now being prominently featured as the latest summer thrill practiced by stylish white people in Southern California. Surfing was not the first Hawaiian cultural practice to influence mainlanders—musicians and hula dancers had been strumming and swaying in the United States since the 1890s—but thanks to George Freeth, it was the first to be successfully transplanted and begin a life of its own, shaped by the people and forces of California.[57]

In ocean rescues, of course, Freeth had demonstrated time and again that lifeguards didn't need to rely on rowboats to do their jobs. They could use their strength as swimmers, and their knowledge of waves and currents, to

By 1911, largely because of Freeth, surfing was being used to promote California beaches as places of fun, leisure, and excitement. *Sunset*, July 1911: J. A. Cahill, "The Girl in the Surf."

Sunset, June 1912: Randal Borough, "A Summer Surf-boarder."

save people from drowning. Through resort advertisements and newspaper reports of the many rescues by Freeth and other lifeguards, Southern Californians were getting the message that not only were the beaches safer than ever but that their rolling waves—ever the cause of danger and drowning—could also be novel sources of fun and excitement. Even if Freeth never returned to the Southland, he had already planted seeds that would forever change California beach culture.

Return to the Islands

Freeth returned to Hawai'i a hero. The Honolulu press tracked him from Los Angeles to San Francisco, mentioning the gold medal and the gold watch that he carried with him. The papers covered his arrival in Honolulu with headlines like "Freeth Comes Home with Laurels for Life Saving."[1] He was declared "the champion life saver of the United States," who had saved scores of lives in California and been honored by the United States government. "He looks like an iron man," reported the *Honolulu Advertiser*, "who could puncture the ocean to any depth, and has a pair of shoulders that might bear up sunken ships."[2]

Before heading directly to Waikīkī with Louis Hammel and L. A. Quinn, who'd traveled with him from Los Angeles, Freeth went to see his family. They were more financially stable now. His youngest sister, Dorothy, had married banker William Campbell the year before, and the two were living east of downtown on Kinau Street with Maggie and Freeth's mother. Maggie had begun her second year of teaching at Honolulu Normal, an institution that trained elementary school teachers. Freeth's father had arrived in Redondo in late October—six weeks after George left—hoping to catch his son before the latter sailed for Honolulu. Freeth Senior had been traveling in the eastern U.S. for the preceding eight months. Perhaps he'd heard about George's gold medal. In an interesting parallel—possibly indicative of an estranged relationship between the two—Freeth Senior had also missed George when the latter traveled through San Francisco on his way to Los Angeles in the summer of 1907.[3] The last record of the two being together was just before George's fifteenth birthday when his father dropped him off in San Francisco before traveling back to Clipperton Island.

Friends and locals welcomed Freeth, Hammel, and Quinn at Waikīkī. They all grabbed surfboards, and Freeth was soon spotted "away out on the crest of the waves, rushing in headlong to the beach."[4] After having acclimated to California's cooler waters, he actually found the surf at Waikīkī too warm. He also described getting used to the strong riptides and fast-breaking surf at beaches that didn't have a protective reef like Waikīkī and where the waves broke much closer to shore. Recounting his first wipeouts in California, he told a reporter, "I wouldn't more than rise to the surface when another one would land on me hard, and I had to double up tight to avoid being pounded to pieces, but after a while I got used to their ways and could ride them without any trouble."[5] Freeth reveals here perhaps a relationship with the ocean that is more indicative of a Native Hawaiian perspective, referring to the waves as having the personality of a sentient being—getting used to "their ways." It's a stark contrast to western narratives of mastery and dominance promoted by mainland writers like Jack London.

After the surf session, Freeth challenged everyone to a swim race from the reef to the sand, which he won. Ever the competitor, he set to organizing a water polo match. A group of army soldiers at nearby Fort Shafter showed interest, so three days later Freeth rolled up to the base with a formidable team of Californian and Hawaiian players. They included Hammel, Archie Robertson (Freeth's cousin and captain of the swim team at the Diamond Head Athletic Club), "Knute" Cottrell (a founding member of the soon-to-be-famous Hui Nalu), and twenty-year-old Duke Kahanamoku.[6] Duke scored four goals in the game, Freeth scored twice, and his team swam to an easy victory. Despite calls in the local papers, no other team accepted their challenge to play that fall, so Freeth's team eventually disbanded for lack of rivals.

Freeth had also reconnected at Waikīkī with Alexander Hume Ford, who made public appeals to have Freeth hired as a lifeguard and surf instructor. "Now that we've got him back," Ford said, "we want to keep him here.... He is known all over the world now and so is surfriding known as the Hawaiian native sport and it would be a great stroke of promotion work."[7]

Unlike water polo, surfing had become more popular in Hawai'i since Freeth had left. Ford had spearheaded the founding of the Outrigger Canoe Club in May 1908, providing the first institutional support for surfing since the reign of King Kalākaua.[8] As Ford mentioned, one of his main goals was to use surfing to promote the Hawaiian Islands around the world. Since Freeth was recognized as the one who had done more than anyone else to popularize surfing in early twentieth-century Waikīkī and had taught Ford himself how to surf, it's not too much of a stretch to see the rise of the Outrigger Club as one of Freeth's important influences. The club not only provided a convenient place for members to store their heavy wooden boards, but it also organized surf contests to develop the athletic abilities of its young men and women.

One of the noticeable trends in surfing during Freeth's absence was the resurgence of the traditional style of riding waves, developed over centuries by Native Hawaiians. Unlike surf contests today, where sharp maneuvers score the highest points, traditional surfing in Hawai'i was a matter of staying upright on the largest wave and gliding all the way into shore. It's true that thirteen-year-old Harold Hustace had regained his title in December 1908 by performing Freeth-like stunts on his shorter board. But the winners of the other three contests between 1908 and 1910—Sam Wight and Kenneth Winter (Freeth's old travel partner), Vincent Genoves, and S. T. Short—all rode longer boards and developed statuesque poses that became the norm at Waikīkī. Iconic Hawaiian surfer Duke Kahanamoku embodied this style into the 1960s.[9]

One might ask if Duke competed in these contests. The Outrigger Canoe Club was initially formed as an amateur group, part of the resort community that wealthy *haole* were building in Waikīkī not only to attract well-heeled tourists but also to enjoy their own luxurious lifestyle.[10] Because Duke and other locals earned money by taking tourists out in canoes and on surfboards, their activities constituted professionalism, or semiprofessionalism, in the eyes of the club founders. The young Native Hawaiian men were thus prevented from vying for the surfing championship trophy—the Clark Cup—awarded at the annual regattas.[11] The lines drawn at the Outrigger Club between amateurs and professionals also encompassed race.[12] Ford himself emphasized this distinction by declaring that the club was "practically an organization for the haole (white person)" while Duke's contemporaneous Hui Nalu ("Club of the Waves") was "composed mostly of Hawaiian youths and part Hawaiians."[13] It's likely that Ford and others built in a sort of protectionism so that the children of white members would have only themselves to compete against. We cannot rule out marketing motives as well. After T. S. Short won the surf contest in June 1910—he'd been surfing for less than a year—the press enthused that people would learn that they too could become expert surfers in a short amount of time at Waikīkī. The *Evening Bulletin* reported, "It means much to Honolulu that a newcomer won the Clark cup for men."[14]

It's also worth noting that the Outrigger Club was ahead of its time by allowing young women to compete—at least young white women. Josephine Pratt took the Clark Cup in the girl's division in 1910, showing that "a girl can learn to ride the surf board as well as any boy."[15]

Freeth wasn't interested in Ford's idea of becoming a surf instructor at Waikīkī and boosting Hawaiian tourism. He had returned home to work as a diver at Pearl Harbor, helping to build the first dry dock for the expanding U.S. naval base. If he didn't get hired there, his plan was to return fairly quickly to California.[16] By November Freeth was indeed working as a diver for the Hawaiian Dredging Company and living on site at Watertown.[17]

The congressmen Freeth had accompanied on their tour three years earlier had seen much of modern and traditional Hawai'i, including the excitement of riding waves at Waikīkī. But the real focus for many of the visitors and locals alike was the development of Pearl Harbor. The United States had first acquired rights to use the area as part of the Reciprocity Treaty of 1887, thereby excluding other countries from establishing a military presence. Amid continued fears of foreign powers taking over the islands and becoming a threat to the United States—England and France both had a long history in Hawai'i, and the Japanese were the most numerous ethnic group—securing Pearl Harbor became a priority for maintaining national sovereignty and developing military supremacy in the Pacific.[18]

Once Congress appropriated funds in 1908 to transform Pearl Harbor from a coaling station into a naval base, the initial clearing of coral to deepen the channel for battleships had to be done by divers.[19] Walter F. Dillingham, president of the Hawaiian Dredging Company, hired Martin Lund and a Hawaiian named Olepau to dynamite the coral thirty feet down. The concussions would kill fish, which brought sharks into feed, so the job was fairly dangerous.[20] After Lund and Olepau had blasted the coral, dredgers followed behind them to scoop the debris out of the channel.

As the clearing of the coral bottom was completed, more divers were needed to help build a dry dock so that battleships could pull in for repairs and cleaning. At this stage of construction, Freeth's work would consist primarily of working in darkness 55 feet beneath the ocean surface. He and other divers built wooden cribs to hold the concrete, which was poured into the space using the "Tremie method": the bottom end of a cast-iron pipe was submerged into the fresh concrete as it poured, thus limiting contact with the ocean water and preventing any washout of the material.[21] The divers, wearing thick suits of canvas and rubber, and sporting copper helmets, guided the pipe and maintained it at the proper depth. The goal was to build a 20-foot foundation of concrete underneath the dry dock itself, which would extend 35 feet below sea level—deep enough to hold the navy's largest battleships.

Once the concrete foundation hardened within the crib, the divers would remove the wooden trusses and build the next compartment. Dry Dock Number One was originally intended to be 820 feet long and 110 feet wide.[22] Freeth had come to Honolulu to help complete this work.[23]

The project ran into problems from the very beginning. The particular mix of seawater at Pearl Harbor at first dissolved the concrete. Divers would apply patches, but the concrete continued to fracture. Divers also had to seal wooden sheet piling that leaked from the pressure of ocean water outside their cofferdam. Water also leaked into the dry dock from the porous coral below, so a system of wooden piles and stronger concrete was eventually devised to keep the dry dock "dry" and to maintain enough pressure on the coral bed to prevent it from buckling. The pile driving had to be done at night because the concussions were too severe for the divers working down there during the day. On the afternoon of February 17, 1913—after two years of construction—the dry dock suddenly imploded from hydrostatic pressure, and the whole project had to be redone. As part of the cleanup effort, Dillingham arranged through his Hawaiian foreman, David K. Richards, to have a Native *kahuna* or priestess bless the site to appease the shark goddess Ka'ahupahau, whom some said had caused the failure because no offerings had been made before the work started.[24] Dry Dock Number One was finally completed on August 21, 1919, ten years after Dillingham first began dredging.

The dry dock wasn't the only problem at the site. Watertown came by its name because the main water pipe—installed hastily, much of it aboveground—leaked so badly.[25] Dillingham had purchased an old hotel in downtown Honolulu and moved it to Watertown for his workers to live in. Freeth either lived in the hotel or set up at one of the surrounding camps segregated by race: white, Chinese, Japanese, or Hawaiian. The structure mirrored common plantation practices in Hawai'i that allowed white owners to pay different ethnic groups unequal wages through a "divide and conquer" strategy.[26] We don't know what wage Freeth earned, but his diving work must have kept him busy. Besides the water polo match in October 1910, local papers make no reference to him playing sports until the AAU swim meet on August 12, 1911. This is a rare gap in team competition for Freeth, especially given his history as one of Honolulu's top athletes.

One picture of him does appear in the *Evening Bulletin* in February 1911. He'd gone down to Waialae Park to watch a baseball game and track meet held by Chinese athletes to celebrate their New Year holiday. He's pictured in a white suit and tie, a big smile on his face. His hands are pushed into his pockets, a gesture that holds open the bottom of his coat just wide enough so that readers can see the gold medal hanging off his belt. The caption below the picture reads in part, "George is justly proud of his medal and wears it most of the time. He says he is back in Honolulu to stay."[27]

~

As with his arrival in Los Angeles, Freeth's move back to Hawai'i coincided with the islands becoming an official chapter of the AAU. Rumblings had begun in March 1910 while Sidney Peixotto, president of the Pacific Athletic Association, was visiting Honolulu with San Francisco's Columbia Park Boys Club.[28] Peixotto indicated that AAU president James E. Sullivan had taken an interest in Hawaiian sports and favored giving the islands their own chapter rather than maintaining them under Peixotto's jurisdiction.[29] The main reason behind giving Hawai'i its autonomy—something Los Angeles had not initially earned—was the territory's great distance from Peixotto's base in San Francisco.[30]

Following the national trend of working to clean up amateur sports, the sporting editor at the *Honolulu Advertiser* declared, "Up to the present time local athletes have been outlaws from necessity and if they don't grasp the opportunity now presented they will be considered outlaws from choice."[31] Hawaiian athletes had been given "outlaw" status partly because of their geographical isolation in the middle of the Pacific. But they were also barred from competing against their mainland counterparts because the AAU didn't allow members to compete against nonmembers. In addition to normalizing the status of Hawaiian athletes, an AAU chapter would help codify the seasons for individual sports. Due to the islands' temperate weather, outdoor sports could be played year-round. The situation led Honolulu attorney and AAU point man Lorrin Andrews to comment that athletics were "all mixed up here. . . . They have no regular seasons for anything."[32]

Meetings began to take place in early spring of 1910, and local organizations were invited to apply for membership. By the time the Hawaiian chapter was officially notified in December that it had been accepted into the AAU, some twenty-five local clubs had joined, including the two longtime powerhouses in aquatic sports: Freeth's Healanis and their archrival, the Myrtles. The Outrigger Club had also joined, and their secretary, Guy H. Tuttle, was elected the first president of the Hawaiian Association of the AAU in January 1911. Their first official tournament took place eight months later in Honolulu Harbor, setting the stage for Freeth's stellar yet bizarre return to amateur sports.

~

Although Waikīkī had become the center of the surfing world by the summer of 1911, and the Outrigger Club was steadily expanding its sports programs, the hub of Honolulu's aquatic competition remained Honolulu Harbor.[33] The boat slips offered long stretches of relatively calm water, and thousands of spectators could stand close to the action on the surrounding piers. The two most important rowing clubs at the time, the Healanis and the Myrtles, both had their clubhouses there, and they'd vied with each other for local honors in the annual regattas since the early 1890s.

Freeth had been associated with the Healanis off and on since 1901, so it was natural for him to compete on their team in the diving competition held at the Alakea Street slip.[34] Understandably, his accomplishments that day have been overshadowed by the extraordinary feats of the young Duke Kahanamoku. The world records Duke broke in the 50- and 100-yard freestyle, and the subsequent controversy from mainland officials questioning the official times and distances in the harbor—all of it served to keep Freeth's performance in the background. Very few had imagined that Duke would leap onto the world stage as dramatically as he did on August 12, 1911.

And practically no one was surprised when Freeth won his event in fancy diving. He'd been a champion diver in the islands, and people remembered his gymnastic grace. He was the last competitor to enter, officially registering the day before the meet.[35] Locals might have done a double-take when they saw his name on the program. Three weeks earlier, the *Honolulu Advertiser* had announced, "Freeth Is Out." The paper explained that his amateur card had been canceled while he was in California, so he wouldn't be allowed to compete.

But four days before the contest, his name suddenly appeared in the paper as a member of the Healanis. The next day, the *Hawaiian Star* published this report:

> It will be decided today whether George Freeth will be allowed to compete in the fancy dive or not. It appears that he applied for registration with the A.A.U. but failed to answer two very important questions on the application form.
>
> One of these was when he last competed at a meeting held under the auspices of the A.A.U., and the other was if he has ever applied for registration with the A.A.U. before?[36]

John Soper, chairman of the registration committee and a member of the Myrtles, questioned Freeth about the missing responses. Freeth told him that "he had never belonged to the A.A.U. or made previous application for registration therein."[37] Satisfied with the answers, Soper gave Freeth his amateur card.

Freeth's answer to the first question was true. But that was because George Braden and his committee in Los Angeles had rejected Freeth's application back in January 1908 and ultimately classed him as a professional in February 1909. The rationale for both decisions was based on Freeth's work as a salaried lifeguard.

If the wording in the *Hawaiian Star* is correct, what drove Freeth to deny his previous application in Los Angeles? We don't know. Since this was the first AAU meet in Honolulu, issues of professional and amateur status were likely still being hammered out. After Freeth's various battles with the AAU in Los Angeles, one can imagine him negotiating that process very effectively. There were athletes competing in the tournament who, like Freeth, had earned money working as swimming, canoeing, and surfing instructors—Duke Kahanamoku, for one. Why should Freeth's status be treated any differently from theirs?

It's also true that Freeth had not been making his living as a lifeguard during the past year, so perhaps he felt justified in his application for amateur status. There were provisions that allowed a banned competitor to return to competition, but an official reinstatement usually only happened after two years of abstaining from all professional activities.[38]

It's true as well that Freeth's ban was in a different sport. He'd made his initial application in 1908 as a swimmer, and his ban the following year came while he was playing water polo. He'd never applied to the AAU to enter a diving competition. As we saw with Braden's decisions concerning the amateur status of Frank Holborow and others, the national organization gave chairmen of local registration committees a great deal of leeway to make decisions on a case-by-case basis. Soper ultimately had the authority to decide Freeth's status, and he allowed him to compete.

What were Freeth's motivations to compete again after working as a diver at Pearl Harbor for most of the year? Among the many possibilities, the chance to appear in the 1912 Olympics looms large. He'd been blocked from trying out in 1908. The diving tryouts for Stockholm were right around the corner—in March 1912—so perhaps Freeth thought his chances of success might improve if he won the amateur diving competition in Hawai'i. American platform diver George Sheldon had won gold in the 1904 Olympics in Saint Louis, so Freeth had an inspiration if he needed one. At the very least, Freeth's victory that day was a testament to his superb talent: without any dedicated practice in the ten months leading up to the competition, Freeth showed up at Honolulu Harbor, rattled off his five regulation dives and three "special" dives, and came out on top.[39]

The upstart Hui Nalu carried off team honors at the tournament, beating both the Healanis and the Myrtles. The Outrigger Club soon found itself on the defensive after Duke's incredible showing, trying to explain why they hadn't accepted him as a member. In a smokescreen that relied on bureaucratic distinctions, a writer for the club (probably Alexander Hume Ford) argued that Duke wasn't a member of the Outrigger Club for a very simple reason: he'd never applied for membership. The writer denied barring Duke because the young Hawaiian had earned money by giving surf lessons to tourists: a club rule stipulated that anyone who made a living out of surfing could not vote or hold office, but "it was expressly stated that he was not called a professional."[40] In any case, the writer continued, Duke was "in the world's championship class and does not care to contest with a swarm of beginners in surfing to have his name engraved on a cup." Even if Duke had been a member of the Outrigger, the argument went, he wouldn't have wanted to compete for the Clark Cup anyway. Besides, the writer concluded, Duke didn't really belong to either the Outrigger Club or Hui Nalu: "Duke Kahanamoku belongs to Hawaii, and all Hawaii is proud of him."

Oscar Brenton, writer of the column "Honolulu News Letter" for the *Maui News*, wasn't fooled by the hairsplitting. He responded that Duke and other young locals had formed Hui Nalu because they were "not too much in love with Ford" after he'd barred them from competing for the Clark Cup.[41] In a later recollection, Hui Nalu founder Knute Cottrell seems to specify a racist element in the young Hawaiians' decision to form the new club: "I heard something said by one of the fellows at the Outrigger Canoe Club at that time which disgusted us quite a bit, so Duke, myself and Kenneth Winter, who was captain of the Club at that time, went over to the Moana Hotel and the three of us started Hui Nalu Club."[42] It would not be until the spring of 1917, as the United States was entering World War I, that Duke became an official member of the Outrigger.

Duke's success in August 1911 would lead, the following year, to his Olympic gold medal in the 100-meter freestyle at Stockholm, an event that brought the kind of attention to the islands that locals hadn't experienced since Annexation Day. For boosters like Alexander Hume Ford and H. P. Wood of the Hawaii Promotion Committee, Duke's triumph represented a golden opportunity to market the benefits of Honolulu and especially Duke's birthplace, Waikīkī. Duke's tremendous talent and his beautiful Native Hawaiian features created wild enthusiasm wherever he went for swimming and surfing—both key components to the development of beach culture on the mainland and in places like Australia and New Zealand. But Duke wouldn't have a sustained impact on California beach culture until the 1920s, when he moved to Los Angeles to pursue a career in swimming and acting.

We don't hear about Freeth again until early November, when the Honolulu papers reported that he'd left for California to get his old job back as a lifeguard in Venice. Freeth departed on the steamer *William F. Herrin* and arrived in Gaviota on November 11. The following month we find him settled not in Venice but at the bathhouse in Redondo. And—no surprise—he's captain of the newly organized Redondo Beach water polo team and arranging a match against a group of all-stars from Ocean Park.[43] He also had his eye on the Olympic tryouts—if not as a diver (his amateur status was shaky in California), then as the manager for his friend and Hui Nalu star Duke Kahanamoku.

8

From Competitor
to Mentor

Freeth had the idea in the spring of 1909—in the midst of his woes with the AAU—of traveling to Hawai'i and recruiting the top swimmers to work as lifeguards in Redondo and play on a professional water polo team. He had a lot of friends among the Healanis and Myrtles, and of course the local boys at Waikīkī. This crew would form the nucleus of a professional water polo league in Southern California and help Freeth accomplish two goals: to raise the level of play in the sport and to avoid any further interference from the AAU.[1] Freeth, as we know, never made that trip. He chose rather to return to Los Angeles from San Francisco and back up his charges of professionalism against area athletes.

But after the sensational success of Duke Kahanamoku and Vincent Genoves at the AAU meet in August 1911 (Genoves had won freestyle events in the 220, 440, and the mile), Freeth revisited the idea. He offered to work as the Hawaiians' manager and spread the news of Duke's world records. His plan was to enter them in the Southern California Swimming Championships and help secure a spot for the two men in the Olympic tryouts.

Once news spread that Freeth had taken on the role of Duke's "unofficial manager," however, Honolulu's power brokers moved quickly to block that possibility.[2] They saw Duke's Olympic bid as a potential advertising boon for the islands, one that needed careful handling. Duke required a coach who not only understood the "wiles and wrinkles" of top competition but who also would ensure that the young swimmer didn't violate his amateur status. "Freeth undoubtedly means well by offering to take Duke under his wing," stated H. M. Ayres, editor at the *Hawaiian Star*, "but it is a safe bet that [Duke] would be classed as a professional within a month after his arrival in California. Freeth sees a chance for the native to make a nice piece of money in California aquatics and incidentally an opportunity to profit himself through intelligent exploitation of Duke."[3] Ayres concluded that if Duke were to have any chance of competing in Stockholm, he needed to leave Hawai'i "under proper auspices." The writer suggested that William T. Rawlins—"an old Yale man"—would be the perfect candidate for the coaching position.[4] The Ivy League schools had long been a training ground for elite young *haole* men in the islands, a tradition that stretched back to the original missionaries who sent their male children back to New England for their continuing education. Walter F. Dillingham, for example—whose company Freeth worked for at Pearl Harbor, attended Harvard; his brother-in-law, Walter F. Frear, who attended Yale, was the territorial governor (1907–1913). Hawai'i was a de facto oligarchy at this time, ruled by a small group of businessmen who shared conservative Protestant values and worked in unison to maintain their influence in all aspects of society. The founder of the *Hawaiian Star*, Joseph Ballard Atherton (born in Boston, Massachusetts), was a member of the safety committee that had overthrown the Hawaiian monarchy in 1893, and his newspaper became the official voice of the new republic. Atherton had also been a president of Castle & Cooke, one of the so-called Big Five companies that formed the nexus of the oligarchy.

So Freeth was up against powerful adversaries. The next day Duke himself gave an interview to the *Hawaiian Star* and supported the choice of Rawlins, who'd been his friend and early supporter. "I don't want to be a professional," Duke said, "and whatever [Rawlins] tells me I will stick to and have nothing to do with those other fellows."[5]

"Those other fellows," of course, meant George Freeth. If anybody was going to profit from intelligent exploitation of Duke, it was going to be the business leaders of Honolulu, not an enterprising lifeguard. Freeth certainly could have guided Duke through the streets and back alleys of amateur competition, but news coverage of his disputes with the AAU in Los Angeles and his hopes of "swelling the professional ranks" had tainted his reputation back in Honolulu.[6] Duke's world-record times in the 50- and 100-yard freestyle had already been disputed by the mainland swimming community. The Honolulu elite didn't want to take any chances that Freeth's troubles might ruin their opportunity to develop a bona fide star for the advertisement of Hawai'i.[7]

As Kahanamoku and Genoves traveled to Pittsburgh for the first round of Olympic tryouts, and then to Chicago for the second round, Freeth pushed to reach Stockholm himself as a diver. He entered the state swimming championships held at the Los Angeles Athletic Club in mid-March.[8] But he'd had an accident while practicing his dives in the Redondo plunge. He wrote to his cousin, Archie Robertson, "I hope my neck will get well pretty soon, because I want to try out for the high and fancy diving for the Olympic team. I was doing a cut-away one and one-half, and hit bottom. It was good-night for me for some time after."[9] The cut-away corkscrew was one of three speciality dives that Freeth had chosen for his routine, beyond the five regulation dives: front dive, front jackknife, back jackknife, straight back dive, and the one and one-half.

Freeth recovered well enough to compete at the state championships in March. But on the night of the contest, the judges suddenly barred him.[10] Though Freeth seemed to take it well—he entertained the crowd in a game of "push-ball" (a milder version of water polo) and put on a diving exhibition—he didn't give up.[11] He found an ally in Wallace Robb, secretary of the local AAU chapter. Robb told Freeth after the contest that he shouldn't have been barred. He offered to write to James E. Sullivan, president of the AAU, and explain the situation. After all, Freeth had won the same competition in Hawai'i, an event sanctioned by the AAU. Robb probably saw in Freeth the same possibility that Honolulu imagined for Duke: the chance that Olympic stardom would bring acclaim to the region. He told Freeth that he'd try to have him entered in the fancy diving event at the Pacific Coast Swimming Championships to be held the following month on Freeth's home turf, the Redondo Bath House.[12]

It would have been a fabulous opportunity for Freeth to display his skills, but his name doesn't appear on the program as a competitor. He was in fact working as a lifeguard at the bathhouse, and Sullivan's rules were clear. Robb wasn't able to get the home office to sanction Freeth's entry. Once again, Freeth was sidelined from his Olympic dreams.

The AAU national committee ended up choosing two divers to compete in Stockholm: George Gaidzick, who'd won bronze in the 1908 Olympics in the three-meter springboard, and Arthur McAleenan of the New York Athletic Club. Neither man advanced to the finals in the high dive. It must have been a consolation to Freeth that his friend Duke Kahanamoku, who ended up winning gold in the 100-meter freestyle, asserted during a visit to Los Angeles after the Olympics, "'I believe George Freeth, our well-known diver, could have beaten all those at Stockholm.'"[13]

～

Freeth continued to compete in the odd swimming and diving contest—especially when Duke came to town—and to put on diving and surfing exhibitions. But his emphasis shifted strongly in the spring of 1912. He threw his energy into helping his young protégés achieve the national and international acclaim that had eluded him as a competitor. His efforts were especially notable because he coached women to championship titles even when the AAU wouldn't admit them as members. Abbie Victoria "Dolly" Mings was Freeth's first female star. At seventeen she'd come in third place in the mile at the Pacific Coast Swimming Championships in September 1911. Once Freeth arrived back from Hawai'i and started working with her, she quickly vaulted to prominence in the shorter distances. She won the 50-yard freestyle at the Olympic tryouts in March and April that Freeth had been barred from. Had American women been able to compete in the Olympics, she certainly could have earned a spot. Two of Freeth's other students, Ludy Langer (age nineteen) and Ray Kegeris (age ten), won the 880 and juvenile diving events, respectively.[14] In August Freeth inaugurated the open-ocean swimming championship in nearby Ocean Park. Langer and Mings (wearing a men's bathing suit) won the two events.[15] Mings completed her season in September by winning the 100-yard freestyle in the Southern California Swimming Championships. Redondo had hosted the event, and the local team also carried off honors in men's diving (Cliff Bowes) and boys' diving ("Jerry" Witt).

Later in September Freeth entered Langer and Bowes in the Pacific Coast Swimming Championships, held at the Olympic Club in San Francisco. Several days before the event, however, the organizers sent a telegram to Leslie Henry indicating that Langer and Bowes would not be allowed to compete. This surprised Henry, since the San Francisco swimmers had competed—all expenses paid—in the same championships in Redondo the previous year. Rumors circulated in the Southland that members of the Olympic Club were afraid of losing against the two young stars.

Freeth decided to go anyway. He put Langer and Bowes on a night train, and they all went up to San Francisco at their own expense. Duke was there, returning from his Olympic success in Stockholm. He gave an exhibition for the San Franciscans, which included a lap against Freeth in the Olympic Club tank. Duke won easily. Freeth, Bowes, and Langer then put on an exhibition themselves, diving and swimming before the large crowds. Perhaps Freeth's connections with Duke and the exhibition softened the northerners' resolve. When race time came on Friday night, Langer and Bowes put on another show. Langer won the 880-yard freestyle, establishing a new Pacific Coast record. And Bowes took first place in the diving competition.[16]

Duke returned to San Francisco the following year for the Pacific Coast Swimming Championships, held at Freeth's old haunts—the Sutro Baths— over the July Fourth weekend. Though Dolly Mings had gotten married to a Santa Ana man named Sydney Droughbough, and Langer was now a student at the University of California at Berkeley, they both continued to train with Freeth. Mings's routine had begun in May with a two-mile run every morning up the beach.[17] Freeth's method of cross-training for his young swimmers—running, diving, and surfing—built their strength and endurance, which gave them an edge in competition. Langer set a new Pacific Coast record in the 880 and came in second to Duke in the 440. It was no surprise that Duke won both the 50- and 100-yard freestyle for Hui Nalu. Cliff Bowes won the high diving event, and Dolly Mings defended her title as the fastest woman swimmer on the Pacific Coast by setting a new record in the 50-yard freestyle. Because women's events were not officially sanctioned by the AAU—President Sullivan thought women had "little or no place in athletics"—Mings swam her events before and after the men's competition.[18]

In August 1913 the Redondo crew dominated the Southern California Swimming Championships, held at the Redondo Bath House. Langer won three events, Mings won two, and Redondo captured the team title by beating out Ocean Park, the Los Angeles Athletic Club, and the San Francisco YMCA.[19] As he'd done with water polo years before, Freeth established Redondo Beach as the top swim team in Southern California. The bathhouse created a glass case to display the collection of medals, silver cups, and pennants won by the team that season.[20]

To show their appreciation to Freeth for guiding them to regional and state championships, several of the swimmers and representatives of the bathhouse held a banquet for him at the Casino on the waterfront. After dinner they presented him with the McClain Cup that he'd helped them win at the Sutro Baths.[21] His response was reminiscent of the time his Venice teammates had given him a gold watch for his twenty-fourth birthday: he was surprised and touched by their thoughtfulness and offered them simple thanks.[22] Freeth was almost thirty years old now, and though his life was largely itinerant, communities adopted him quickly because he not only dedicated himself to keeping everyone safe in the water, but he also invested himself in the success and potential of their young people. In appreciation for all of his efforts, one citizen wrote a rousing tribute in the local paper for his birthday that year:

> Many visitors at the beach have wished for an opportunity to express appreciation of the work of Mr. Freeth at the bath house.
> We have been entertained by his skill, rejoiced by his chivalry, inspired by his courage and awed by his sublime heroism.
> Redondo Beach is fortunate to have in her midst a teacher of aquatic sports who is so perfectly the exponent of that which he teaches.
> Long may he live—this large souled, fine grained, noble hearted Freeth.[23]

The comment "rejoiced by his chivalry" catches our eye, as if the writer were a woman. If so, it's a quick peek into how they might have viewed him in his day-to-day interactions as a lifeguard and a swimming and diving instructor: his gallant and courteous behavior. Such tributes imply, at heart, a generous and gentle nature.

~

During this same period Freeth intensified his development of surfing in Los Angeles. There were two hotbeds of surfing in the world at this time: Waikīkī and Santa Monica Bay. Both of them had George Freeth in common. Freeth had reinvigorated surfing in the islands by reminding Native Hawaiians and *haole* alike what could be done on a surfboard. He gave public exhibitions and lessons to promoters like Alexander Hume Ford, who went on to found the Outrigger Canoe Club. With Freeth's knowledge Jack London had added cachet to the sport and encouraged his western readers: "Get in and wrestle with the sea; wing your heels with the skill and power that reside in you; bit the sea's breakers, master them, and ride upon their backs as a king should."[24] Freeth brought a less combative version of this message to Southern California and used surfing to promote himself and whatever product his employers were trying to market: resorts, bathhouses, even railroad excursions. In late January 1912, Freeth put on a surfing exhibition in the chilly winter surf at Redondo Beach for locals and several hundred excursionists on the "Balloon Route"—a one-dollar, round-trip trolley ride from downtown Los Angeles through Hollywood, Santa Monica, Playa Del Rey, and Redondo Beach. "The surf was running good," reported the *Redondo Reflex*, "and Freeth took his surf-board out and took a number of spectacular rides on the huge breakers."[25] Ever since landing in Redondo in December 1907 and giving a surf exhibition, Freeth had shown that riding waves could be a year-round sport in California, not simply a summer recreation.

The *Los Angeles Times* announced May 5 as the opening of the 1912 surf-bathing season and predicted that "the surf-board will be as popular as ever this year and some of the first raters will use the big scoot-board which is larger and can accommodate two persons."[26] The *Times* didn't specify Freeth as the shaper, but it's likely he modified his eight-footers into the longer tandem boards that he'd seen at Waikīkī the year before. Freeth later turned this model into the first surfboard to be commercially marketed: a forty-pounder shaped from Oregon pine, the wood soaked in oil to delay waterlogging. The sporting goods store Dyas-Cline put the board on display in its downtown Los Angeles location and had already received several orders by the time the announcement came out.[27]

Surfing gained enough popularity in the summer of 1912 for Frank Holborow—Freeth's former water polo teammate and now head swimming instructor at the Los Angeles Athletic Club—to write an article for the the *Los Angeles Times* on safety precautions to take in the surf. Holborow instructed beginners how to prevent their boards from being knocked away by the waves and injuring other bathers. He also described how riders should lie on a board so that they themselves didn't get hurt.[28] Holborow had lifeguarded with Freeth in Venice and represented the first generation of Southern California surfers who were already spreading the knowledge that Freeth had given them.

That summer was a banner year for surfing in Los Angeles. Holborow's club swimmers were surfing and setting the swimwear style in Venice—the new colors were solid blue or gray, with the elite swimmers donning silk bathing suits. Meanwhile Freeth was making headlines in Redondo for teaching Dolly Mings and other young women how to surf. An article in the *Los Angeles Times* published a sketch of Freeth standing on a board and presented his detailed lessons that surfers still use today: don't let the board get between you and the wave, and never let your surfboard go—it might harm another surfer or swimmer. Freeth's great influence on the spread of surfing in Southern California is captured by the reporter's words: "When you hear Freeth describe how to ride a surf board you feel as though you could do it."[29] One of Freeth's contributions to surfing in California was to democratize the sport. He made people believe that anybody could learn how to ride waves at their own beach, and he took the time to show them how to do it.

Freeth's work with children was especially important. Young people generally have more freedom than adults to spend their weekends and summers at the beach, and they learn more quickly because they place fewer limitations on themselves. Freeth calmed any fears they may have inherited about the ocean from a previous generation and gave these young Californians a new connection to nature that helped form their own identities and that of the region. Kevin Starr has observed in his broad history of the state, *Americans and the California Dream: 1850–1915*, that noteworthy Californians of the period "put forward their love of the outdoors as the key component in the structure of their regionalism."[30] To John Muir's Yosemite, Jack London's Sonoma Valley, and Mary Austin's desert landscape, among others, we can add George Freeth's Southland beaches. Freeth may have been Hawaiian, but California became his adopted home. It would be another two decades before a new generation of Californians wedded regional identity to beach culture—on the shores of Palos Verdes, San Onofre, and Malibu—but that engagement began years before on redwood surfboards that George Freeth built.

Freeth made sure that young women always felt at home on the beaches. They played and trained on the same heavy planks as the young men. "No one seems content merely to jump the breakers," the *Times* article reported about the Redondo girls in the summer of 1912, "or lounge on the sand in a stunning bathing suit." Under Freeth's guidance, nascent California beach culture had the opportunity to develop surfing along the traditional Hawaiian model, with both sexes participating equally. California did not pursue this model, and it wasn't until the 1950s that female surfers started gaining broader numbers.[31]

As an aside, we can mention that "a stunning bathing suit" was indeed becoming an official part of the beach scene. Miss Lydia Anderson, an employee of Jacoby Brothers' merchandise store in downtown Los Angeles, won the substantial sum of two hundred dollars (over five thousand dollars today) in a bathing suit contest that summer at Venice. Many of the contestants were reportedly aspiring actresses trying to land roles in the budding Hollywood movie industry. When Jacoby's held their annual picnic at Redondo in late July, Anderson and three other women who'd entered the Venice contest arrived to compete in their swimwear. "A number of the races were run by four charming girls from the store, in stunning bathing suits," reported the *Los Angeles Times*, "and none of the events seemed of much interest unless these fair contestants took part."[32] As Victorian attitudes about the body steadily faded in the early twentieth century, so did lengthy hemlines on women's bathing suits. Such contests ran counter to the beach culture activities that Freeth developed for young women—swimming and surfing—and quickly overshadowed them as a way to draw visitors out to coastal resorts. Freeth's model appeared only later in the century, with women competing in surf contests in California beginning in the late 1950s and female lifeguards initially being hired in the early 1970s. During the heyday of bikini contests at surfing events in the 1980s and 1990s at Huntington Beach, female surf contestants often found themselves competing unfavorably against their runway counterparts, who typically received much more attention and press. Both models persist as part of beach culture today, though surfing's rise in popularity among women over the past several decades, both recreationally and competitively, marks a fortunate return to Freeth's more equitable vision.

When the young men in Redondo read that Mings and the others were "probably the only women in the country who ride the surf board, and but few men have learned the art of handling the board," their competitive drive probably kicked in. Many of them had already been surfing with Freeth, especially lifeguards Ludy Langer and Merle Reed. But later that fall they did something completely expected yet utterly groundbreaking: they organized

"Sennett Bathing Beauties" at Venice Beach, June 1917. Film producer Mack Sennett hired young women to perform in bathing suits for his silent films and to enter beauty contests at local beaches. By the early 1910s, bathing suit contests were lending Hollywood glamour and sex appeal to California beach culture. Security Pacific National Banks Collection/Los Angeles Public Library.

themselves into California's first surf club. They adopted the name of Duke's Waikīkī club, Hui Nalu, and six of the fourteen members were scheduled to give their first exhibition on a Sunday in November. The club built their own surfboards, and Freeth took charge of instruction.[33]

As Freeth was guiding his Redondo swimmers to championship titles and planting the seeds of California surf culture, he was also innovating lifesaving equipment to improve rescue times and techniques. He introduced the "torpedo tube" to Los Angeles beaches in the summer of 1912, the basic form of which remains the standard in lifeguarding today. The novel shape allowed lifeguards to swim through the surf with much less resistance than the typical ring-shaped life buoy. Freeth's addition of flexible steel wire rather than rope to secure the torpedo likewise decreased interference from floating kelp and strong currents. The torpedo itself was hollow and made of copper: forty-two inches long and eight inches wide. A lifeguard attached the tube to a belt slung

June 10-19?
Venice Parade

around his waist and swam out to a drowning victim. A handle at each end allowed both swimmer and lifeguard to hang on without the former grabbing the latter and complicating the rescue. Two onshore lifeguards manned the portable reel that unwound the wire and then hauled the lifeguard and victim back to shore. Freeth would have seen a rudimentary version of this device during his time on the East Coast, where members of the Atlantic City Beach Patrol carried out rescues along the New Jersey shore.[34]

Freeth demonstrated the device on opening day of the summer season. Fifteen thousand people reportedly came out to Redondo in mid-June. Most of them arrived on Huntington's trolleys, but the more well-to-do traveled by automobile. Henry Ford had introduced his Model T in 1908, and driving quickly became a national obsession for those who could afford the $850 price tag (about $22,000 today). The automobile would become critical to the development of California beach culture in the 1920s and 1930s, giving surfers the ability to travel off the beaten path in search of waves. In Southern California, Redondo embraced the fad fairly quickly by grading boulevards to connect the beach with downtown Los Angeles. In front of thousands of spectators, Freeth swam out six hundred feet and brought a man back to shore in three minutes in what the *Los Angeles Times* called "a spectacular

A spectator's-eye view of a bathing-suit contestant parading through a crowd of men circa 1915 in Venice or Santa Monica. The gaze and close proximity of the men, along with the woman's own downcast eyes—at least at the snap of the shutter—give the impression less of glamour than of a gauntlet. USC Digital Library. California Historical Society Collection.

exhibition in the surf."[35] Somebody filmed the rescue, because ten days later the Garrick Theatre in downtown Los Angeles was advertising the "Freeth Life Saving Device" as part of its entertainment program.[36]

Despite the success and publicity that Freeth had brought to Redondo—including introducing the ukulele that summer as part of the beach scene (the Broadway show *The Bird of Paradise*, with its ukulele-playing Hawaiian princess Luana, had created a fad for *hapa haole* music earlier that year)—he resigned from the bathhouse in late November, presumably due to low wages.[37]

Ludy Langer and Freeth manning Freeth's torpedo tube and wire-reel innovation, Redondo Beach c. 1913. Courtesy Los Angeles County Lifeguard Trust Fund, Witt Family Collection.

It was reported that he shipped his surfboard to Long Beach, where he was negotiating with the manager of the local bathhouse to relocate there.[38] This opportunity apparently fell through, because he started working for Southern California Edison, likely putting his telephone lineman experience to good use as the electric company expanded its services around Los Angeles.[39]

Freeth's impact as a lifeguard can be more fully gauged when we consider what happened in his absence. William Britton, a young clerk for the Southern Pacific Railroad in Berkeley, was visiting Los Angeles with two of his coworkers. They'd been working in Tucson, Arizona, for the past month taking inventory and were scheduled to complete a similar task in Los Angeles. Because Britton liked to swim, he'd been enjoying the area plunges. It was a Sunday, and the three decided to visit the Redondo Bath House. Britton was diving with one of the other young men when he suddenly stopped and pulled himself onto the low concrete wall that separated the diving pool from the main tank. There was a fountain at the center of the wall, a popular place for bathers to sit and relax. Britton told his friend Johnson that his head felt "awfully funny." Johnson took another dive off the springboard, but when he surfaced, Britton was gone. He thought perhaps Britton had left for the beach. So Johnson got out of the pool and went looking for him. Later he returned to the bathhouse, got dressed, and he and the third man, named Dopking, waited around for Britton to show up.

The plunge closed at six that evening. As the staff began to clear out the dressing rooms, they found Britton's clothes along with several personal letters and his Southern Pacific ID card. Because this happened frequently, manager Bryon Minor told his employees to keep the building open until Britton returned. When Britton didn't come back to claim his clothes or effects—he'd also placed his watch and eight dollars in their safe box—they did a search of the beach. It was February—off-season—and not many guests had swum in the plunge that day. Because two lifeguards had been on duty all afternoon at the bathhouse, Minor feared that Britton had gone to the beach and drowned in the surf.

Johnson and Dopking waited until 8:30 that night. When Britton didn't turn up, they weren't alarmed. They figured he'd taken an earlier trolley back to the Antler Hotel in downtown Los Angeles. So they left. Because Johnson and Dopking were staying at a different hotel, they didn't look for Britton when they arrived back in the city.

The next morning Minor began the routine of having the bathhouse tanks emptied and the salt water replaced. They found Britton's body in eight feet of water, faceup. The autopsy showed that his right lung had hemorrhaged before he drowned, probably from hitting the water on his last dive. Because of the two lifeguards on duty, Minor hadn't considered the possibility that anyone could have drowned in his plunge. They would have found the body on Sunday afternoon, explained the *Redondo Breeze*, but the fountain's shadow had concealed it.[40]

One simply can't imagine such an accident occurring with Freeth on duty. He was too aware of the dangers that water posed, too alert for signs of trouble. The bathhouse management agreed. One week later, Freeth was back working at the plunge. The pattern would repeat itself throughout his career as a lifeguard in Southern California: rather than being maintained on duty to prevent drownings, he was often hired only after a deadly accident forced a business owner or city council to prioritize public safety.

Freeth kept bathers safe once again and packed the galleries of the bathhouse with his aquatic stunts. The chamber of commerce decided on an early date to open the 1913 season—Easter Sunday—to celebrate the new roller coaster on the waterfront, the "Lightning Racer," and the paving of Pacific and Catalina avenues, the two main automobile routes into town.

But Freeth was still struggling to earn a wage that fairly compensated him, and he threatened to quit again. It's another reminder of how Freeth, and the lifeguards who followed in his path for the next two decades, had to subsist on low wages and itinerant work until coastal towns established year-round lifeguard service.

An article titled "Keep Freeth Here" in the *Redondo Reflex* laid out the logic, and the humanity, of putting Freeth on the city's payroll:

> Can the citizens of Redondo Beach afford to let Freeth leave? In all the eight years that he has served as life guard on the coast he has not lost one life that he sought in the ocean waves. The city maintains a police force to look after the welfare of the pedestrians; a fire department for protection, and why should they not set aside a fund for a life guard. With a salary of say forty dollars a month together with his salary at the bath house would be some inducement to keep a man, like Freeth, known the length and breadth of this continent for his heroism, in Redondo Beach. The saving of one life, were it some one near and dear to you, would fully repay all that it costs.[41]

Freeth had his champions, and Redondo had citizens who encouraged the city to consider investing in a professional lifeguard service, which the trustees eventually did. That summer Freeth was paid twenty-five dollars a month to be a "police officer on the water front," a position similar to the one he'd briefly held in Venice years before.[42]

The extra salary at least gave Freeth some breathing room, and he turned his attention back to lifeguard equipment. He wasn't satisfied with the advances he'd made with the torpedo tube. He wanted to shave even more time off his rescues. The metal buoy and portable reel system was effective, but you couldn't run it down the beach very easily. And lifeguards often wasted precious time on false alarms, as when a Mrs. M. J. Kennedy lost her footing and slipped into the surf a mile north of the bathhouse. Freeth and Merle Reed ran down the beach after the alarm sounded only to be greeted by Mrs. Kennedy's drunk companion, who told Freeth that the lifeguards weren't needed and that he "had better beat it."[43] The *Los Angeles Times* reported indignantly that two policeman on the same call—Marshal John Keppel and Officer Gipe—"both of whom are heavyweights, had nearly brought on apoplexy by their long run, but not so much as a 'thank you' was tendered by the angry bather."[44]

The Redondo Bath House invested one thousand dollars in the latest resuscitation device that year: a Draeger pulmotor with an airtight rubber mouthpiece that pumped oxygen into the lungs of victims and maintained their breathing. Freeth came up with the idea of using a three-wheeled motorcycle to haul the pulmotor and other lifesaving equipment to beach rescues. His innovation would not only extend the reach of lifeguards into neighboring towns but also allow them to respond to emergencies in record time, thus saving more lives.

In April 1913 Freeth and other bathhouse employees held an exhibition in the plunge to raise the initial funds for the vehicle. By the first day of summer, local business owners had kicked in enough money to secure the motorcycle and outfit it according to Freeth's specifications. The motorcycle could hold several lifeguards and a victim lying on top of a six-foot box that stretched along the sidecar; the pulmotor, first-aid kit, and medicine chest were all stored inside the box. The reel with fifteen hundred feet of wire was mounted on the back. The motorcycle reportedly reached speeds of seventy miles an hour.[45]

Freeth began daily training runs along the coast—north to Hermosa and Manhattan beaches, and south to Clifton-by-the-Sea in the shadow of Palos Verdes. He told a reporter that riding a surfboard was easy compared to driving the motorbike, but the *Redondo Breeze* dismissed his comment: "George just hates speed like a prima donna hates publicity."[46] He proved the effectiveness of the machine when he raced up to Manhattan Beach one afternoon in August—"Clad only in a light green bathing suit"—and helped rescue and resuscitate a swimmer who'd been caught in a riptide by the pier.[47] Later that month in an exhibition, Freeth saved a swimmer who'd been covertly placed two and a half miles north of the bathhouse and two hundred yards offshore. He made the rescue and round trip in fifteen minutes—with four traffic delays—further demonstrating the speed and effectiveness of the "Mile-A-Minute" motorcycle.[48] No longer would he and other lifeguards compromise a rescue by having to run down the beach.

Freeth's novelty captured the attention of filmmaker Mack Sennett, famous for, among other things, his work with Charlie Chaplin and the Keystone Cops. Sennett filmed Freeth and Ludy Langer conducting a rescue using the motorcycle in Redondo Beach. A basic plot was developed in which a woman fell into the surf after being chased by her "overly-amorous date." A couple of Keystone Cops filled out the story with their slapstick antics. Once the woman's date sounded the alarm, Freeth and Langer rolled to the scene on the motorcycle. Langer hooked himself to the torpedo buoy and swam out to the woman while Freeth played out line from the reel. When the woman reached shore, she was carried to the stretcher on the motorcycle and driven to a nearby location, where she was hooked up to the pulmotor and revived. After recovering enough to knock out her date with a police baton, she ended the film with a grateful kiss for Freeth and Langer.

They filmed over three days in early July, producing a six-minute educational comedy that introduced Freeth's innovation to the world and captured, as the film title indicated, "The Latest in Life Saving" techniques.[49] The basic outline of the story may have come from Freeth himself. The summer before, he had asked his diving protégé Cliff Bowes to don a woman's blonde wig and bathing suit to catch a masher who'd been bothering women on the beach. After the disguise lured the man to Bowes, the lifeguards grabbed him and dunked him in the surf several times. Once the man promised not to return and bother anymore women, they put him soaking wet on the next trolley back to Los Angeles.[50]

Duke and his fellow Hui Nalu swimmers were in town for the filming. They'd come to Southern California to compete against the Los Angeles Athletic Club. After the meet they trolleyed out to Redondo to visit Freeth and Dolly Mings. Duke tried surfing at Redondo, but the swell was down so he beached his board and spent the afternoon bodysurfing. It was his first trip to Los Angeles, and he liked what he'd seen so far. He only wished the waves had been better in Redondo. He told the local papers that he planned to scout other beaches in the area because a surf session would "remind him of home."[51] Duke ended up in Long Beach the following week and was able to have his first full surf session in Southern California, giving an exhibition in front of a couple thousand beachgoers.[52]

On the afternoon of September 11, a call came in from the Pacific Electric Power Plant north of the bathhouse. Three-year-old Wilfred Schultz had wandered away from his grandmother and tumbled into the surf, where he was quickly pulled out to sea. Freeth and George Mitchell took the motorcycle onto Pacific Avenue and got as far as Emerald Street, right behind Huntington's pavilion, when a man selling newspapers loomed up in front of them. Freeth swerved the bike to avoid running him down. He hit the curb and smashed into a telegraph pole. Though the child was eventually saved with the help of Cliff Bowes and Merle Reed, Freeth fractured his right ankle in the accident. Mitchell, riding on the back, sustained minor bruises and scratches.

They took Freeth to the local doctor, who set the bone, and then Mitchell's parents took him into their home until he was well enough to get around on crutches.[53] Freeth still planned on taking his Redondo swimmers to the big meet in Portola the following month at San Francisco's Sutro Baths. This was the annual West Coast Championship between the northern and southern chapters of the AAU, but Duke and other members of the Hawaiian swimming clubs had also been invited.

At the end of September, however, Freeth got an offer he couldn't refuse: the Los Angeles Athletic Club (LAAC) was looking for a new head swimming instructor. Not only was the LAAC the most prestigious athletic club in the region, but winter was coming on. Freeth probably didn't want to find himself working for the Edison Company again because of low bathhouse wages. The Redondo City Council didn't help matters when the public properties committee didn't recommend paying off the rest of the motorcycle after the accident.[54]

The *Redondo Breeze* reported that Freeth left town the evening of September 30 on crutches. "He will be missed in this city," the article read. "The Redondo Breeze, along with his many friends, wish Freeth the best of success in his new position with the Los Angeles Athletic Club." Freeth made loyal friends wherever he lived and worked. He had put Redondo on the sporting map, and in many ways his success and accomplishments were also theirs. Though he'd be working every day in downtown Los Angeles, he still planned on living in Redondo.[55]

Crutches and all, Freeth had less than a month to organize his new swimmers into a competitive squad for the meet at Portola.

9

Coaching Duke

The trolley ride to the central depot at Sixth and Main took about an hour from Redondo. From there it was a quick walk over to Seventh Street and the entrance to the LAAC, the city's oldest private club. Its members included the wealthiest landowners, the nucleus of whom had transformed Los Angeles from an agrarian community at the edge of the continent to a bustling, modern metropolis. When the club was founded in 1880, Los Angeles had a population of about eleven thousand. By the time Freeth walked into the lobby on October 1, 1913, the city was pushing four hundred thousand. In little over a month, William Mulholland would officially open the Los Angeles Aqueduct, which provided a critical water supply from the Owens Valley for the city's dynamic growth. To the south, the Port of Los Angeles at San Pedro, whose main channel had been dredged and widened, began welcoming the large maritime vessels that connected Los Angeles to the rest of the world and assured its continued modernization.

Matching the city's bustling expansion, the LAAC had moved into a brand-new building the previous year, a glorious twelve-story monument to comfort, convenience, and luxury. Members enjoyed a steakhouse with its own butcher shop and bakery on the second floor, the main dining room and lounge on the third floor, and additional private dining rooms on the fourth floor along with a banquet room, a library, and a twelve-table billiard hall. Athletics proper began on the fifth floor with enough space for three thousand lockers and a cluster of Turkish bath facilities that area plunges had popularized: steam room, cooling room, dry-heat room, shower, and massage rooms. A good chunk of the floor space held massive girders that cradled the incredible accomplishment on the sixth floor: a plunge 100 feet long, 32 feet wide, and 10 feet deep that held 1.5 million pounds of water.

Skylights and large windows lit up the white ceramic tile surrounding the plunge, whose water was replaced every other day. The filtration system in the basement could fill the tank in four and a half hours through the mouth of the marble gargoyle sitting at one end of the pool. No expense was spared to create facilities that would, the club owners hoped, house the top swimming team in the country. Freeth had been hired specifically to accomplish that goal.

The seventh floor held a balcony for spectators to watch the swim meets. The space doubled as an indoor track—ten laps to a mile—where members could look down on Seventh Street and Olive as they huffed and puffed. The seventh floor also offered punching bags and rowing machines. Floors eight and nine sported handball and squash courts with galleries above. The top three floors housed over a hundred rooms and suites where members could lodge in the lap of luxury, high above busy streets clacking with trolleys and honking with the novelty of automobiles.[1]

How could Freeth have said no to Leslie Henry, chairman of the club's swimming committee? The fact that the club even *had* a swimming committee was already a mark of prestige. The club was rife with committees: chess, billiards, handball, boxing, squash, football—you name it, they had a committee for it. They also competed in basketball, wrestling, indoor golf, and track and field. They had their own magazine, the *Mercury*, for which Freeth wrote articles on water safety and encouraged members to sign up for lessons with him.

We get an idea of Freeth's work hours by looking at those of his predecessor, Frank Holborow. Holborow offered swim classes every day over the lunch hour and from 4:00 to 6:00 P.M. Members could also make appointments with him for lessons on weekends or any day outside of normal class hours.[2] In addition, of course, Freeth would be responsible for developing swimmers to compete in the club championships and the major AAU tournaments throughout the year. Leslie Henry had indicated soon after hiring Freeth that the club had its eye on winning the Panama-Pacific Games in July 1915, a competition that would celebrate the completion of the Panama Canal and bring the nation's top swimmers to the Sutro Baths. Henry called Freeth "the best swimming instructor in this country" and promised, "It will be the endeavor of Instructor Freeth and the committee to develop between now and that time the greatest team of aquatic stars that the west has ever known, and one that will be hard for any team in this country to beat."[3]

Freeth worked as head swim instructor at the Los Angeles Athletic Club in downtown Los Angeles from October 1913 to February 1915. Photo by Bach, *Mercury*, December 1913. Huntington Library, San Marino, California.

So Freeth had his work cut out for him. Beyond the necessity of earning a living wage, the challenge of building a nationally ranked swim team must have piqued his competitive drive. He'd already become the top lifeguard and water polo player on the West Coast. He had few equals in diving and surfing. Now he had the chance to extend his success on the national stage—perhaps even farther, to the next Olympics. Berlin in 1916 must have crossed his mind once or twice. Now almost thirty years old, he'd reached the peak of his professional reputation in Los Angeles. From the very first day, he must have set his sights on recruiting Duke Kahanamoku to the club. With Duke, Ludy Langer, and Cliff Bowes on the roster, the LAAC would be hard to beat at the Panama-Pacific Games. The first step in accomplishing that goal would be to get Bowes up to San Francisco for the Portola meet and to reconnect with Duke and Langer.

∾

Duke arrived in San Francisco in mid-October with six members of the Hui Nalu and George Cunha from the Healanis. Thanks to Duke's explosive talent, the team that had officially formed in 1911 to compete in the first AAU meet in Honolulu had quickly become the most dominant club in the West. Duke swept his freestyle events at the Sutro Baths: the 50-, 100-, 220-, and 440-yard races. He anchored the relay race at the end of the meet, which his team also won. Langer won the 880 swimming for the University of California at Berkeley. Cliff Bowes won the high diving event. Freeth had also brought two young divers from Redondo: Ray Kegeris (age twelve) and Tommy Witt (age seven). Kegeris would go on to win a silver medal in the 100-meter backstroke at the 1920 Olympics.

It must have been an odd sensation for Freeth to watch Duke and Langer compete to such acclaim in amateur athletics. As a friend and coach, he certainly would have been proud of them. As a former competitor, he must have wondered how they'd managed to fly below the AAU's radar for professionals. Incredibly enough, Duke had admitted upon arriving in San Francisco that the people of Honolulu had given him a house after he'd returned from the Olympics. The residence in Waikīkī for Duke and his large family had strategically been placed in a trust. As Duke biographer David Davis writes, "The primary factor, it was later revealed, was to preserve his 'status as an amateur athlete to the end that he would not, by reason of acceptance of the gift, be deemed a professional athlete for purposes of national and international athletic competition.'"[4] Duke was fortunate to have a legal team behind him managing his amateur status. Recall the AAU rule that had triggered Freeth's ineligibility years before: an athlete was allowed to compete unless someone filed a protest. Apparently no one did so against Duke.

Neither did anyone protest against Ludy Langer, who'd worked as a lifeguard with Freeth in Redondo the summer before and had even showcased that profession in "The Latest in Life Saving." By this time Langer was the Pacific Coast champion in the 880 freestyle. As had been the case with Frank Holborow back in 1909—and certainly with Duke and Langer—established champions were given more leeway when it came to professional status. Freeth had certainly been a diving champion, but his need to earn a living had worked against him when it came to decisions of who would be allowed to compete as an amateur and who wouldn't. His high visibility as a lifeguard, especially after his rescue of the seven Japanese fishermen, perhaps cemented his ban. Freeth could have chosen to work off the beach—and had done so on several occasions—but his love of lifeguarding, and the desperate need he saw to develop the service, always pulled him back to duty. His personal loss in terms of potential individual honors in amateur sports turned out to be an immense gain not only for the people whose lives he saved but also for the development of lifeguarding in California and beaches around the world.

When Duke had arrived in San Francisco for the Portola meet, he'd been asked about moving away from Hawai'i. He replied that he had no intention of opening up a swimming school in California. "The people of the islands have been very generous to me," he said, "and I have no intention of deserting my home."[5] But Freeth had other ideas for the young Hawaiian.

The next big meet was the following summer over the July Fourth weekend, again at the Sutro Baths. This time the national powerhouse Illinois Athletic Club had been invited to compete. Duke's prominence had slipped some in the intervening year. In February 1914 at Honolulu's Mid-Pacific Carnival, he'd lost the 50-yard freestyle to "Bab" Small of San Francisco's Olympic Club. Later that year, in June, he lost the 50 again at the annual AAU match in Honolulu Harbor. Though Duke won both the 100- and 220-yard freestyle at the Sutro Baths, he lost the 50 to Arthur Raithel of the Illinois Athletic Club. This was the third time in less than five months that he'd lost the short-distance race. In the 880 Duke came in second to Ludy Langer, who also captured the 440 in world-record time. By the end of the meet, Freeth had managed to boost the LAAC from a dismal sixth place the year before to a respectable third. The Hui Nalu, triumphant the previous year at Portola, had to make room for the new champions from the Illinois Athletic Club.

When the Hawaiian team climbed aboard the *Sonoma* to return to Honolulu, Duke remained behind. Perhaps his losses that year and the subsequent public criticism in the newspapers of his being past his prime (at twenty-three years old) made him rethink Freeth's earlier offers.[6] By mid-July 1914, Duke was living in Los Angeles and training at the LAAC.[7] It was an amazing coup for Freeth to lure Duke away from Hawai'i and the Hui Nalu. Back in 1912 the Honolulu elite had blocked Freeth from training Duke for the Olympics, fearing for Duke's amateur status. Now Freeth was on the cusp of realizing the club's dream of building the strongest swimming squad in the country.

The first thing Freeth had to fix was how Duke started his races. The pool at the LAAC is thirty-two feet wide. The two men lined up on the side and raced across the tank. Freeth beat Duke every time. In such a short race, the dive was the most crucial part, and Freeth's feet were hitting the water seven feet beyond Duke's. Freeth then laid a pole in the water six feet from the edge: if Duke's dives weren't long enough, he'd crack his shins on the pole. Duke soon learned to use the tremendous driving power of his legs to leap over the pole and improve the distance on his starts.

Next were Duke's turns. Freeth discovered that Duke was surfacing too soon after pushing off the wall, again losing the full benefit of his powerful legs. With a little practice, Duke was soon shooting nearly twenty-five feet underwater and moving more efficiently into his stroke. With the new and improved Duke, along with Langer and Bowes, the *Los Angeles Times* predicted that the club would be "a sure winner" at the national swimming championships at the Sutro Baths in 1915.[8]

∽

Because Duke had switched clubs, amateur residency rules required him to wait four months until he could compete for the LAAC. In the meantime he worked on his dives and turns, gave exhibitions, and explored Southern California. His star appeal as the world's fastest swimmer gave surfing a boost in the region, prompting the *Los Angeles Times* to declare, "Surf board riding, practically unknown to the California Coast until Duke Kahanamoku and George Freeth introduced it, is fast becoming a fad with both men and women."[9] Though Freeth had been giving exhibitions and lessons in Southern California for seven years by then, and had founded the state's first surf club, Duke still captured top billing in news reports. Duke's tremendous talent, his youth, his good looks, his regal name, and his humility—all of it created excitement and drew attention wherever he went. His long-lasting fame and exploits at Waikīkī eventually earned him the title "The Father of Modern Surfing." Had Freeth not died so young, he might have carried that honor himself.[10]

On a Sunday afternoon in mid-September, Duke put on a wave-riding show for members of the South Coast Yacht Club at Corona del Mar, a harbor town in Orange County, south of Los Angeles. He'd been the guest of honor that weekend and returned the favor by giving members canoe rides when the swell came up at the mouth of Newport Bay. He then borrowed a surfboard from a local man named Felix Modjeski and gave an exhibition for a couple of hundred people watching from their boats and lining the bluffs along shore. Very much like Freeth, he did headstands and dove off the back of the board to entertain the crowd. Due to his long rides, estimated at a quarter of a mile, the *Santa Ana Daily Register* stated that Duke had given "a far better exhibition of surf board riding than has been the case at any other point along the coast."[11]

Freeth had already ventured into Orange County with his surfboard several months earlier, giving an exhibition in Huntington Beach at the opening of their new municipal pier.[12] Though Freeth was in San Francisco over the July Fourth weekend that year for the swim meet at the Sutro Baths, his impact on the growing popularity of surfing could be seen in that weekend's advertisements for a "surf board riding exhibition" at Newport Bay and "surf board contests" in Redondo Beach.[13] The town of Seal Beach, just north of Huntington Beach, welcomed the Minnesota State Society with a picnic at the end of July. The planned festivities included a "surf-board race . . . the first of its kind on the Coast," in which the competitors rode into shore from twenty-five yards out.[14] In August the *Los Angeles Times* ran a picture of Miss Jeannette Kinney from Seal Beach standing on a surfboard. The paper declared her one of Southern California's "most proficient surf-board shooters" and added that the early-morning sessions were the result either of parental disapproval because of the dangers involved or simply a matter of young surfers not wanting to have an audience while they were learning to ride the waves.[15]

Because the wooden boards were heavy and hard to maneuver, the dangers were real. A week after Jeannette Kinney's picture appeared in the paper, seventeen-year-old Grace Hamilton was rushed to the Seaside Hospital after a surfboard accident in front of the Long Beach bathhouse. She'd been riding prone on a wave when the nose of her board struck the sand, jamming her stomach into the tail. The blow knocked her out, and they feared she might die from her injuries.[16]

Despite occasional accidents, the exhibitions of Freeth and Duke helped surfing take hold in Orange County as it had done along the Santa Monica Bay. At the boat-racing carnival in Ocean Park that fall, where both Freeth and Duke competed, a reporter noted that the lifeguards who'd entered had an advantage because they'd learned to ride the waves in boats just as they did on their surfboards.[17] Freeth's cross-training methods for his lifesaving crews had given them critical skills in reading ocean waves so that they could conduct their rescues more effectively. Surfing's growth in the early years was a by-product of this training, spreading from the lifeguards to local enthusiasts and general beach visitors. For the next four decades in California, as surfing steadily grew from a novelty to a lifestyle, the best surfers in the state were always lifeguards. If we count Duke as an honorary member of that group—he in fact saved numerous lives while living in California—the group includes Charlie Wright and Tom Blake in the 1920s, and Pete Peterson through the 1930s. After World War II a younger crew innovated both activities into the 1960s, including Tommy Zahn, Joe Quigg, Matt Kivlin, Phil Edwards, Greg Noll, Buzzy Trent, and Mike Doyle, to name a few. These circumstances worked against the development of a female surf population, since women weren't allowed to be lifeguards. Los Angeles County didn't hire a female lifeguard until the summer of 1974. One of the tests that eighteen-year-old Wendy Paskin (a non-surfer) had to pass was paddling a surfboard through large waves at Hermosa Beach to rescue a two-hundred-pound man. Freeth would have understood Paskin's reasons for taking on the challenge. She told a reporter that it was fun and the money was good. "I get $5.12 an hour," she said. "That's real good for a girl."[18] Swimming and surfing star Mary Ann Hawkins did become an "unofficial entry" in the lifeguard competition at Hermosa Beach in 1938, the only woman among 150 applicants. And though her performance was "on a par with the swimming prowess of the regular contenders," according to James K. Reid, superintendent of the Los Angeles County Department of Recreation, she was not hired for the position.[19]

～

The LAAC's dream of a national championship took a hard blow when Duke suddenly left for Honolulu in early November 1914 and then traveled to Australia and New Zealand on a swimming tour. It wasn't immediately clear from reports if he would remain a member of the LAAC or return to the Hui Nalu. Perhaps he didn't know himself.[20] One thing remained certain: Duke's training with Freeth had put the young Hawaiian back into gold-medal form. He not only beat the top Australian, Hawaiian, and American swimmers down under, but he also established a new world's record in the 50-yard freestyle by finishing just under fifty-four seconds. By the time Duke's victories were reported in Los Angeles in January 1915, the media still referred to him as a member of the LAAC. Freeth commented that "by the time he got through with the Duke he would be able to cut his mark down to 52 seconds or better."[21]

At the time, Freeth was preparing his members for the club championships and lobbying in the *Mercury* for compulsory swimming instruction in the public schools. He believed that "fully eighty per cent of the accidental drownings in the United States could be avoided if the victims were taught by competent instructors how to take care of themselves and overcome fear in the water."[22] A critical supplement to Freeth's development of surfing in Southern California was his day-to-day instruction of swimming. Surfing's popularity absolutely depended on a widespread knowledge of swimming and Freeth's ongoing mission to demystify the dangers of the ocean. He reached out to community members—high schools and women's clubs—to give demonstrations of lifesaving that would make them and their families feel safer at the beach.[23] To stimulate more interest in swimming among downtown businessmen, he started offering free instruction over the noon hour and from five to six in the evenings.

In late January 1915 William T. Rawlins, president of the Hui Nalu, reported in the *San Francisco Examiner* that Duke would be competing that summer at the Sutro Baths as a member of the Hawaiian team.[24] Little more than three weeks after that announcement, Freeth resigned from his position at the LAAC.[25] In late winter he visited San Francisco and gave an interview to a reporter at the the *San Francisco Chronicle*. Freeth indicated that Duke had sent him a letter from Australia and that the young star confirmed his plans to swim for Hui Nalu. If Freeth was bothered by the news, he covered it well. He spoke about the possibility of Duke shaving even more time off his world record: "From my intimate acquaintance with the Duke, I know that on former occasions he has beaten the best of them practically upon strength, and with the style which he has now acquired, I look for him to lower his own mark to something in the neighborhood of fifty-two seconds."[26] Duke's new "style," of course, came as result of his work with Freeth, though Freeth was gracious enough not to blow his own horn. He took the opportunity to praise the accomplishments of another one of his protégés, Cliff Bowes, who had gone to Honolulu to compete in the Mid-Pacific Carnival.

In addition to giving interviews, Freeth enjoyed the Hawaiian Pavilion at the Panama-Pacific International Exposition, which had begun in late February.[27] The territory had allocated one hundred thousand dollars to the exhibit, a live advertisement for Hawai'i. Over eighteen million people are estimated to have visited the fair in 1915, and their exposure to hula dancing and Hawaiian music created a nationwide fad for steel guitars, ukuleles, and *hapa-haole* tunes.[28] Supplementing Freeth's development of surfing in Southern California, a community of expat Hawaiians would transplant island music and dance the following decade through their work in Hollywood films, recording studios, and the growing café scene in Los Angeles. Their sustained influence in broadcasting Hawaiian culture to young Californians became critical for the growth of beach culture in the 1930s.

As for Freeth's own plans, he said they were "not yet formulated." He floated the idea of moving to San Francisco. If he didn't do that, he would "undoubtedly return to Honolulu."[29] Another report from a Los Angeles paper captured more of the adventurous Freeth: "He intends to charter a schooner and cruise among the South Sea Islands. It is the plan to take motion pictures of the sights on the trip. Owen R. Bird and D. A. Bary, two well-known Los Angeles writers, will be included in the party."[30]

It's hard to know why Freeth had decided to resign. With Duke no longer the LAAC's star performer—or projected star performer, since he hadn't actually competed for the club—perhaps Freeth saw a dream slipping away and felt it was time to leave. One can't imagine him resigning if Duke had chosen to return to Los Angeles in April after his tour of Australia. But Freeth could be impulsive. He had worked at the LAAC for fifteen months. Maybe it was time for a change.

After giving swimming and surfing a boost in Australia and New Zealand during his visit, Duke rejoined the Hui Nalu at Waikīkī and didn't return to Los Angeles until the early 1920s.[31] Freeth returned to Redondo after visiting San Francisco, making the seaside town his center of activity once again. But his own time in Los Angeles was coming to a close.

~

Freeth bided his time until summer and then did what he did best: he picked up a lifeguarding job for the City of Redondo. He was also given "police duties." One paper reported, "His uniform is a bathing suit, and he is supposed to preserve order both in and out of the water and also save lives."[32] The position recalls his situation two summers before when Redondo had paid him twenty-five dollars a month to be "a policeman on the waterfront." This was in addition to his bathhouse pay and was undoubtedly meant to ensure that he wouldn't quit. Freeth earned eighty dollars a month in his new position (just over two thousand dollars today).[33] His hiring marks an important trend in Los Angeles. The beaches themselves were drawing increasingly larger crowds during the summer, and towns like Redondo wanted to ensure visitor safety beyond the bathhouses. Three lifeguards had been hired several days before Freeth: Fred Teschke, athletic manager at the University of Southern California, was working his fifth season; Percy Furlong, a student at UC Berkeley with Ludy Langer, was in his second year; and Ray Henderson—described as "a fine all-the-year-round lifeguard"—completed the force. The town hired additional lifeguards as needed for special occasions.

Freeth's duties seemed to be more focused on the beach than those of the other lifeguards. The city council instructed the marshal to turn Freeth's own innovation—the lifesaving motorcycle—over to him to conduct rescues.[34] In truth, Freeth had already begun preserving order in the water before his official start date by rousting a sunbathing sea lion. The creature had gotten into someone's boat anchored in the bay. Freeth grabbed a length of rope and swam out. Once he neared the boat, he dove under and popped up close enough so that when the sea lion raised its head at him, he lassoed it around the neck. A tug-of-war ensued between man and animal: Freeth tried to haul the sea lion ashore, and the animal struggled to remain in the water. Freeth finally towed his prize to the beach after nearly an hour, but he'd been badly bitten on the hand and leg. The man and beast ended up having their picture taken together that afternoon in a local photography studio.[35]

The funny thing is, Freeth knew exactly the kind of fight he was in for when he'd grabbed that rope. He'd done the same thing the year before at the opening of the Hermosa Beach Pier. That day he'd enlisted the help of Cliff

Freeth (*in the bow*) and Redondo lifeguard Fred Teschke—"the two best surf boat chauffeurs on the coast"—practicing for competition. *Los Angeles Times*, July 14, 1915. Courtesy Los Angeles County Lifeguard Trust Fund.

Bowes, Ray Kegeris, and Tommy Witt to put on a diving exhibition for the large crowd of visitors. But the boys stopped diving when they spied a sea lion in the water. The creature had gotten a hook and line stuck in its mouth earlier that day, and several boys in a nearby skiff were throwing things at it and trying to hit it with their oars—probably to prevent it from stealing any fish they'd hooked.

Freeth dove off the pier and managed to hoist the sea lion into the skiff, scattering the boys into the water. When all was said and done, one of the boys had been bitten on the leg, and Freeth had bites on his hands, arms, and legs. The sea lion turned into something of a mascot for the Redondo Bath House and escaped at least once into the tanks, where Freeth and others finally had to drain the pool to recapture it. The *Los Angeles Times* snapped a picture of the two together, Freeth squatting down in his suit and tie and

"George Freeth and his captive sea-lion." *Los Angeles Times*, May 18, 1914.

hanging on to the sea lion by the tail.[36] Beyond any duty to keep the peace, Freeth must have enjoyed the challenge of capturing a sea lion in front of an admiring crowd, wounds notwithstanding.

Ten days after Freeth started lifeguarding again in Redondo, he had the distinction of saving the same woman twice. Miss Frances Curtis, a clerk from Trinidad, Colorado, first got into trouble at the bathhouse. She was learning to swim in the largest pool and injured herself, so Freeth had to pull her out. The second incident occurred when she jumped into the surf north of the bathhouse and was being carried out to sea in a riptide when Freeth once again swam to her rescue.[37]

That summer a few of the players from the 1908 championship water polo team decided to reunite as Southern California organized a new league. In the first preseason game played against Long Beach, "a large crowd of lusty fans" filled the Redondo plunge.[38] Freeth took up his normal position as goalie. In a hard-fought game that ended with Redondo on top four to zero, team captain A. L. Walton pulled Freeth from the game at the end of the first half for "being too rough."[39] Play also had to be stopped several times so the men could change their bathing suits, which had been nearly torn off of them.

By the time Redondo and Long Beach held a rematch two and a half weeks later, Freeth had resigned his position as lifeguard and was reportedly visiting San Francisco again where the Panama-Pacific fair was still taking place.[40] If he'd managed to keep Duke on the LAAC squad, the club certainly would have been the star of the meet: Duke won freestyle events in the 50-, 100-, and 220-yard races; Langer won the same events in the 440, 500, and 880, breaking three American records; and Cliff Bowes came in a respectable second place in diving. By this time it was apparent to most people that there would be no Olympic Games in Berlin due to the outbreak of World War I the previous summer. Duke, Langer, and many others would have to wait another four years to chase their gold-medal dreams.

Freeth had lasted only six weeks as a lifeguard and police officer in Redondo. At their meeting on August 2, the city council recommended hiring two lifeguards to replace him: Vera Ostendorf and Bo Barkley.[41] Without Freeth as goalie, the local water polo team lost to Long Beach four to zero and Long Beach went on to win the championship that year. It's not clear if Freeth went to San Francisco to watch the swim meet. The same local newspaper that had reported his departure for San Francisco also mentioned that he would tour the East afterward—Chicago and New York—to give swimming demonstrations.[42] If Freeth in fact did go to see Duke, it would have been a short visit. Duke left for the islands on August 3, the day after Freeth reportedly left for San Francisco.

Though Freeth seemed to like the idea of setting his sails for new horizons, he settled in Redondo and more or less fell off the radar until the following summer. He may have been able to live off family money. His father had died in May of the previous year. Freeth Senior must have received a terminal diagnosis sometime near the end of 1913. He made his will on November 22 of that year in Los Angeles and then traveled to New York and made his way back to England, where he died on May 5, 1914.[43] It's interesting that Freeth Senior listed Los Angeles as his place of residence in the will. This would have been around the time when George was hired at the LAAC, so it may be that father and son managed to spend time together after all.

Freeth Senior had inherited income from the estate of his own father, Major General James Holt Freeth, after this latter's death in 1904. Freeth Senior left that continuing income to his wife, Lizzie. Upon her death, his entire estate was to be sold and divided up among his five children, whose addresses he listed on the will. According to that document, in 1913 his oldest son, Willie, was working for Standard Oil Company and living at Millers Station, north of San Francisco. Charlie was still living in Philadelphia and working at Ridgeway Refrigerator Company. Maggie and Dorothy were both in Honolulu. Dorothy and William Campbell had had a son in February 1913 and named him in honor of George.[44] Maggie had gotten married to Ralph Clark in May 1915.

Lizzie was reported as having spent from three to six months on the mainland during the first part of 1916, so perhaps she had a chance to see Willie and George, and maybe Charlie too.[45] If she had received income from Freeth Senior, it's possible she gifted some to her sons.[46] Freeth Senior may also have given George money before he left for England in November 1913. Although Freeth Senior's probate wasn't settled in Los Angeles until 1938—twenty-four years after his death—his estate totaled just over six thousand pounds, or about five hundred thousand dollars adjusted for inflation. So the income from the estate of James Holt Freeth was substantial.

Freeth's name popped up from time to time in the local papers. In early February 1916 he was in San Francisco training Ludy Langer at the Lurline Bath House for an upcoming meet in Honolulu.[47] The following month he reportedly issued a challenge to swim against the captain of the Venice lifeguards, A. L. McCullen.[48] Around this time Redondo had started looking into hiring a beach lifeguard, because spring was a dangerous season for swimmers. Though Carl Blumberg, a lifeguard at the bathhouse, was being considered, the local paper affirmed that "our friend Freeth" would be a better man for the job, "providing he would take the position."[49] So Freeth was hanging around Redondo, just not inclined to work. At the annual ocean race in June that year at Ocean Park, Freeth was reported "too busy and perhaps not enough interested to consider the swim."[50]

Freeth does seem to have lost interest in all things swimming and lifeguarding in Redondo. The town papers reported upcoming swim meets, the formation of a women's swim club, and young female ocean swimmers who could challenge records set by Dolly Mings. But Freeth's name is nowhere to be found among the announcements. Ludy Langer was working out regularly in Redondo that summer, paddling an eight-foot surfboard every morning as part of his preparation to defend his swimming titles in St. Louis and New York City. But Langer doesn't mention his friend and mentor.[51]

And yet Freeth's life was about to change drastically. The small newspaper blurb that mentions his departure on July 6 for San Diego to pursue "athletic interests" belies the renewed fame he would find in that city, his final port of call.[52]

A New Beginning in San Diego

Freeth hit the San Diego swimming community like a burst of fireworks. Rumors spread in early July that the San Diego Rowing Club, founded in 1888 on the San Diego Bay, might have a chance of landing the coach of Duke Kahanamoku and Ludy Langer. Langer himself, recently graduated from the University of California at Berkeley, had written a letter to the club on Freeth's behalf. He and Hawaiian George Cunha of the Healanis were reportedly interested in relocating to San Diego if they could find employment.[1]

All the local papers tracked the story. The *San Diego Sun* called Freeth "probably the most widely known and most popular swimming coach in the country." If he were hired, they said, "there will be a revival of interest in swimming."[2] The *San Diego Union* expressed even greater hopes: "San Diego is to become the swimming capital of the Pacific, and therefore, of the world." The *Union* mentioned that the rowing club board would hold a special meeting to consider Freeth's offer. The paper also reported that club members were talking about raising money themselves to offset any difference between Freeth's asking price and what the club could afford.[3]

This latter detail might have been a red flag concerning the club's finances, but Freeth must have known what he was getting himself into. He spent a couple of days at the club surveying the talent and, perhaps most importantly, adjusting expectations of how soon they could become competitive. "San Diego has fine prospects of becoming a swimming center," he said, but it would take a year or two before it could become a national powerhouse.[4]

The club decided to offer him a contract for two months—until September 15, when they promised to consider an extension. Along with his pay of seventy-five dollars a month (about eighteen hundred dollars today), he was given the privilege of supplementing his income by offering private lessons at Los Banos, a nearby bathhouse on Broadway in downtown San Diego. His hours at the club were similar to those he'd worked at the LAAC: every day from 11:00 A.M. to 1:30 P.M. and from 4:00 to 6 P.M.

Once Freeth was hired, the *Evening Tribune* crowed that San Diego had "secured the highest class man available on the coast as instructor."[5] "Expect Big Things from Water Coach," echoed the *Sun*.[6] The *Union* ran a picture of Freeth along with his advice on how swimming promoted good health—ideas common enough today but at the time certainly a novelty. Freeth said that in addition to developing one's strength and confidence, and building up the cardiovascular system, swimming supplied "the body with a tonic that restores waste and invigorates jaded nerves."[7] After a quiet year in Redondo, Freeth himself was invigorated enough to take on building another swim program in another Southern California city.

The same night that Freeth was hired, the rowing club also joined the Amateur Athletic Union. The club had offered to host the state swimming championships over Labor Day weekend that year. Freeth was hired specifically to prepare club swimmers for that meet, which is why his contract only went through mid-September. How the club fared at the tournament might determine whether or not his contract was renewed. He had less than two months to prepare the team.

His move to San Diego and his new position followed a pattern similar to that of his arrival in Los Angeles back in 1907: he was hired essentially to boost the area, much as the Panama-California Exposition at Balboa Park had been created to promote San Diego itself. San Diego was growing fast—a population of about sixty thousand when Freeth arrived—and the city wanted to market itself as the first U.S. port of call north of the newly opened Panama Canal. San Diego was in direct competition with San Francisco, whose celebration of the canal's opening—the Panama-Pacific Exposition of 1915—had been intended to advertise its own spacious harbor as the most favorable destination for northbound ships. Ever since the gold rush of 1848, followed by California statehood in 1850, San Francisco had been the western center of industry, culture, and population. Los Angeles would overtake its northern counterpart in this latter category by 1920 and was quickly developing its port at San Pedro. Los Angeles had already bumped San Diego as the primary western terminus of the transcontinental Santa Fe Railroad back in 1887, so San Diegans were sensitive to hints of second-class status in Southern California. San Francisco had the recognized powerhouse in swimming in 1916—the Olympic Club—complete with star Norman Ross, who would go on to win three gold medals in freestyle events at the 1920 Olympics: the

400-, the 1500-meter, and the team relay (with Duke Kahanamoku). Hiring Freeth was the San Diego Rowing Club's first step in trying to elbow its way into state and national prominence.

Freeth's first order of business was to recruit men and women for the Labor Day meet, so he sent out a call in the local papers. When he wasn't at Los Banos giving private swim lessons or working with the local talent on their turns, he was down at the club's boathouse on Steamship Wharf at the foot of Fifth Avenue.[8] Although ocean temperatures in San Diego average some dozen degrees cooler than those in Honolulu during the summer, Freeth must have felt right at home training swimmers in the harbor.

On weekends he roamed beyond the calm waters of the bay to the Coronado Peninsula, hunting for waves. "I am lonesome for the surf, and for a surf board," he told the *Sun*, "and this is one grand little opportunity for me to indulge in my favorite pastime. . . . I am making several boards, and if the tide is right at the cove Sunday, I will try to show the crowd something in water fun that has been sort of neglected in and around San Diego."[9]

San Diego offers better quality surf in the summer than the Redondo area—south swells aren't blocked by the Santa Catalina and San Clemente islands—so it's no surprise that Freeth was eager to catch waves soon after landing. His comments offer a rare glimpse into his emotional state—"lonesome for the surf, and for a surf board." One can't help but recall the ending of the novel *Gidget*: "All things considered—maybe I was just a woman in love with a surfboard." Without draping Freeth in too much Hollywood kitsch—*Gidget's* author, Frederick Kohner, was a screenwriter—the Hawaiian's words express a deep connection that all surfers feel for the sport, especially when waves are absent from their daily lives. He also expresses a quintessential Hawaiian quality by calling surfing his "favorite pastime," a description captured in western accounts of the sport from Captain Cook's mariners to writers like Mark Twain.[10] We have to wonder: Why wasn't Freeth surfing in Redondo? What happened to his surfboard?

In any event, he made himself a couple of boards and took them out to Brickyard Cove, a beach along the isthmus connecting the mainland to Coronado Island. The rowing club was hosting a Sunday picnic there for some sixty members, including wives and "sweethearts." The group had also invited their counterparts from the San Diego Yacht Club, who turned up later that day after a morning race. The affair turned into what the *Union* called a "Hawaiian water carnival" with Freeth giving surf lessons to "the whole party."[11]

Surfing had been introduced to San Diego as early as 1893 when John Ahia and several other Hawaiians gave exhibitions for the La Jolla Park Hotel. Ahia had been hired principally as a fisherman to provide fresh seafood to the guests but earned money on the side by surfing. The hotel's manager, Hamilton Johnson, had previously been part owner and manager of the Hawaiian Hotel annex at Waikīkī, so he understood the appeal that surfing would have for visitors. H. P. Wood, later secretary of the Hawaii Promotion Committee, had been in San Diego since 1889 and was appointed the Hawaiian consul for San Diego around this time and would certainly have known Johnson. The Hawai'i–San Diego connection goes back to the early life of Alta California as a Mexican territory. Hawaiians were hired by merchants for their expertise in launching and landing rowboats in heavy surf. The best-known description of such activities comes from Richard Henry Dana's memoir, *Two Years before the Mast* (1840), where the author befriended a group of Hawaiians who helped ensure that loads of cattle pelts were safely transferred to merchant vessels trolling the California coast. Many surfers can't help but imagine that the Hawaiians, cobbling together a spare life near the beach, had taken advantage of the abundant surf to practice their national pastime.

If we were inclined to go back even further, the Kumeyaay, Tongva, and Chumash peoples thrived for thousands of years in the southern region of what is now California before Spanish colonization began in 1769. Their light reed boats—the tule balsas—and the larger plank canoes exclusive to the first two tribes were staples of work, trade, and travel.[12] The Yurok, living farther to the north, constructed similar vessels.[13] It's not hard to imagine coastal Native Americans steering these craft in the waves for pleasure too. They certainly had the expertise.

Freeth appeared in a San Diego newspaper report as early as 1907. The *Evening Tribune* mentioned the possibility of Freeth coming "for the purpose of instructing the people of this vicinity in the art of surf riding."[14] We'll recall that Freeth had passed through San Diego with his father in the summer of 1898 on their way to Clipperton Island. The two had traveled back from Clipperton in the fall and spent the night in downtown San Diego at the Hotel Brewster. Perhaps Freeth had initially considered a short stint in the area after surfing in Los Angeles in 1907. The report from the *Tribune* turned out to be true, just nine years too early.

The next mention of surfing in San Diego is connected to the Hawaiian Village exhibition at Balboa Park in September 1915. A troupe of hula dancers and musicians took time out from entertaining visitors to offer a luau of sorts at La Jolla Cove: a clambake along with music, dancing, and exhibitions of swimming, diving, and surfing.[15] Because the Balboa Park exhibition continued until New Year's Day of 1917, these Hawaiians were probably the surfing "experts" behind advertisements that also appeared in June 1916 to draw visitors out to La Jolla.[16] This was a month before Freeth's arrival at the San Diego Rowing Club. It's been reported that Duke Kahanamoku took part in these Hawaiian Village exhibitions, but Duke's first visit to the area actually wasn't until July 1922, when he competed in a swimming tournament at Coronado Tent City.[17]

Once Freeth settled in San Diego, it didn't take him long to discover La Jolla's waves for himself. The rowing club picnic had gone so well at Brickyard Cove that officers approved a request for him to make two more surfboards—the "cost not to exceed $5.00"—and bring them to a swim competition in early August that ended at La Jolla.[18] Freeth's swimmers won first and third place in the mile-and-a-half race. Afterward Freeth gave an exhibition of diving and surfing.[19] That same weekend two club members—Elliott Burns and Junior Dula—captured first and second place at the annual rough water swim at Ocean Park.[20] Freeth's training had made an immediate impact on the club's reputation as their swimmers began to win regional competitions, and his surfboards soon migrated beyond Brickyard Cove and La Jolla. Club members Jimmy McIntosh and Bill Pringle, who'd gone to Ocean Park for the race (McIntosh came in fourth), took boards with them and surfed at Ocean Park; another member, William O'Farrell, tried one of the boards at Mission Beach, just south of La Jolla.[21]

Freeth ventured farther up the coast and introduced the sport at Del Mar. When Richard Barthelmess, writer of the "Rowing Club Gossip" column in the *San Diego Sun*, wondered in print about Freeth's "great attachment" for Del Mar, Freeth told him the beach had the "greatest breakers in California." Barthelmess quipped, "Surf breakers or heart breakers? Prof. Geo."[22] (Freeth and other instructors of the era were often called "professor.") The blurb captures how quickly Freeth had been accepted into the rowing club community. Barthelmess, a club member—in perhaps a rare reference to a romantic relationship for Freeth—felt comfortable enough to give him a bit of ribbing in the paper. We see similar humor in the column on Valentine's Day the following year:

> Prof. Gawge Freeth has agreed to teach all club members and their ladies the art of diving and swimming each Thursday night at Los Banos.
> A number of swimmers have promised to bring their lady admirers.
>   Pretty soft for Prof. Freeth, hey?[23]

The mild insinuations of romance show not only that Freeth had been accepted as "one of the guys" but also that any relationships would not have especially been a problem for him in terms of race. Though known to be Hawaiian, his lighter skin allowed him social liberties that might not have been acceptable for darker-skinned *kānaka maoli* (Native Hawaiians), even Duke Kahanamoku, who had to confront racism as he traveled through the United States.[24]

Surfing in the San Diego area was not only a way for Freeth to have fun and entertain people, but he always used the sport as an effective training routine for his swimmers and lifeguards. He also understood that surfing was a great marketing device for his swimmers: having them ride surfboards in front of large beach crowds would bring them attention and help build local support for the upcoming swim meet.

But turning his swimmers into surfers wasn't enough; Freeth wanted them to become lifeguards too. And he wanted to share his knowledge of lifesaving techniques with the community. Two weeks after he was hired at the San Diego Rowing Club, he visited the local Rotary Club to give a lecture on swimming and lifesaving.[25] Three days later he gave a demonstration before a large crowd on the latest techniques to subdue, rescue, and resuscitate a drowning victim. Although he quickly reviewed how this could be done with lifeboats, torpedo buoys, and pulmotors, his focus that particular day was how to save a life without the aid of technology.

He started off by showing the crowd wrestling grabs like the "hammer lock" that allowed one to safely restrain a victim. He then showed them how to tow a victim through the water by grabbing his hair or clothing and using a scissor kick. Once they reached land, the victim could be bounced across a knee to expel water from the lungs. Or with the help of another person kneeling on all fours, the victim could be rolled over that person's back.

Freeth demonstrated how to pump a victim's arms and push on his diaphragm to get him breathing again. He recommended the technique be done twenty times a minute and continue for a minimum of two hours: pumping, pushing, rubbing, chafing, rolling—anything to get the victim to respond. Freeth told the crowd that he knew of one victim who'd been restored after being unconscious for three and a half hours.

He then demonstrated for the crowd the latest swimming strokes and explained why some were more effective than others. His own preference was for the American crawl, which Ohio-born swimmer Charles Daniels had used to win gold medals in the 1904 and 1908 Olympics. The stroke itself triggered a national fad in swimming during the early decades of the twentieth century, its motions "regularly related," as Olaf Stieglitz notes, "to ultimate modern ideas of speed, efficiency, and streamlining." Swimming was particularly appealing to (and marketed at) white, middle-class Americans because of its dual benefits of fitness and leisure. Stieglitiz observes that "its popularity rested on the fact that one could spen[d] a day at the beach but still claim to go swimming."[26] The ease of learning the stroke certainly helped propel the growth of beach culture, especially with enthusiasts like Freeth providing demonstrations and instruction.

Once Freeth concluded his demonstrations, he did indeed invite his audience to the beach—Mission Beach—where his club swimmers put on a surfing show. The papers mentioned that arrangements had been made to have Freeth filmed while he was riding waves, though it's not known if this ever took place.[27]

~

Fresh from their victory in Ocean Park in early August, the Rowing Club sponsored Freeth and two swimmers, Elliott Burns and Charles Shields, to travel back up to Los Angeles later that month to compete in the national championship one-mile ocean swim. Record holder Ludy Langer would compete for the LAAC along with members of San Francisco's Olympic Club and the New York Athletic Club. The *San Diego Union*, in an article titled "San Diego Takes Important Place in Pacific Coast Aquatics," vaunted Freeth's impact on the local team: "Since Coach George Freeth has assumed charge of the club swimmers there has been a marked advancement in their work, and Freeth, a coach of vast experience, believes he will be able to develop a few champions."[28] Though he'd been working with Burns and Shields for only a month, the two came in a respectable third and fourth place behind Langer and Norman Ross.[29]

Next up on the summer schedule for Freeth was the state swimming championships held at the San Diego Rowing Club. Once again Freeth garnered high praise in the local papers for having his squad put up "a game fight" against the more established clubs. Though the San Diego team came in last place, glimpses of future success were seen in young Jimmy McIntosh, who stole second place from the LAAC with a come-from-behind effort in the relay race.[30]

Immediately after the meet, Freeth helped boost another sport in San Diego: aquaplaning, an early version of waterskiing. He and Frances Cowells, a female swimmer from the Olympic Club who had established an American record in the 50-yard backstroke, gave an exhibition in San Diego Harbor. They took turns being towed by a motorboat while standing on a wooden board that was four and a half feet long, eighteen inches wide.[31] Freeth, of course, wasn't satisfied with merely standing on the board. He flipped upside down into a headstand, and pictures of him and Cowells made the front page of the *Union*.

When mid-September rolled around, the club decided not to renew Freeth's contract due to a "shortage of funds."[32] He was costing them seventy-

Looking fit and relaxed, Freeth shows off his balance as he helps introduce the sport of aquaplaning to San Diego in 1916. San Diego History Center.

five dollars a month, and the next big swim meet in San Diego wasn't until the following July 4, when Coronado would host the Pacific Coast Championships. Even if the club had fared better than last place at the Labor Day tournament, it's not clear if Freeth's contract would have been renewed. He may have suspected as much. Winters were always a lean time for men in his line of work. Richard Barthelmess reported in his "Rowing Club Gossip" column that Freeth planned to stay in Coronado if the LAAC didn't offer him a job first—"kidnap him," in the words of the writer. Barthelmess also hinted at conflicting voices on the club's board and insisted that Freeth deserved more credit than he'd received for the swimming victories that past summer. He ended his column with a public plea: "Don't leave us, George."[33]

With more time on his hands, Freeth turned to an old standby: water polo. A four-team league was starting up, but Freeth's professional status quickly became an issue. Bill Pringle, one of Freeth's surf protégés, also represented the local branch of the AAU, which had recently formed in San Diego. He warned players that they'd be barred from swim meets if they played water polo without joining the national organization. He also reminded them that playing against professionals—namely Freeth and another man, named McKinnon—would also make them ineligible. Once again Freeth's work as a lifeguard was cited as the reason for his professional status.

The sponsor of Freeth's team, Theo Aldrich, protested the hardball tactics of the AAU. He argued in the *Union* that young people should be allowed to compete in sports without having to join a national organization or pay membership dues. One reporter noted that while "there was no great rush to get aboard the A.A.U. bandwagon," some of the players "were a little shaky about defying the governing body."[34] Freeth, likely tired of his struggles with the AAU, agreed to Pringle's request not to play in the league. Ultimately he didn't want to cause any eligibility problems for the high school students or members of the rowing club. So the games went on without him.

Around this time, news of Jack London's death made headlines around the world. The famous writer had died at the age of forty on his ranch in Northern California. Freeth's connection to London was reported in the *Union*, which reprinted London's account of meeting Freeth in the waves at Waikīkī.[35] It had been nine years since the two had surfed together. Charmian London, visiting Hawai'i with Jack in 1915, had commented that they'd heard Freeth "was teaching swimming and surf-boarding in Southern California." She noted that the "newest brood of surf-boarders" at Waikīkī "had learned and put into practice angles never dreamed of a decade earlier."[36]

Her comments were likely drawn from Lorrin P. Thurston's "Surf-Board Riding in Hawaii," published that year in *Mid-Pacific Magazine*. Thurston had been among the first group of boys to learn surfing at the Outrigger Canoe Club in 1908. The boards he described riding in 1915 were essentially the same model that Freeth used throughout his life. But the younger generation had found that they could "slide" twice as fast by turning and riding sideways along the face. As Thurston wrote, "Six years ago they stood up on the surfboards and came straight in; now they go off on a slant, sliding diagonally along the front of the wave."[37]

Native Hawaiians had long known how to ride surfboards at such angles, so the latest generation was rediscovering these techniques. Freeth himself could certainly turn a surfboard, but his preference was to use the deck like a springboard to perform jumps, flips, and twists. His reputation might have fared better in the twentieth century had surfboard styles not moved away from his shorter, wide-nosed boards. Duke's preference for longer, heavier craft—in vogue at Waikīkī because they caught waves easier, rode waves longer, and could be used to tandem with guests—became the norm in California from the 1920s until the late 1960s. The most iconic surf breaks during those years—Corona del Mar, the Palos Verdes Cove, San Onofre, and Malibu—all provided to one extent or another the long rides surfers enjoyed at Waikīkī.

The style of riding longer boards also followed Duke's influence of the statuesque pose, which London captured well in his famous account from 1907: "He is impassive, motionless, as a statue carved suddenly by some miracle out of the sea's depth from which he rose. And straight on toward shore he flies on his winged heels and the white crest of the breaker." This was the opposite of Freeth's highly kinetic style. Freeth's shorter boards were actually better suited to the quick-breaking surf at most California beaches. But Duke and Waikīkī were such dominant forces in California surfing starting in the 1920s that Freeth's shorter boards, and his acrobatic rides, faded in popularity like trolley rides and public bathhouses.

Freeth's position was similar to that of Duke's after his Olympic fame: someone who attracted admiration and praise wherever he went yet never knew where his next dollar might come from. But Freeth didn't need a lot to survive. And when given the choice, he often seemed to prefer a spare life by the beach rather than the workaday world of financial security. We can certainly see in his life the kernel of what would become "the beachboy lifestyle" that transitional figures like Tom Blake would later popularize in California from his time at Waikīkī in the 1920s and 1930s. This lifestyle essentially boiled down to prioritizing his life around the beach—working and playing, training and teaching—rather than devoting himself to raising a family or accumulating wealth. Freeth shared this proclivity with the Waikīkī beachboys, most of whom also lived from hand to mouth in the off-seasons. Renowned beachboy Alan "Turkey" Love, who started working the beach in the late 1930s, recalled that tourism in Hawai'i "only had two seasons, winter and summer. In between there was nothing. And I mean nothing."[38]

Freeth had to improvise to maintain this lifestyle. Though no longer on contract, he stayed connected to the San Diego Rowing Club during the winter months by organizing "aquatic rallies" at Los Banos to help prepare club swimmers for the July Fourth meet at Coronado.[39] Alongside the standard distance and relay races, he added novelty events to make the rallies more entertaining: "a blindfold dash," an obstacle course where swimmers had to punch through life buoys anchored in the tank, and a "follow-the-leader" diving contest, which Freeth led himself.[40] This latter event reminds us why he was such an admired and influential coach, especially for young people:

he swam and dove right alongside them, creating a fun and challenging atmosphere for them to learn and excel. He also recruited women divers to the club by offering them free lessons every Thursday night.

Freeth also found work in the club lunchroom, showing off an unexpected talent. He cooked for club members and gave the meals exotic names— "cannibal goulash" and "porpoise soup"—and earned such accolades as "chef extraordinary" and "concocter of culinary masterpieces."[41] Richard Barthelmess, now president of the rowing club, mentioned in his "Rowing Club Gossip" column that Freeth had generously treated a number of his hungry friends to a meal in late February. Reinforcing the fellowship that Freeth had found in this community, Barthelmess added, "Let us know when you feel that way again, Gawge."[42]

Freeth's reputation for cooking spread beyond the rowing club. In early April he was hired to cater a fishing tournament at Del Mar sponsored by the local sporting goods store, Cycle and Arms. They dubbed him "president of the feed squad," and his surf protégé Bill Pringle, who also worked at Cycle and Arms, took charge of the bait for contestants.[43] Pringle, who'd recently been reappointed to oversee AAU affairs in San Diego, convinced Freeth to serve on the seven-man committee with him.[44] We don't know how long Freeth held this position, but it was a surprising twist given his embattled relationship with the AAU over the years. He was certainly well versed in the ins and outs of amateur competition—mostly on the outs, unfortunately for him.

Freeth lived east of downtown at 1240 C Street during the year 1917, home of "The Best Apartments," the catchy slogan of proprietor E. C. Best.[45] Freeth was used to smaller rooming houses during his years in Redondo Beach, and though there were some twenty others living in the apartments around him now, they represented much the same population as his other lodgings: working-class men and women trying to make a life for themselves in Southern California.[46] Among Freeth's neighbors were Fred Albright and George Noe, meat cutters; E. J. Browne, a cook; Ruth Favel, a chocolate dipper for the candy makers Showley Brothers; Mrs. Alice Neff, a dressmaker; Mrs. Estelle Stewart, a "waiter" at the Jewett Hotel; Harry and Emma Hill, who worked as a tailor and a buyer, respectively; and Cleve and Lela Lewis (he was a splicer for Pacific Telephone and Telegraph). It was a mobile population, much like Freeth himself. Looking at city directories in years preceding and following 1917, one doesn't find many of the same names at the Best Apartments.

As the spring of 1917 arrived, Freeth turned his attention back to the beach. The *Evening Tribune* reported in late March that he'd be working at Coronado that summer. The paper went on to explain that Freeth had been consulted about hiring a lifeguard crew to patrol area beaches: two men at Ocean Beach, one at Mission Beach, and another at La Jolla. Ernest Davies, secretary of San Diego's Civil Service Commission, planned to have Freeth organize a series of physical tests to ensure that the applicants were capable of performing their duties at the highest level. Freeth came up with the following program: the men had to dive from a height of 25 feet, swim half a mile in thirty minutes, swim 150 yards through the surf and tow a body back to shore, dive 10 feet underwater and retrieve a 20-pound weight, row a lifeboat out through the waves, and, finally, demonstrate two methods of artificial respiration.[47]

Had the event actually taken place, it likely would have been the first official beach lifeguard testing program in Southern California. Unfortunately Davies resigned in early June, and the fate of Freeth's program remains unknown.[48] It's safe to say that Freeth based this program on training methods he was already using—along with surfing—so informally it was already in place. By early June, Freeth was in charge of swim instruction and general aquatic entertainment at Coronado Tent City, a popular summer resort on the outer edge of San Diego Bay. He'd also been rehired by the San Diego Rowing Club to prepare their swimmers for the July Fourth event competition.[49] This was part-time work, two nights a week, until the day of the tournament. The LAAC had beaten the club badly at an impromptu swim meet in mid-May: Freeth had taken seven swimmers up to Los Angeles, and the Mercurymen had won every single event.[50] In addition to the challenge of getting his swimmers into shape for the state championships, the United States had entered World War I in late April. Freeth had to try to pull together a team with young men everywhere enlisting in the army and navy.

11

Chief Lifeguard

Corporal J. H. Sherman manned a recruiting office at Coronado Tent City on Sunday, June 3, 1917, during opening weekend of the resort. Among the estimated ten thousand visitors, he was hoping to recruit 150 men for the Fifth and Sixth companies of coast artillery.[1] The U.S. Marines had established barracks at Balboa Park during the Panama-California Exposition, and the army's Camp Kearny, eleven miles north of San Diego, was little more than a month away from serving as a jumping-off point to World War I battlegrounds.[2]

Freeth was thirty-three years old in the summer of 1917 and still more than a year away from his own registration in the third round of selective service. As the war geared up for Americans, Freeth geared up for a full summer of activity as Tent City's lifeguard, swimming instructor, and all-around master of aquatic entertainment. John D. Spreckels had founded Tent City in 1900 as a way for the rising middle class to experience a taste of resort life. While the grand Victorian-style Hotel del Coronado (also owned by Spreckels) catered to the wealthier guests—movie stars, East Coast elites, U.S. presidents—the five hundred tents and thatched-roof cottages stretching south of the hotel created a mini-city where the slender of purse could bask in the sun and enjoy amusement-park amenities. Tent City had its own restaurants, grocery store, merry-go-round, bowling alleys, shooting gallery, a pool hall, theater, bandstand, and dancing pavilion. It had a police department and even a newspaper, the *Coronado Strand*. One could rent a fully furnished tent or pick and choose camping items à la carte: cots, tables, oil lamps, and beds. A trolley cut down the middle of Tent City to transport visitors up and down the beach, and one could reach the resort by ferry or automobile.[3]

Coronado Tent City looking north toward the grand Hotel del Coronado. Courtesy Coronado Public Library.

Much as Redondo Beach had been developed by Henry Huntington, so San Diego had its own wealthy booster in John D. Spreckels, eldest son of Claus Spreckels, who'd had such a strong influence on King Kalākaua and the development of the sugar industry in Hawai'i. Beyond the Hotel del Coronado and Tent City, John D. Spreckels owned the Oceanic Steamship Company, which transported passengers, mail, and freight from the mainland to Hawai'i, Australia, and New Zealand (Freeth had first arrived in California on the company's ship *Alameda*). Spreckels had invested millions into the development of San Diego proper: the streetcar system, newspapers (he owned both the *San Diego Union* and the *San Diego Evening Tribune*), railroads, and water and electric companies. Spreckels himself had lived in Hawai'i in the late 1870s and invested in his father's sugar plantation, known as Spreckelsville, on Maui. As Tent City's lifeguard, Freeth was essentially a Spreckels employee.

The San Diego Rowing Club members—one of whom had cracked, "Looks good to see our ol' coach, George Freeth, among the Tent City moguls for the summer"—planned to picnic at Tent City with the San Diego Yacht Club during opening weekend. The yacht club wanted to prevail upon Freeth "to demonstrate with the surfboard, as per usual."[4] Freeth had been giving surf exhibitions at Ocean Beach with Bill Pringle the previous month as part of the Ocean Beach Booster Club's efforts to attract visitors. Other events included bathing suit contests and racing Harley-Davidson motorcycles along the beach.[5]

But Freeth didn't have much time to surf once Tent City opened. His organizing skills came in handy as he oversaw a program of swimming, diving, boat races, and general water fun for the next three and a half months. Tent City would close up in September, so at least Freeth knew when he'd have to start looking for his next job.

In the meantime he put in long days at the outdoor saltwater pool, giving free swim lessons to women and children, sometimes as early as 6:00 A.M. "Freeth is not enthusiastic about getting up at such an unseemly hour," reported the *Union*, "but he has been known to do it frequently as an accommodation to those who desire to learn the art of swimming before the crowds of bathers and onlookers arrive."[6] The pool normally opened at 10:00 A.M. and didn't shut down until the evening. Sometimes his days were extended when the resort hosted one of its midnight bathing parties.

Freeth also organized special water carnivals reminiscent of those he'd competed in at Honolulu Harbor. He held swimming and rowing races, including events with canoes, single sculls, and four-oared barges. He added novelty events like canoe-tilting contests to entertain the crowds. He did his part by giving diving exhibitions, which turned into good advertisement for Tent City when pictures of his acrobatics were published in the *San Diego Union*.[7]

Freeth was still coaching club swimmers two nights a week for the upcoming Pacific Coast Championships over the July Fourth weekend. Given the club's part-time practice sessions beginning in late May, their last-place finish behind San Francisco's Olympic Club and the LAAC was fairly predictable. Two of Freeth's swimmers, Charlie Shields and Elliott Burns, managed a couple of second places in the 220- and 880-yard freestyle races, respectively. But the star of the meet was future Olympian Norman Ross of the Olympic Club, who swept everyone else by winning seven events. Freeth was able to reconnect with several of his protégés during the competition: Gerald Witt and Ray Kegeris, from his Redondo Beach days, and women's national diving champion Aileen Allen, whom Freeth had coached at the LAAC.[8] Ludy Langer wasn't at the meet. He'd moved to Honolulu after graduating from UC Berkeley in 1916. Langer found work as a civil engineer at Pearl Harbor and would join the army by the end of the year.

The saltwater pool at Coronado Tent City (c. 1920), where Freeth spent the summer of 1917 as head swimming instructor. Courtesy Coronado Public Library.

After the state tournament Freeth continued with his packed schedule at Tent City. The outdoor saltwater pool was open seven days a week and reported by the *Union* to be "the most frequented spot in the resort for women and children bathers." The same paper noted that Freeth had gained a reputation for turning timid beginners into "enthusiastic swimmers . . . ready to become expert divers."[9] Though Freeth had many dramatic rescues during his career, so much of his contribution to lifesaving came in the day-to-day work of prevention: teaching people, one at a time, to feel confident in the water so that they could avoid trouble and actually enjoy the many pleasures offered by the ocean.

Tent City welcomed an unexpected visitor that summer: one August afternoon, a sixty-foot whale swam into San Diego Bay, flipped a motorboat over its back, and then managed to beach itself on a shallow sandbar. Freeth, on lifeguard duty, got hold of a .30–30 rifle from somewhere and was "about to make a determined stand" when the whale managed to thrash itself loose and escape. Freeth later pulled a large chunk of its hide off the bottom of the motorboat. Friends told him that, considering his reputation of performing "most any conceivable act in the water"—including catching fish with his hands—he should have swum out to meet the creature. Freeth replied that "he wasn't going to play 'Jonah' for any whale."[10]

He remained active in and around Tent City as summer came to a close. He appeared in films at the local theater aquaplaning on San Diego Bay.[11] He

visited the Coronado City Council and lobbied for more-effective lifesaving equipment at Tent City, showing them pictures of his tripod setup and the three-wheeled motorcycle. Over Labor Day he helped the local Boy Scout troop win top honors in the swimming events at their annual competition against other area troops. He also competed in a lifeguard swim race after Labor Day, when Tent City threw a special picnic for all of its employees.[12]

Once Tent City closed for the season, Freeth ventured north to Redondo and stayed with his old lifeguard friend George Mitchell, who'd been on the back of the motorcycle years before when Freeth had broken his ankle. The *Redondo Reflex* reported that Freeth was "awaiting a call from the New York Engineers Corps to go to the front at any time."[13] This was a bit premature for Freeth, who was probably in town scouting lifeguard opportunities either at the beach or the bathhouse. He ended up returning to San Diego in early November and taking his old job as a swimming instructor at Los Banos. His friends were encouraged to go down and see him sporting a new mustache— "some humdinger," according to the "Rowing Club Gossip" column.[14] Freeth was pinching pennies by this point and couldn't afford to pay for lodging. The rowing club voted on his thirty-fourth birthday to let him stay in the captain's room "for a short time."

There were no lifeguard jobs to be had for Freeth at the local beaches. The La Jolla Chamber of Commerce had managed to convince the San Diego Police Department to budget for a year-round lifeguard at their beach, a position filled in late October by Hiram Barton.[15] But the other beach cities were less proactive, and budget woes limited lifeguard hiring to the summer season: June 1 to October 1. That was unfortunate for local draftsman James A. Webster, who drowned at Ocean Beach in mid-December while beachgoers watched helplessly from shore.[16]

The San Diego Rowing Club allowed Freeth to stay at their clubhouse for seven weeks altogether and then asked him to move out two days after Christmas.[17] He welcomed the new year by hitting up his friend Bill Pringle for a sales job at the Cycle and Arms sporting goods store.

~

Freeth passed the winter and spring at Cycle and Arms, popping up now and then in the "Rowing Club Gossip" column.[18] He stayed in contact with Duke Kahanamoku, who wrote Freeth a letter saying he was eager to come to the mainland and compete in swim tournaments. Freeth gave advance notice of Duke's arrival through the newspapers and predicted that his friend would be the star of the tour and return to Honolulu a champion. Freeth added that he wasn't doing much swimming himself in San Diego. He told a reporter that he was a member of "a big corporation" and had "'won a home' with the president."[19] Freeth liked to talk a good game, but the last comment might suggest that he was living with Pringle. At some point during this time, Freeth ended up living several blocks from Cycle and Arms at the New Southern Hotel on Sixth Street.[20]

That spring, while Duke and other Hawaiian swimmers were supporting the Red Cross on their sixteen-city tour of the United States and parts of Canada, Ocean Beach's lack of a lifeguard service was about to change Freeth's life. On April 21 fourteen swimmers were rescued over three hours by two policemen and one former policeman. Heeding calls that bathers at Ocean Beach were in trouble in a heavy "tide rip," the men—Frank Merritt, Glen Freese, and Edward Schlitz—managed to row a lifeboat out. Despite being capsized numerous times, they were able to haul all the bathers into shore safely. That Sunday rescue was merely a prologue, however: exactly two weeks later, thirteen men drowned at Ocean Beach in one day, ten of them members of the military.

In response to the April 21 rescue, San Diego's city council had met on May 4 and approved hiring Louis Chauvaud as a lifeguard at Ocean Beach.[21] Chauvaud had lifeguarded there the four previous summers, but he was quickly overwhelmed on May 5, his first day on duty. About 250 people were in the water that afternoon. The water temperature was chilly, sixty-four degrees, but the current remained calm until about 3:30 P.M.

Eight soldiers walked down to shore at the foot of Santa Monica Street. Chauvaud alerted them to a fast-moving current that had started running north along the beach. He told them that it was too dangerous to enter at that point and ordered them to go back.

The soldiers weren't about to take orders from any civilian. "Mind your own business," they said, "and go to hell."

Chauvaud told them to stay within fifty feet of shore. Instead, they went straight out to the breakers "and led the crowd out."[22]

Chauvaud followed. The current quickly knocked him off his feet as he made his way out. He ran into four bathers who had started to swim back, and two grabbed hold of him. After a severe struggle, he managed to get both of them ashore. He swam back out, grabbed a woman, and brought her in to safety.

Over the next two hours, seventy people were rescued. Two of the police officers who'd been part of the April 21 rescue—Merritt and Freese—arrived on the scene. Apparently they'd taken a late lunch. They began saving bathers with lifeboats, though the waves capsized them time and again. Soldiers, civilians, and off-duty policemen formed human chains and manned lifelines to pull people to safety.

Despite the many heroics from people on the beach, seven soldiers from Camp Kearny lost their lives. Three seamen from the navy's North Island, adjacent to Coronado, also drowned. Among those ten, Private Charles Humphrey from Bakery Company No. 323 had died trying to rescue another bather; Machinist's Mate Henry P. Hanson of North Island had reportedly saved between five and eight people before succumbing himself.

Only two bodies were recovered that day—those of Humphrey and Private Hugh Burr from the machine gun battalion. It took nearly an hour to get Burr to shore, by which time it was too late to save him with a pulmotor. Humphrey had been swept north into Mission Bay. They worked on him for an hour and a half without success. The remaining victims were taken by the sea. Their clothes remained behind in the dressing rooms of the bathhouses to mark their identities.

San Diego's chief of police, S. P. McMullen, closed Ocean Beach the day of the drownings and posted guards to keep watch all night for any bodies that might drift in. Search parties also fanned out to Sunset Cliffs, immediately south of Ocean Beach, and as far north as Pacific Beach, on the other side of Mission Bay.

The next day McMullen wrote to Mayor Louis J. Wilde and the city council, requesting they join him at Ocean Beach to inspect the site themselves. A large group arrived that afternoon to conduct the investigation, including four city council members, Chief McMullen, two officers representing the army and navy, and a number of Ocean Beach locals. They interviewed Chauvaud, Merritt, and Freese to gain firsthand information of how the tragedy had unfolded. The group tried to determine the source of the problem to prevent it from happening again, but there were no easy answers. Many of their comments reveal their limited knowledge of beach and ocean conditions in general. They hardly knew which questions to ask.

The navy representative, a Lieutenant Cushman, asked about the lifeboats, the number of oars in each boat, and the length of the oars. Councilman Bard asked Chauvaud if he had warned the first group of eight soldiers. Councilman Fay asked if Chauvaud's bathing suit showed his authority. Councilman Moore, who presided over the investigation, asked if the south wind had had any effect on the riptide. They wanted to know other things: Were the bathers good or poor swimmers? Wasn't it true that men who manned lifeboats were liable to be thrown into the surf and unable to help? How many life preservers were stationed at the beach? How long had Chauvaud worked at Ocean Beach?

They also wanted to know about the rescue on April 21, but Chauvaud replied that the current had been completely different that day. Councilman Moore asked him if the conditions at that moment were more dangerous than they'd been the day before. Chauvaud said he didn't know—he hadn't been in the water that day. He indicated that conditions at the beach changed so often that determining the safest place to bathe had to be done every day.

The committee asked for recommendations. Officer Freese suggested anchoring a float in the surf and running a V line to the beach where bathers would be safe to swim. Lieutenant Cushman added that lifeguards should be given the authority to arrest anybody attempting to enter the water outside of the V line. Ocean Beach resident H. G. Gottesburen said it would be better to anchor two pylons out in the surf and run lifelines to the beach—a float in the surf would only encourage novices to swim out and dive off of it. Another citizen suggested installing a rope gun on the beach and firing buoys at drowning bathers. Officer Merritt recommended building a fence to section off the most dangerous part of the beach; police officers and military police could patrol the fence on Wednesdays, weekends, and holidays, and anybody bathing north of the fence would be arrested. Councilman Moore concluded, for his part, "Unless it is absolutely necessary to stop swimming here now, something should be done, and done immediately."[23]

To make sense of the information—and the conflicting advice—the council contacted Freeth. He'd given a number of surf exhibitions at Ocean Beach the year before, so he was familiar with the conditions. He visited the site and presented a number of safeguards to the council. He tended to agree that anchoring a float out in the surf would "only induce poor swimmers to go farther out than they should."[24]

The city council ended up hiring Freeth as chief lifeguard for seventy-five dollars a month and following all of his recommendations. They purchased a three-wheeled motorcycle with the stretcher and rescue-reel assembly. They installed a tripod with the reel, wire, and torpedo buoy at the foot of Santa Monica Street, where the thirteen people had drowned. They installed another tripod assembly at Mission Beach. They ordered new lifeboats built to Freeth's specifications—his personal preference was the Swamp Scott Dory, a two-person boat. The city also required all the bathhouses to purchase similar lifeboats, and they closed the beach for the rest of the month until everyone complied.

But Freeth understood that Ocean Beach needed more than lifesaving equipment: the beaches needed lifeguards who had been properly trained to use the gear during emergencies. This was especially true for handling lifeboats in heavy surf. Freeth reserved one of the new lifeboats for rescues, and the other as a training vessel. Two weeks before opening day, he gave a demonstration of the new equipment and crew for city council members. He supervised the lifeguards and police officers who'd already been hired—Chauvaud, Merritt, and Freese—and brought in young Jimmy McIntosh from the San Diego Rowing Club as a "victim" to be rescued. Freeth's demonstration was so impressive that the city council considered putting him in charge of all the lifeguards at San Diego beaches.[25]

Ocean Beach finally opened on May 30, much to the relief of the bathhouses and other businesses. The city had been promoting itself intensively as a weekend destination since 1913 when it opened Wonderland Park, which could be reached in twenty minutes by trolley from downtown San Diego. Wonderland Park boasted a roller coaster, casino, dancing pavilion, zoo, and dozens of concessions. The resort suffered, however, when the Panama-California Exposition opened in 1915 and drew visitors away. Wonderland Park closed the following year after a flood permanently damaged the roller coaster.[26] As part of various weekend programs to draw visitors back to the resort, Freeth began surfing at Ocean Beach in the spring of 1917. After the drowning tragedy of May 5, Ocean Beach officials came up with the idea of a massive four-day treasure hunt to advertise opening weekend.

Secret committees fanned out across the beach each night and buried thousands of coupons in the sand. These were placed into oilskin envelopes and tubes to protect them. The donated prizes were announced in the papers ahead of time to stoke excitement: a washing machine, gold cuff links, an eighteen-dollar vanity bag, two hundred dollars in cash, hotel stays, free admission to the dance hall and pool room, and dozens of other services and prizes—haircuts, meals, dental visits, a starter bank account, merry-go-round rides. Hundreds of bottles of root beer and White Ribbon temperance beer were also buried for treasure seekers.

The crowds came, and Freeth was ready with his lifeguard crew, to which he'd added two of his top swimmers from the rowing club: Charlie Shields and Elliott Burns. In addition, Ocean Beach resident H. G. Gottesburen organized a volunteer lifesaving corps to supplement the lifeguards. On top of their lifeguard duties, Freeth's crew gave swimming, diving, and surfing exhibitions during the four-day celebration.[27]

Although the military commander at Camp Kearny continued to ban soldiers from swimming at Ocean Beach because of the drownings, the resort tapped into wartime patriotism by holding drills, flag-raising ceremonies, and various public addresses. A lingering reminder of the dangers still present came in the form of a body discovered by fishermen in the kelp beds several miles offshore. It was believed to be one of the victims from May 5. Freeth and Louis Chauvaud took charge of the corpse and brought it down to the San Diego coroner.[28]

Overall Freeth couldn't have chosen a more ideal summer for himself. He was working on the beach once again at a job he loved. He had a supportive city council behind him that funded all the lifesaving equipment he'd need to keep bathers safe for the rest of the season. The crew and equipment Freeth had assembled certainly served as a model for any beach town that wanted to protect its citizens and visitors. San Diego had acted decisively after the tragedy of May 5, true enough. But like most cities, they didn't feel obligated to protect bathers year-round. San Diego would not fund a county-wide lifeguard service until 1942.[29]

Working his third summer in San Diego, Freeth had found more than another job at the beach. He'd found a community. He'd registered to vote as a Democrat earlier that year, perhaps a sign that he intended to stay long-term.[30] He'd also remained close with members of the rowing club. They'd quickly taken him in two summers before, and Freeth continued to deepen those friendships through work and social events. He'd hired club members Charlie Shields and Elliott Burns as lifeguards at Ocean Beach, not only because of their skill in the water but also to keep them in top swimming form. He did the same for Jimmy McIntosh, his young protégé, who told the papers during the July Fourth swim meet the previous year, "I owe all my success to

Summer 1918 at Ocean Beach, where Freeth was hired after thirteen men drowned in one day, ten of them members of the U.S. military. Freeth had innovated the idea of using a motorcycle as part of his rescues in Redondo Beach in 1913. Bishop Museum Archives.

the coaching of George Freeth."[31] Freeth had McIntosh appointed lifeguard at Ocean Beach in mid-July. Instead of working out at the San Diego Rowing Club every day, McIntosh trained at the beach with Freeth. The routine was later acknowledged as the reason why McIntosh was able to break the club record in their swim competition in late September.[32]

It was also a great summer of surfing for Freeth. After nearly a dozen years of giving exhibitions in California, he still drew large crowds. Advertisements for Ocean Beach in the local papers urged visitors to "See Champion Freeth ride the surfboards."[33] As he'd done in Venice back in 1907, Freeth also gave free surf lessons to beachgoers and used the sport to keep his lifeguards fit

Freeth at Ocean Beach with San Diego Rowing Club swimmer Jimmy McIntosh, June 1918. The surfboard and lifeboat represent the twin activities around which California beach culture developed. Freeth's deep tan and relaxed demeanor would become hallmarks of future California surfers.

and to teach them about waves and currents. By midsummer his exhibitions were so popular that Ocean Beach hired him to surf every afternoon for the rest of the season.[34] He performed his normal routine while riding waves—standing on his head, lying down, doing dives. On July 14, in front of a reported crowd of four thousand, he was inspired to add a new move to his repertoire. The *San Diego Union* wrote, "Riding on the crest of the wave in the usual manner, Freeth suddenly leaped, clearing the board by at least three feet, turned a somersault, regained his balance on the board again, then completed his stunt with a dive. The trick was a thriller, and evoked a storm of applause."[35] Even considering the acrobatic aerials performed on today's waves, it's incredible to imagine a surfer doing a backflip on an eight-foot board in the middle of a ride and then continuing to surf. Freeth was thirty-four years old—still putting on a show for the crowd, still innovating and having fun on his surfboard.

When Jimmy McIntosh joined the lifeguard crew, Freeth updated his exhibitions to keep the shows interesting. He started tandem surfing with McIntosh—the two riding one board—and he and the other lifeguards gave free bodysurfing lessons every morning.[36] Surfing received a big boost in mid-August when a dozen soldiers from Honolulu joined Freeth in the waves. They were part of the Thirty-Second Infantry Brigade at Camp Kearny. "With 13 surfboard riders racing to the beach on the crest of the breakers at one time," reported the *Evening Tribune*, "visitors to Ocean Beach yesterday enjoyed a rare and wonderful sight."[37] It's safe to say the "regiment of surfboard riders" was the largest crowd of surfers that had ever paddled out together in California.

Perhaps because of the Honolulu surfers, rumors spread that the army had lifted the ban on bathing at Ocean Beach. Freeth reportedly set about organizing "surfboard riding races" with the new arrivals. Lieutenant Colonel Harry D. Blastland, commander of the Thirty-Second Infantry and acting commander of Camp Kearny, had to republish his orders in the *Union* that his soldiers were still forbidden to bathe at Ocean Beach or enter the water for any reason.[38]

So the surfboard races never happened. Freeth continued to perform without the soldiers. He relied on Jimmy McIntosh and the other lifeguards to join him in exhibitions over Labor Day. In mid-September he registered for the military himself—in the third round of selective service for men eighteen through forty-five. His military registration card listed his address as 1940 Abbott, so he'd been living at Ocean Beach since being hired as a lifeguard. While Freeth awaited orders, the local sandbars suddenly shifted, providing an early example of how good surf attracts tourists.

During the first week of October, the waves changed from "sharp breakers" into "long, rolling breakers," which, according to Freeth, permitted "surfboard riding feats which have heretofore been impossible." This was a boon for Ocean Beach businesses so late in the season. They quickly organized a special weekend program that featured Freeth riding the Waikīkī-style waves each morning and afternoon.[39]

In early November Freeth appeared on a list of alternates for men shipping out to Kelly Field in Texas, and to Camp Lewis in the state of Washington. The armistice was signed on November 11, however, so Freeth was never called up to duty. Though far from the European battlefields, Ocean Beach displayed constant reminders of the war. Army engineers had been working since early July to place pontoons across the channel at Mission Bay, and crowds came to Freeth's beach every day to watch the soldiers work.[40] Announcements for Freeth's surfing appeared in the papers alongside the Overseas Honor Roll of soldiers who'd been killed or wounded in action and those who'd died of disease.[41] The disease itself—a virulent strain of influenza—traveled with the soldiers from Europe to San Diego in the second wave of the pandemic, bringing the deadliest aspect of trench warfare back to the States. It was the second worst epidemic in U.S. history, first hitting Boston in late August 1918. More U.S. soldiers died of disease—about 57,000—than were killed on World War I battlefields. While an incredible 50 million people are estimated to have died of the flu worldwide, 675,000 Americans succumbed in three waves of the disease in 1918 and 1919.[42] With no vaccine to prevent flu infection, and no antibiotics to treat secondary infections like pneumonia, communities resorted to the same measures that have been used to fight the latest pandemic of COVID-19: personal hygiene, quarantine, and wearing masks.

Military officials understood that quarantine was the most effective way of battling the epidemic. But Army Chief of Staff Peyton March "invoked the exigencies of a war of attrition" to maintain troop transport to Europe.[43] Since Russia had pulled out of the war in 1917, Germany no longer had to fight on two fronts; the U.S. military believed that quickly building up a massive fighting force in Europe was key to defeating the Central Powers. President Woodrow Wilson ultimately deferred to March's judgment, and the transports continued despite widespread sickness.

The flu hit Camp Kearny on September 21, 1918. Over the next six weeks, during the deadliest period of the epidemic (the second wave), the San Diego City Council passed a number of resolutions to encourage citizens to comply with local Board of Health orders: wearing gauze masks in public and obeying quarantine laws. But when the United States signed the armistice, quarantine laws were impossible to enforce. Americans celebrated in the streets, which helped fuel the final wave of the epidemic. The flu grew so bad in San Diego that the city council was forced to "establish an absolute quarantine upon all places within the City" from December 4 to December 11. The council also required "the universal use of gauze masks within the City" until midnight, December 18. This order was later extended to Christmas Eve. Local bathhouses requested an exception for bathers swimming in their pools, which the city council granted.[44]

Freeth was working at Los Banos in mid-December. The water temperature in San Diego Bay was too chilly for rowing club swimmers, so they trained every morning in the bathhouse pool. Jimmy McIntosh trained with them and had started coaching under Freeth's tutelage. The club swimmers were preparing themselves for the upcoming swim meets in 1919.[45]

Freeth had escaped both the war and the first two waves of influenza. However, he fell sick in the first week of the new year. On January 15 he was admitted to the Agnew Hospital and Sanitarium in downtown San Diego.

Last Breath

At a meeting of the San Diego Rowing Club on Thursday, March 13, the officers held a discussion regarding Freeth's long stay in the hospital. Club secretary Charles Weldon had been giving them regular updates on Freeth's condition.[1] Freeth had battled the flu for eight weeks—a nearly miraculous period of time for a disease that could kill a healthy person within twenty-four hours if pneumonia took hold. Death rates around the country had been staggering. When the flu hit the army's Camp Grant in Illinois, for example, fourteen soldiers died on Tuesday, October 1, 1918; thirty died on Wednesday; forty-six on Thursday; seventy-six on Friday; and more than two hundred died over the weekend. Acting camp commander Colonel Charles B. Hagadorn, despondent over the high death toll—he'd lost more than five hundred men—committed suicide with his pistol on October 7. Camp Grant ultimately lost over a thousand men to the epidemic. In the last two weeks of that same month, over seven thousand people died in Philadelphia; more than nine thousand died in New York City.[2]

But Freeth was on the mend, and the club officers decided to set up a relief fund until he could return to work. They sent announcements through the local papers informing friends and admirers up and down the coast about Freeth's condition and requested their help. "The big, genial fellow is just pulling through an attack of influenza which has kept his life in doubt for the [p]ast 10 weeks," announced the *Evening Tribune*. "Some of the young men he has taught and helped here and know his charming personality want to tide him over, help him get on his feet and going strong again." The *San Diego Union* put Freeth's picture in the paper and added that he was just now getting about but was "still too weak to engage in his regular vocation." The

Union listed some of Freeth's famous rescues and mentioned his work with Duke Kahanamoku at the LAAC.[3] Duke himself had come down with the flu in Washington, D.C., the previous summer, but he'd managed to recover and eventually made his way home, some twenty pounds lighter and looking like "a ghost."[4]

The subscription worked. Within two days Weldon had collected over one hundred dollars from well-wishers. He expected another hundred to arrive shortly. The *Union* reported that young rowing club members were dropping off donations of five and ten dollars apiece: "All expressed pleasure at the chance of helping one who has done so much for the rowing club and for beach cities on the Pacific."[5] The announcements reached San Francisco and Honolulu. In Redondo Beach the Elks started organizing a swim tournament to raise a purse for Freeth.[6]

Two weeks after the announcement, however, Freeth still couldn't shake the bug. Ludy Langer, receiving news of Freeth's illness, decided to visit him. Langer had been discharged from the army months before and would soon be traveling to Honolulu to train for the upcoming swim season. At first the doctors didn't want to let him in—Freeth had contracted pneumonia—but Langer pressed, and the staff finally relented.

Sixty years later, Langer described his brief visit: "He was very ill and didn't say much. He liked his drinks every night, gin fizzes mostly. But he always had sense enough to work them off the next day. I just talked about that and the old days and once or twice I got a smile out of him."[7]

On Sunday afternoon, April 6, Freeth asked the staff to take him up to the roof of the hospital. They had a garden above the fourth floor, bordered by palm trees. He wanted to feel the sun's warmth and look out at the ocean. He saw sailboats and steamships down in the harbor. Although the beaches lay beyond San Diego Bay, he reportedly watched and listened to waves roll in.[8] As Duke had said about his own recovery from the flu, "I needed the sun. I needed the surf."[9]

Freeth returned to his bed and passed a quiet night, the fresh air doing him good. The next morning about ten o'clock he suddenly felt a change for the worse in his heart and informed his nurse. He told Maud Burns (wife of club member E. J. Burns), who had helped care for him during his hospital stay, "I guess the old pump is pretty bad." He asked her to contact his mother and to tell her that he'd been "thinking of her and [his] sisters all the time."

Late that night Mrs. Burns was still by his side. Freeth thanked her for everything she'd done for him. Because there was no cure for the flu, all Mrs. Burns—or any doctor, for that matter—could do for Freeth was ease his suffering and make him comfortable.

An hour later, at 11:20 P.M., after nearly three months in the hospital, Freeth passed away at the age of thirty-five. His death certificate listed the following cause: "Influenza—Suppuration; Pleurisy (Empyema); Acute Dilatation of Heart with a contributory factor of Lobular Pneumonia." In lay terms—and bitterly ironic considering his life's work—Freeth's lungs became inflamed and filled up with liquid, causing his heart to give out due to lack of oxygen in the bloodstream. In essence, he drowned.

~

The hospital sent a cablegram to Lizzie in Honolulu letting her know about her son's death. Freeth's sister Dorothy replied that it would be impossible for the family to come to San Diego and take charge of the body. She told them to have it cremated and send the ashes to Honolulu.[10] The family held a public ceremony on May 4, interring him at Nuʻuanu Cemetery.[11]

Members of the rowing club took charge of the funeral arrangements in San Diego. They accepted ninety dollars from Freeth's friends in Redondo Beach to help pay expenses. Richard Barthelmess, who'd been collecting donations for Freeth along with Charles Weldon, wrote in his "Rowing Club Gossip" column, "George's untimely death cast a feeling of deep sorrow over his great circle of close friends at the S.D.R.C."[12] They set the funeral for Saturday, April 12, in the chapel of Johnson-Saum Funeral Home.[13]

Eugene Estoppey, a local gardener and endurance athlete who had trained with Freeth, created a special floral arrangement for the ceremony. He intertwined poppies and other local flowers into the shape of a life preserver to honor his friend. The casket, laden with flowers, was carried by six members of the rowing club: E. J. Burns, Neil E. Brown, E. B. Gould Jr., Richard Jessop, Richard H. Barthelmess, and Charles E. Weldon.[14]

Attorney Charles E. Sumner, a two-time president of the rowing club, gave the eulogy that afternoon. In front of hundreds of mourners, he offered the club's "loving tribute" to Freeth, whom he referred to as "a brave, fearless, tender gentleman."[15] Sumner reminded those gathered that Freeth had been captain of the Volunteer Life Saving Corps at Venice and head swimming instructor at the LAAC before taking on the same role at the San Diego Rowing Club. Freeth had "trained and turned out the greatest swimmers in the world," Sumner said, a statement that would be confirmed the following year when Duke, Langer, and Ray Kegeris won gold and silver medals at the 1920 Olympics. Sumner mentioned how Freeth had also excelled at diving and water polo; "as a surf board rider," he added, "he had no equal in this country."

Sumner then read from a *Los Angeles Examiner* article that described Freeth's heroics in rescuing the seven Japanese fishermen in December 1908, an event that came to define Freeth for his bravery and his revolutionary technique of swimming through storm surf to save lives. He noted that Freeth received a Gold Life-Saving Medal for this act—the highest honor the U.S. government bestowed upon a lifesaver. But it was what Sumner called Freeth's "humanitarian application" of his skills that had always sparked people's admiration and appreciation for the Hawaiian.

Sumner recalled how San Diego had sought Freeth's expertise after the drowning of thirteen men the year before and remarked that after the city hired him, no lives were lost at Ocean Beach under his watch. Sumner added that since Freeth had left the job, several drownings had been reported at area beaches. He described Freeth's long illness and his stay in the hospital. Freeth's "last hour," he said, "comported with the whole tenor of his life; he met the grim messenger in the same brave way that he had met all the situations in life. In death, as in life, his courage increased with his peril."

"His qualities were not limited to the good he has done to humanity in surf and wave," Sumner continued, "but his even temper, his cheery smile, his sunny disposition, radiated and brought comfort and warmth to all about him. I have never seen him ruffled, or out of sorts, nor have I ever seen him exhibit anything but the best of good nature and kindly feeling for his fellow."

Freeth was not a success based on what Sumner called "the sordid yard stick of commercialism." But he was a success "measured by his courage, his daring, and his heroism . . . Measured by the higher and purer qualities of heart and soul."

Sumner concluded his eulogy by speaking directly to his fallen friend:

George, the San Diego Rowing Club appreciates what you have done, and loves you for it. For thirteen weeks we have received almost daily reports as to your condition . . . and during the entire time of your sickness we hoped and prayed for your recovery.

And now, in behalf of the six hundred members of the San Diego Rowing Club, I bid you good-bye. May this, your last earthly sleep be attended by that sweet peace and repose which always comes with the consciousness of a life well spent.

~

The news of Freeth's death carried to New York, where an obituary in the *Tribune* several weeks later not only testified to his national reputation but also captured well the legacy he had established for succeeding generations:

The recent death of George Freeth, former coach at the Los Angeles A.C., deprived swimming of one of its ablest and most enthusiastic promoters.

A national authority on all branches of watermanship and a close student of the science of natation, Freeth launched on a successful career many a champion, including Ludy Langer. But sport never caused him to overlook the most important purpose of swimming, lifesaving, and every pupil was taught the best methods of rescue and resuscitation. Directly, or indirectly, a great number of lives must stand to his credit, for he personally performed frequent rescues, several under such dangerous conditions that they won him medals for bravery. He will prove a sad loss.[16]

The lives that stood to Freeth's credit, based on several newspaper reports before his death, numbered between two and three hundred.[17] The *Tribune's* observation of Freeth's authority "on all branches of watermanship" became what is known as the "waterman tradition" that emanated from Hawai'i and which Freeth established in California. In order to better save lives, Freeth trained his lifeguards to become expert in all manner of aquatic skills and ocean craft: swimming, diving, water polo, surfing, bodysurfing, rowing, and resuscitation. He honed their skills through coaching and competition to make them the most effective lifesaving force on the Pacific Coast.

True to his Hawaiian roots, Freeth's legacy always included a waterwoman tradition as well. Lyba and Nita Sheffield, who had trained under Freeth in Venice (their father, Dr. Homer Sheffield, was a surgeon in the Volunteer Life Saving Corps), later organized the Girls' Life-Saving Corps when they became students at the University of California at Berkeley. As mentioned earlier, they wrote a textbook, *Swimming Simplified* (1920), in which they promoted swimming and lifesaving both as healthy exercise and worthy of inclusion in every school curriculum. Freeth had advocated this message not only while he worked at the LAAC but also while back in his early days at Venice when he and Dr. Sheffield gave resuscitation lessons to students visiting from a Los Angeles high school. Freeth created such a devoted following, especially among young people, because his idea of education always included *physical* education: when he and Sheffield finished their lesson, Freeth got the students into the plunge, where they played a game of water basketball.[18] The Sheffield sisters devoted two chapters of their book to lifesaving and resuscitation techniques. In a tribute to Freeth, they included pictures of him surfing and posed with Ludy Langer on the Mile-A-Minute three-wheeled motorcycle.[19]

Surfing in California had high and low notes the last summer before the Roaring Twenties. World War I was over, the flu had run its course, and young Southern Californians were drawn to the popular sport. Though Freeth had done so much to encourage people to enjoy riding waves, the occasional tragedy served as a reminder of the ocean's inherent dangers. In mid-June three friends—Basil Schmidt, T. McNallan, and Lucien Higelin—walked to the end of the Silver Spray Pier in Long Beach with their surfboards. They had the idea of dropping them over the railing and leaping off the pier to avoid paddling out through the large waves, which they wanted to ride. Seventeen-year-old Schmidt made the fifteen-foot dive and hit the water on his stomach, which stunned him. His friend Higelin, diving in after, held Schmidt above the surface until he grew exhausted and had to save himself by swimming to his surfboard. Despite an intensive search by lifeguards, Schmidt had disappeared. A woman raised the alarm the next day when Schmidt's body bumped into her as she swam in front of the Long Beach bathhouse.[20]

But such incidents hardly slowed the public's enthusiasm for surfing. A big article on the sport's popularity appeared the following month in the Sunday edition of the *Los Angeles Times*. Vance Veith, who'd followed Freeth as head swimming instructor at the LAAC, was pictured riding a wave alongside Eleanor Fields. The caption championed the growing public enthusiasm for personal transporation: "Drive Down to One of the Beaches in Your Automobile and Try to Do This." The article—"Surf-Board Riding Is Some Sport"—mentioned Freeth, provided some history on the sport, explained how to ride waves, and described the different types of boards one could use. The writer even revealed surprising details about how the tide impacted catching waves, information that surfers still rely on today: "Low tide is all right if you enjoy a gentle push, but the best time is between tides when the breakers are of medium height and have a long roll."[21]

The *Times* ran a report that same month about the "debonair" silent-film star Tom Moore, who had just finished filming *Heartsease* and was spotted on one of his surfboards at a local beach—"a picturesque figure as he emulates the husky Hawaiian on the risky water conveyance, from which he hardly ever falls."[22]

Duke Kahanamoku, of course, would own the 1920s when it came to surfing and Hollywood. He moved to Los Angeles, where he swam competitively, acted in numerous films, and gave the "royal sport" a tremendous boost. In the San Diego area, lifeguard Charlie Wright picked up Freeth's mantle in the early 1920s and gave regular surf exhibitions at Mission Beach with his partner Mary Powers. The *San Diego Union* reported, "Wright claims the American championship as a surfboard rider."[23] Following Freeth's legacy, women like Eleanor Fields and Mary Powers were not an unusual sight in the surf. Freeth's connection to that legacy, however, and his seismic contributions to beach culture in general, fell deeper into shadow with each passing year.

The surfing and lifeguarding traditions that Freeth launched introduced a generation of young people to the many possibilities open to them at the beach: pleasure, livelihood, competition, and personal well-being. The culture that developed around these ideals spread across Southern California in the ensuing decades, each generation adding its own flourishes. Technological innovations would be key to this development. The growing popularity of automobiles allowed Californians to range beyond Henry Huntington's network of electric trolleys, further opening up the coastline to pleasure and adventure. The automobile also permanently changed some of Freeth's old haunts: by the end of the 1920s, Abbot Kinney's original canals were all filled in to make room for traffic flow and parking. The growth of beach culture also depended on what Peter Westwick and Peter Neushul have called the "intersection of broad political, economic, and environmental interests."[24] The discovery of oil fields in Southern California, for example, filled the beaches with great iron derricks, and California ultimately had to choose recreation over petroleum so that beach culture and tourism could flourish in the state.[25]

Los Angeles County surpassed a million people in the 1920s, two million in the 1930s, and boasted 40 percent of California's entire population by 1940 as it reached toward three million. The county began buying long tracts of beach along its seventy-five-mile coastline to support and encourage recreation among this booming population, from Sequit Point north of Malibu to its southern border in Long Beach. In 1926, when the county started the process of developing these sites with lifeguard service, they chose a most historic location: Venice Beach, where Freeth had demonstrated the training methods that would eventually be adopted by the Los Angeles County Lifeguards, currently the largest professional lifeguard service in the world.[26] The heart of California beach culture as we know it today developed in Los Angeles County and its southern counterparts—Orange County and San Diego County—coastal communities where George Freeth, a transplanted Hawaiian and California's original beachboy, roamed, surfed, and saved lives.

Freeth certainly played his part in the early marketing schemes to promote the coast, what we would call today the "beach lifestyle." It's hard to know what he would think about where that ideal has ended up in the twenty-first century, much of it—clothing, décor, designer accessories—only tangentially related to the activities he dedicated himself to. Were we to look for core values among those who cultivate a life by the beach today, I think we would find them in the basic pursuits that Freeth and his aquatic descendants engaged in: teaching others about the dangers of the ocean and working to ensure that everyone can safely enjoy its many pleasures.

Notes

Introduction

1. Assembly Bill No. 1782, Chapter 162, California Legislative Information, https://leginfo.legislature.ca.gov/faces/billNavClient.xhtml?bill_id=201720180AB1782.

2. For Freeth's particular link to the origins of California beach culture, see Westwick and Neushul, *World in the Curl*, 66–68, and Laderman, *Empire in Waves*, 34.

3. *Evening Bulletin* (HI), October 8, 1907.

4. *Daily Surf* (CA), July 20, 1885. See also Finney and Houston, *Surfing*, 81–82.

5. *Los Angeles Herald*, August 18, 1889; *Los Angeles Times*, August 12, 1892; *San Diego Union*, July 30, 1893; *Hawaiian Star*, December 20, 1893; *Los Angeles Herald*, July 6, 1895 (keyword "surf").

6. London, "Riding the South Seas Surf," 1907.

Chapter 1. A Pacific Ocean Childhood

1. See the University of Hawai'i eVols: "Thomas Alexander Kaulaahi Cleghorn" (http://hdl.handle.net/10524/48595) for information on Freeth's maternal line (70–71). Lepeka was the daughter of American merchant Eliab Grimes and a Hawaiian woman named Uilani. William Lowthian Green's obituary (which does not mention Lepeka, since the two never married) can be found at George F. Nellist, ed., "The Story of Hawaii and Its Builders," published by the *Honolulu Star Bulletin*, 1925, http://files.usgwarchives.net/hi/statewide/bios/green25bs.txt. Green became a member of the Hawaiian League, a group of American and European businessmen who compelled Kalākaua to accept the Bayonet Constitution of 1887. Under duress from the league, Kalākaua had asked Green to form a new cabinet, a body in which Green himself served as minister of finance and premier until ill health forced him to resign in 1889. See Lorrin A. Thurston's *Memoirs* for Green and the Hawaiian League (158).

2. For Sir James Freeth (General), see en.wikipedia.org/wiki/James_Freeth. Information on the military career of James Holt Freeth (Major General)—including his postings, promotions, marriage, and the birthdates and birth places of his children—is drawn from Britain's National Archives, catalogue reference WO 25/3913. See "HMS *Conway* 1859–1974" (hmsconway.org) for information on the history of the training ship and a list of the cadets and their prizes. Freeth Senior's birth registration (born December 15, 1854) was obtained from the General Registrer Office for England and Wales: Reference Volume 02A, page 169 (accessed at https://www.gov.uk/general-register-office). James Holt Freeth was stationed in Ireland from December 1858 to May 1863. There is mention of "family correspondence" (uncorroborated) from a genealogical page owned by Doug Borthwick, Freeth Junior's great-grandnephew, indicating that Freeth Senior was born on board a ship in St. George's Channel on the way to Cork, Ireland. Family tree information on Ancestry.com lists Freeth Senior's youngest sister, Blanche Delia, as having been born in Cork on July 28, 1863; this was almost two months after James Holt Freeth departed to Ceylon for four years, so it appears that Freeth Senior's mother stayed in Ireland to have the baby. She may have remained there with some or all of the children or later joined her husband in Ceylon.

3. On the maternal side, Freeth Senior's mother, Louisa Margery Armstrong, came from Montreal. She married James Holt Freeth in October 1845 while he was stationed in Canada (October 1844 to April 1847). In an article Freeth wrote for the *Evening Herald*, he stated that his father was "a native of Cork, Ireland" (see Moser, *Pacific Passages*, 153–54). Freeth's death certificate listed "Ireland" under "Birthplace of Father." Misinformation about Freeth's background can also be traced to John H. "Doc" Ball's influential *California Surfriders: 1946*, which introduced Freeth as "Irish-Hawaiian." See Ball's reprinted edition, *Early California Surfriders* (11).

4. "Article from *The Evening Herald*" by George Freeth, in Moser, *Pacific Passages*, 153–54.

5. Freeth's birth announcement in the paper gave no first name but simply mentioned that "a son" was born on November 8 to the wife of G. D. Freeth (*Daily Bulletin*, November 10, 1883).

6. *Evening Bulletin*, November 16 and 17, 1883; *Pacific Commercial Advertiser*, November 17, 1883.

7. *Pacific Commercial Advertiser*, April 3, 1880.

8. George Senior and his older brother Edward, who also trained on the *HMS Conway*, had continued the family tradition of military honors. Edward won the gold medal of the Mercantile Marine Service Association "for the greatest proficiency in all branches of training and education." George Senior, in addition to winning this medal himself, captured the Queen's Gold Medal in 1872. This coveted prize, inaugurated by Queen Victoria in 1864, was awarded annually to the cadet who displayed the finest all-around qualities of a sailor, as determined by the commander and voted on by the cadets. Information on Freeth's awards can be found in Durand, *Elizabeth College Register* (248), and on his official cadet record (kindly provided to me by

Alfie Windsor). The HMS *Conway* website (hmsconway.org) provides descriptions of the awards under the link "Slop Chest" and subsequent link "Cups & Prizes."

9. *Liverpool Mercury*, July 5, 1873. Freeth Senior's appointment in the Royal Naval Reserve on April 2, 1873, and his exit on March 2, 1880, are recorded in the Admiralty's Officers' Service Records for the Royal Naval Reserve (The National Archives: Catalogue Reference ADM 240/19/8).

10. See *The San Francisco Directory* for 1876–1878: https://archive.org/details/sanfranciscodire1876lang/page/n92.

11. *Honolulu Advertiser*, March 8, 1884.

12. Freeth and Peacock held a mortgage on the *Allie Rowe* for $3,500; it was owned by E. C. Rowe (*Evening Bulletin*, February 9, 1886).

13. The deeds that passed from Green to Lizzie can be found in the Registrar of Bureau of Conveyances, Deed Records, 1846–1900, at Honolulu's Bureau of Conveyances: Green's purchase of the lot on Fort Street in 1861 (book 14, 450–52); his purchase of the lot at Kālia in 1862 (book 15, 81–82; Royal Patent 2607, apana 4); placement of the Kālia property in trust to Lizzie and her brother William in 1864 (book 18, 348–49); Lizzie's purchase of a quarter-acre lot adjacent to the lot in Kālia (for $300) in November 1879 (book 63, 152–53; Royal Patent 7063, Land Commission Award 1407); Lizzie's acquisition of the Fort Street lot (book 61, 439) and the Kālia lot held in trust for her (book 61, 440) in December 1879; the Freeths' mortgage of the two lots in Kālia and the Fort Street lot to Alex J. Cartwright in December 1884 (book 89, 463–65); and the Freeths' default on the mortgage in July 1887 (book 89, 463–65).

14. *Evening Bulletin*, October 30, 1888.

15. See Lane, J. C., *Directory and Hand Book of the Kingdom of Hawaii* (217). Accessed at eVols, University of Hawai'i at Mānoa, https://evols.library.manoa.hawaii.edu/handle/10524/19436.

16. For Alexander's birth, see *Honolulu Advertiser*, March 30, 1885; his death is listed on findagrave.com.

17. The Freeths were also connected to Hawaiian royalty through George's grandmother Lepeka, who had three daughters with Archibald Scott Cleghorn after she left William Lowthian Green. Cleghorn, a Scottish businessman, later married Miriam K. Likelike, the sister of Kalākaua. Their daughter, Princess Victoria Kai'ulani, was heir to the throne until her death in 1899 at the age of twenty-three. So Freeth's mother was the half sister, as it were, of the three Cleghorn women, who themselves were the half sisters of Princess Kai'ulani.

18. *Honolulu Advertiser*, August 8, 1885; *Evening Bulletin*, October 24, 1889.

19. *Hawaiian Gazette*, May 14, 1909.

20. Information on the North Pacific Phosphate and Fertilizer Company can be found at the Hawai'i State Archives (listed as the Pacific Chemical and Fertilizer Company, 1890–1956; M-476). The archives also hold ledgers, minutes, and correspondence with the minister of interior who approved the lease of Laysan and neighboring Lisiansky.

21. *Evening Bulletin*, February 2, 1893.

22. Hugo Schauinsland, in *Atoll Research Bulletin Nos. 432–34*, 29.

23. The Freeths departure on the *Mary L. Ames* for Laysan on July 2, 1892, is recorded in *Passengers Leaving for Foreign Ports April 2, 1891–June 29, 1895*, at the Hawai'i State Archives. Only two children are listed (along with twenty Japanese), so the other three (perhaps the boys) sailed on a different ship. The *Honolulu Advertiser* (September 8, 1893) lists the Freeths returning from Laysan with all five children.

24. My description of Laysan is drawn from Ely and Clapp, *Atoll Research Bulletin* 171, 3–19, which provides records of the island as it existed in the 1890s.

25. Lencek and Bosker, *The Beach*, 177.

26. *Hawaii Holomua-Progress*, October 9, 1894. The Freeth children and Robertson shared the same grandmother (Lepeka). Freeth's grandfather with Lepeka was William Lowthian Green; Robertson's grandfather with Lepeka was Archibald Scott Cleghorn. See also *Los Angeles Herald*, February 28, 1909. The quotation from the *Holomua-Progress* is odd because Freeth Senior and the two boys are also reported as having returned in mid-November (*Honolulu Advertiser*, November 13, 1894).

27. Rothschild, *Avifauna of Laysan*, x.

28. Ibid., 58. For additional references to Freeth Senior and a general history of Laysan, see F. Walker, *Log of the Kaalokai*, and Ely and Clapp, *Atoll Research Bulletin*.

29. Peter Pyle, "Nomenclature of the Laysan Honeycreeper *Himatione [sanguinea] fraithii* in *Bulletin of the British Ornithologists' Club* 131, no. 2 (2011): 116–17.

30. *Evening Bulletin*, January 15, 1892. For descriptions of the guano work, see Ely and Clapp, *Atoll Research Bulletin*, 25–26.

31. Mining information can be found at the Hawai'i State Archives under "North Pacific Phosphate and Fertilizer Company."

32. Population figures come from Nordyke and Matsumoto, "Japanese in Hawaii," 165.

33. See J. C. Lane, *Directory and Hand Book of the Kingdom of Hawaii* (172, 347) accessed at eVols, University of Hawai'i at Mānoa, https://evols.library.manoa.hawaii .edu/handle/10524/19436.

34. *Evening Bulletin*, April 1, 1895.

35. *Honolulu Advertiser*, July 12, 1901. For a description of Holstein's death, see the same paper for May 15, 1894.

36. *The Independent*, July 23, 1895.

37. *Hawaiian Star*, February 25, 1902.

38. *Honolulu Advertiser*, October 26, 1895.

39. *Honolulu Star-Bulletin*, June 2, 1951.

40. Freeth held the position from May 10 to November 7, 1898. On this latter date he recommended that Benjamin Edward Holman, who replaced Freeth as superintendent of Clipperton for the Pacific Islands Company, assume the position of inspector. See México, *Isla de la Pasion*, 31, 53.

41. *San Francisco Call*, July 3 and October 9, 1898.

42. Willie had been sent to train aboard the HMS *Conway* (like his father and uncle

Edward) in 1895; Charlie had left the islands in 1897 to study marine engineering at the Hillman Ship & Engine Building Company in Philadelphia.

43. *San Francisco Call,* September 29, 1898.

44. *San Francisco Call*, December 31, 1899.

45. From October 1898 to January 1902, when Freeth's name appears as a competitor at the Sutro Baths, his name does not appear in the Honolulu papers. There are two exceptions: December 8, 1900, and January 12, 1901. In both cases, Freeth's name appears in the Sutro programs (and the *San Francisco Call*), but he is also listed in the Honolulu papers as playing soccer. The conflict is a mystery. Several times Freeth won events at Sutro and his name was not listed in the program, so perhaps these two dates are examples of his name appearing in the program without his competing.

46. One can find Freeth's name in the local papers and in various Sutro Baths Programs in the Adolph Sutro Collection, San Francisco History Center (box 5, folders 17–86).

47. For background on Adolph Sutro and the baths, see James P. Delgado, Denise Bradley, Paul M. Scolari, and Stephen A. Haller, "The History and Significance of the Adolph Sutro Historic District: Excerpts from the National Register of Historic Places Nomination Form Prepared in 2000," https://www.nps.gov/goga/learn/historyculture/upload/sutro_history.pdf; *San Francisco Examiner*, March 15, 1896; Stewart and Stewart, *Adolph Sutro*, 189–90.

48. See the Sutro Baths program for July 9, 1899 (San Francisco History Center, Adolph Sutro Collection, box 5, folders 51–62).

49. *San Francisco Call*, July 31, 1899.

50. The Freeth divorce records can be found at District Court (O'ahu First Circuit), at the Kapolei office (p. 44, no. 2695).

51. *Honolulu Advertiser*, November 10, 1900; *Honolulu Republican*, July 13, 1900.

52. *The Independent*, July 18, 1900.

53. *Pacific Commercial Advertiser*, January 28, 1901.

54. On Regatta Day: *Honolulu Advertiser*, September 23, 1901; football: *Hawaiian Star*, October 5, 1901; Sutro's: *San Francisco Call*, December 22, 1901, and January 18, 1902.

55. *Honolulu Advertiser*, August 18, 1903.

56. "Article from *The Evening Herald*" by George Freeth, in Moser, *Pacific Passages*, 154.

Chapter 2. Renewing a Royal Sport at Waikīkī

1. *Los Angeles Times*, July 14, 1912.

2. "Article from *The Evening Herald*" by George Freeth, in Moser, *Pacific Passages*, 154.

3. Helpful histories of surfing covering this era include Finney and Houston's *Surfing,* 21–59; Warshaw, *History of Surfing,* 14–37; Laderman, *Empire in Waves*, 8–17; and Westwick and Neushul, *World in the Curl*, 7–30. For surfing's continuity among

Native Hawaiians, see Clark, *Hawaiian Surfing*, 33; Walker, *Waves of Resistance*, 26–31; and Moser, "Endurance of Hawaiian Surfing."

4. *Hawaiian Star*, September 3, 1903.

5. *Hawaiian Gazette*, April 29, 1902.

6. Kūhiō was fourteen years old in 1885; Edward, sixteen; and David, seventeen. Edward Keliʻiahonui died of typhoid in 1887.

7. Titcomb, *Native Use of Fish in Hawaii*, 92 (accessed through ulukau.org.). For an account of traditional rituals surrounding surfing, see "Hawaiian Surf Riding (1896)" in Moser, *Pacific Passages*, 125–31.

8. For samples of Hawaiian gods and surfing (Māmala, Ka-ehu, Ka-hiki-lani), see Moser, *Pacific Passages*, 26–33.

9. *Honolulu Advertiser*, October 13, 1904, and February 16, 1905; *Hawaiian Star*, October 4, 1901.

10. *Evening Bulletin*, December 8, 1905.

11. Haynes, "Waves of the Future," 27. The author attributes these features to brochures put out by L. E. Martin, a water sports equipment manufacturer, who called Freeth "The Pacific Norseman."

12. Freeth's World War I registration in September 1918 provides the height, hair, and eye color information (accessed at ancestry.com). Photographs of Freeth standing next to his friend and protégé, Olympic silver medalist Ludy Langer—listed as five foot eight—show them to be of similar height.

13. *Honolulu Advertiser*, December 8, 1905. The article reported that Freeth left "yesterday," but he in fact played in a football game on December 9 before leaving. Mrs. Freeth's bankruptcy: *Evening Bulletin*, December 22, 1905.

14. *Honolulu Advertiser*, August 5, 1903, and December 2, 1904. For ownership of the Emma Street house, see *Honolulu Advertiser*, June 21, 1902.

15. *Evening Bulletin*, December 12, 1905; Freeth's departure: *Honolulu Advertiser*, December 13, 1905.

16. For Freeth's work and address, see Husted's *Directory of Honolulu and Territory of Hawaii 1905–6*. For the Mutual Telephone Company's station at Nawiliwili, see https://www.qsl.net/ah6rh/am-radio/hawaii/history.html. One of the company's charter members in 1883 was Archibald Scott Cleghorn, so Freeth's employment was loosely family related.

17. *Hawaiian Star*, May 16, 1906.

18. *Hawaiian Star*, December 26, 1906.

19. *Hawaiian Star*, October 11, 1906.

20. *Honolulu Advertiser*, September 17, October 2, and October 17, 1905.

21. *Hawaiian Star*, December 31, 1906.

22. *Los Angeles Herald*, July 22, 1910.

23. See *Pacific Commercial Advertiser* (June 29, 1897) for previous mention of a water carnival at Honolulu Harbor.

24. *Pacific Commercial Advertiser*, March 26, 1905.

25. *Honolulu Advertiser*, April 23, 1905.

26. *Honolulu Advertiser*, April 27, 1905.

27. *Evening Bulletin*, April 24, 1905.

28. *Honolulu Advertiser*, April 27, 1905.

29. *Pacific Commercial Advertiser*, December 27, 1906, and February 17, 1907.

30. *Honolulu Advertiser*, July 3, 1907.

31. *Hawaiian Star*, January 3, 1907.

32. *Hawaiian Gazette*, February 19, 1907. The article indicates that water polo hadn't been played in the islands before, but see the *Evening Bulletin*, February 1, 1901, for a match played by the Healanis that week.

33. *Hawaiian Star*, October 1, 1906.

34. *Hawaiian Star,* September 27, 1906.

35. For overviews of tourism in Hawai'i during this era, see Trask, *Native Daughter*, part 3; Desmond, *Staging Tourism*, 34–59; I. Walker, *Waves of Resistance*, 57–67; Laderman, *Empire in Waves*, 17–40; Lawler, *American Surfer*, 30–35; and Wood, *Displacing Natives*, 45–52.

36. *Hawaiian Star*, October 27, 1906. For more information on the Hawaii Promotion Committee, see Moser, "Hawaii Promotion Committee and the Appropriation of Surfing."

37. *Hawaiian Star*, October 27, 1906.

38. *Honolulu Advertiser*, March 19, 1907.

39. *Honolulu Advertiser*, March 17, 1907. For an interesting article on the five Hustace brothers using surfboards to save lives at Waikīkī, see *Honolulu Advertiser*, July 21, 1908.

40. See the article on the following year's contest in *Honolulu Advertiser,* July 20, 1908: "Harold Hustace, the champion surfer of last year, turned in vain on his diminutive board to ride backward and did his usual fancy stunts, but the great, long boards of Kenneth Winter and Sam Wight kept the waves long, long after the smaller boards disappeared behind the rollers."

41. The *Evening Bulletin* (December 7, 1908) called Hustace "the world's greatest amateur surfboard rider."

42. *Evening Bulletin*, June 12, 1907. The article misspells his name as "Freith."

43. See Moser, *Pacific Passages*, for accounts by Twain (117) and London (137–46).

44. London, *Our Hawaii*, 76–81.

45. *Evening Bulletin*, May 29 and May 30, 1907.

46. See Charmian London, *Our Hawaii* (52–81), for details of meeting Ford and surfing at Waikīkī.

47. *Pall Mall Magazine*, July to December 1908 (326–31).

48. The story first appeared in *Lady's Realm* (December 1908) and was later included in London's collection *The House of Pride and Other Tales of Hawaii* (1912).

49. London, "Aloha Oe," *Lady's Realm*, December 1908, 175.

50. London, *Our Hawaii*, 53. The note "Ford's story" appears on the manuscript of "Aloha Oe" in the Huntington Library.

51. London, "Aloha Oe," *Lady's Realm,* December 1908, 172.

52. London, *Our Hawaii*, 104.

53. *Pacific Commercial Advertiser*, June 30, 1907.

54. London, "Riding the South Seas Surf," *Woman's Home Companion*, October 1907, 10.

55. *Evening Bulletin*, May 3, 1907; *Ke Aloha Aina*, May 4, 1907.

56. *Honolulu Advertiser*, June 23, 1907. See the same paper (June 2, 1907) for a description of Freeth holding up Ford's surfboard.

57. Ford, "Surf Riding for the Motion Picture Man," 278.

58. London, "My Hawaiian Aloha," *Cosmopolitan*, September 1916, 170.

59. *Pacific Commercial Advertiser*, June 2, 1907. The standard history of surfing and Ford's influence begins with Ben R. Finney and James D. Houston's *Surfing: The Sport of Hawaiian Kings*: "Under the leadership of Alexander Hume Ford, this group promoted surfing's potential in a new Hawaii" (70). This work is based on Finney's master's thesis, "Hawaiian Surfing: A Study of Cultural Change" (University of Hawai'i, 1959). In the revised edition of the book, *Surfing: A History of the Ancient Hawaiian Sport*, Ford's role is emphasized even more: "He took it upon himself to personally boost its revival and popularization" (60). In *Empire in Waves*, Scott Laderman gives a nice overview of popular histories that support and expand upon Finney and Houston's comments (18–19).

60. Ford, "Our Japanese Territory," *Collier's*, 12–13.

61. See Walker's *Waves of Resistance* (10–11) for his theory of *ka po'ina nalu* (the surf zone) as a space of Native Hawaiian identity and resistance.

62. "Article from *The Evening Herald*" by George Freeth, in Moser, *Pacific Passages*, 154.

63. For a discussion of this tradition, see Desmond, *Staging Tourism*, 66–67.

64. *Pacific Commercial Advertiser* and *Hawaiian Star*, July 3, 1907; *San Francisco Call*, July 4, 1907; *Evening Tribune* (San Diego), July 11, 1907.

65. For the beginnings of this tradition, see Timmons, *Waikiki Beachboy*, 25–30; Clark, *Hawaiian Surfing*, 69–73.

66. Winter had Native Hawaiian ancestry through his maternal grandmother, Akula Kainana Mana [or Manu] Kahooneiaina Rives, who married Thomas J. Mossman in 1855.

Chapter 3. A Waterman in Los Angeles

1. *Hawaiian Star*, August 2, 1907.

2. *Pacific Commercial Advertiser*, October 18, 1907.

3. *Evening Bulletin*, October 8, 1907.

4. D. J. Waldie, "A Walk along Long Beach's Gaudy, Tawdry, Bawdy Pike," https://www.kcet.org/shows/lost-la/a-walk-along-long-beachs-gaudy-tawdry-bawdy-pike.

5. *Los Angeles Times*, July 5, 1907.

6. *Los Angeles Herald*, May 8, 1907.

7. *Los Angeles Herald* and *Los Angeles Times*, May 3, 1907.

8. Ibid.

9. *Santa Monica Outlook*, May 14, 1907.

10. *Los Angeles Times,* May 15, 1907.

11. *Los Angeles Herald*, May 27 and 31, 1907.

12. *Los Angeles Herald*, June 14, 1907.

13. *Los Angeles Herald*, June 15 and 20, 1907.

14. For a good introduction to *hapa haole* music, see Cooley, *Surfing about Music*, 31–37.

15. *Los Angeles Herald*, July 14, 1907.

16. *Santa Monica Outlook*, May 4, 1904, and May 2, 1905.

17. For general information on the Venice resort, see Alexander, *Abbot Kinney's Venice-Of-America*, 24–28; Alexander, *Venice, California*, 15–27; "Abbot Kinney a Great Wonder," *Santa Monica Outlook*, July 10, 1905.

18. Alexander, *Abbot Kinney's Venice-Of-America*; *Los Angeles Herald*, July 5, 1905.

19. *Hawaiian Gazette*, June 11, 1877.

20. *Los Angeles Herald*, June 25, 1895.

21. *Los Angeles Herald*, July 1, 1895. Although the waves didn't cooperate on the first day of the event (June 30), a report from July 4 noted "surf-riding" as one of the attractions of the day and stated, "It was the most successful Fourth of July Redondo ever celebrated" (*San Francisco Call*, July 5, 1895; see also "Summerers at Redondo," *Los Angeles Herald*, July 7, 1895). The program continued for several days after the fourth with more mention of the "native Hawaiian surf riders," seeming to indicate that the group managed to catch a few waves and put on a show (*Los Angeles Herald*, July 5, 1895).

22. "Report of the Chamber of Commerce Secretary," *Pacific Commercial Advertiser*, June 22, 1907, and "Promotion Work Bringing Results," *Pacific Commercial Advertiser*, July 11, 1907.

23. *Pacific Commercial Advertiser*, June 22 and July 11, 1907.

24. Mak, *Creating "Paradise of the Pacific,"* 54, 67.

25. *Los Angeles Herald*, August 4, 1907.

26. An article in the *Buffalo (NY) Courier* from May 25, 1902, lists Colonel J. Wesley Jones as the founder of the group, which was incorporated in 1890. See also Pelletreau, *History of Long Island*, 37. The organization was funded by the state legislature beginning in 1894.

27. *Evening Bulletin*, October 8, 1907.

28. *Los Angeles Herald*, October 8, 1907.

29. *Santa Monica Outlook*, November 9, 1907.

30. *Santa Monica Outlook*, November 27, 1907.

31. Alexander, *Venice, California*, 37.

32. *Los Angeles Herald*, December 19, 1907.

33. *Santa Monica Outlook*, December 24, 1907; *Los Angeles Herald*, December 25, 1907.

34. *Los Angeles Herald*, October 26, 1907; *Redondo Reflex*, December 26, 1907; *Redondo Reflex*, January 9, 1908; *Los Angeles Times*, January 9, 1908.

35. Flamming, *Bound for Freedom*, 271–75. For a slightly different version, see "Resort Was an Oasis for Blacks until Racism Drove Them Out," *Los Angeles Times*, July 21, 2002. See also Jefferson, *Living the California Dream*, 29–103.

36. Culver, *Frontier of Leisure*, 60.

37. Westwick and Neushul, *World in the Curl*, 64.

38. U.S. Geological Survey, "Seafloor Mapping," Pacific Coastal and Marine Science Center, updated 2021, https://walrus.wr.usgs.gov/pacmaps/la-persp4.html.

39. *Los Angeles Herald*, March 17, 1907.

40. *Los Angeles Times*, July 14, 1912.

41. Thorpe, *Henry Edwards Huntington*, 182, 188, 210; Friedricks, *Henry E. Huntington*, 2–7.

42. Thorpe, *Henry Edwards Huntington*, 205–209.

43. Friedricks, *Henry E. Huntington*, 90–91.

44. *Redondo Reflex*, July 4, 1907.

45. Arthur C. Verge corrected the Huntington myth in "George Freeth: King of the Surfers." The story began in Doc Ball's *California Surfriders: 1946* and was repeated in Haynes, "Wave of the Future" (1976), and Hinch, "Man Who 'Walked on Water'" (1980), among other places. Additional writings on Freeth that derive from Verge's work include "Bronzed Mercury: George Freeth," in *Legendary Surfers*, vol. 1 (ch. 9), by Malcolm Gault-Williams, and "Reinventing the Sport" by Joel T. Smith. It's not likely that Freeth met Huntington before he started working at the Redondo Bath House in December 1907. Huntington had left for the East Coast on his annual extended business trip on September 9, 1907. He did not return to Los Angeles until early May 1908 (*Los Angeles Herald*, September 10, 1907, and May 5, 1908).

46. *Los Angeles Herald*, July 2, 1909. Later meetings between Freeth and Huntington seem questionable. Freeth left for Hawai'i the following year (September 1910). By that time Huntington had "retired" from day-to-day work in his transportation, utility, and real estate ventures and focused on the cultivation of his ranch in San Marino and the acquisition of art and books. See Thorpe, *Henry Edwards Huntington*, 238.

47. *Los Angeles Times*, December 29, 1907; *Los Angeles Herald*, January 4 and January 14, 1908; *San Francisco Call*, May 6, 1908.

48. *Los Angeles Times*, January 26, 1908; *Los Angeles Herald*, January 26, 1908. The AAU meeting took place in downtown Los Angeles at the Federation Club on January 25, 1908.

49. *Los Angeles Times*, February 13, 1908.

50. *Los Angeles Times*, February 1, 1908. The report notes that the times were slow because the pool was only ninety feet long, which required the swimmers to make an extra turn.

51. *Los Angeles Herald*, December 8, 1907.

52. *Los Angeles Times*, January 5, 1908.

53. *Los Angeles Herald*, April 9, 1908.

54. *Los Angeles Herald*, July 23, 1908.

55. Korsgaard, *History of the Amateur Athletic Union*, ch. 11 ("Maintaining Amateurism"), 250.

56. The *Los Angeles Times* reported interest in organizing a league on both November 3, 1903, and March 24, 1905. The *Times* also reported (October 18, 1905) a match between Bimini and Ocean Park for "the championship of Southern California," but it appears this was only a single game. For the formation of league play, see *Santa Monica Outlook*, September 2, 1907, and *Los Angeles Times*, January 9, 1908.

57. *Los Angeles Herald*, January 18 and 23, 1908.

58. *Los Angeles Herald*, April 14, 1908.

59. The *Official Handbook of the Amateur Athletic Union of the United States* (1907) lists eight-minute halves, but reports of the games themselves often vary that time by several minutes. Most of Freeth's games seemed to have seven-minute halves.

60. *Los Angeles Herald*, March 21, 1908.

61. *Official Handbook*, 103–104. The team in Long Beach played an adapted "English-Scottish" version of the game, where players could throw the ball to score. See *Los Angeles Herald*, July 30, 1908.

62. *Los Angeles Herald*, August 11, 1907.

63. *Honolulu Advertiser*, February 3, 1907.

64. *Hawaiian Star*, February 12, 1907.

65. *Hawaiian Star*, February 5, 1907.

66. *Los Angeles Herald*, July 21, 1909.

67. In 1909 Freeth dove twenty-five feet in Ocean Park to fix a tackle to the intake pipe of the saltwater plunge, "staying under water several minutes during the feat" (*Los Angeles Herald*, September 13); in 1911 he dove twice in water "over thirty-nine feet" to retrieve his Gold Life-Saving Medal, which he'd dropped from a wharf in Redondo (*Santa Ana Register*, December 7).

68. *Los Angeles Herald*, April 11, 1908; *Redondo Reflex*, May 7 and 21, 1908.

69. Surdam, *Century of the Leisured Masses*, 46.

70. *Los Angeles Herald*, May 31 and July 31, 1908; *Redondo Reflex*, May 14, 1908; *Official Handbook*, 65–66.

71. *Redondo Reflex*, June 11, 1908.

72. *Los Angeles Times*, June 7, 1908.

73. *Redondo Reflex*, July 16, 1908; *Los Angeles Herald*, July 19, 1908. The trophy presentation took place on July 13.

74. *San Francisco Call*, August 25, 1907.

75. Ibid. See the *Long Beach Tribune* (August 20, 1906) for a description of Venice lifeguard Ed Burns, who struck a swimmer who had grabbed him by the throat.

76. Haynes, "Wave of the Future," 31.

77. *Redondo Reflex*, February 27, 1908.

78. *San Francisco Call*, August 25, 1907.

79. The *Honolulu Advertiser* (August 25, 1907) reported on an "artificial respirator"

patented by a Professor George Poe of Virginia, who had success reviving animals. He was apparently placing the respirator on the market and predicted, "It is only a question of time when all life-saving stations and ambulances, as well as hospitals, will be equipped with them."

80. *Redondo Breeze*, August 10, 1912.

81. *Santa Monica Outlook*, June 15, 1908. An article from the *Venice Vanguard* found in the collection of the Redondo Beach History Museum indicated that Freeth was "due back in Venice" the week of June 11, 1908.

82. The *Los Angeles Times* (June 21, 1908) reported the cost of the bathhouse at $150,000; the *Los Angeles Herald* (June 22, 1908) reported twenty-five thousand visitors. See also Alexander, *Abbot Kinney's Venice-Of-America*, 41.

83. *Los Angeles Times*, June 22, 1908.

Chapter 4. The Rescue

1. *Los Angeles Times*, June 21 and September 10, 1908.

2. *San Diego Union*, July 29, 1893. A couple of early references to surfing in California are worth mentioning. On August 18, 1889, the *Los Angeles Times* reported that one A. H. Smith, "formerly of the Sandwich Islands, now of Pomona, has organized a 'Surf Board Club' at the latter town, and is having a number of the Hawaiian surf boats made to use among the breakers at Santa Monica. Mr. and Mrs. Smith went down to Santa Monica yesterday to make a first trial." The *Los Angeles Times* also reported on August 12, 1892, that a man in Santa Monica "was using a surf board on Wednesday and came in very successfully and gracefully with the breakers."

3. *Ka Nupepa Kuokoa*, September 30, 1893. The Hawaiian reads: "He oiaio paha, owau ke oki loa o ka ike ole i ka heenalu ilaila (Hawaii), aka nae owau ka helu ekahi i ka heenalu o Kaleponi nei"; on racial equality: "He aina maikai keia, he kaulike na mea a pau. Ua like no au me na poe e ae e noho nei iloko o keia Hotele"; for payment: "o ko'u uku heenalu, he $10 o ka la hookahi." I am indebted to John R. K. Clark for sending me the reference. Translation by Keao NeSmith. Ahia came from Kona, Hawai'i (*Hawaiian Gazette*, August 15, 1893).

4. *Hawaiian Star*, December 20, 1893, and *Ka Makaainana*, January 8, 1894. The *Star* indicated that Apu was from Kaua'i, yet the *Pacific Commercial Advertiser* from January 4, 1894, reported that he was from Ni'ihau. There is similar confusion with Kapahee in the papers.

5. *Los Angeles Times*, July 5, 1908; *Los Angeles Herald*, August 7, 1908; *Los Angeles Times*, September 10, 1908.

6. *Los Angeles Herald*, July 27, 1908.

7. *Los Angeles Times*, July 4, 1908.

8. *Los Angeles Times*, June 22, 1907; *Los Angeles Herald*, July 25 and 31, 1908; *Los Angeles Herald*, August 4 and 13, 1908; *Santa Monica Outlook*, September 15, 1908; *Los Angeles Herald*, September 22, 1908.

9. *Los Angeles Herald*, July 31, 1908.

10. *Los Angeles Times*, August 13, 1908.

11. *Los Angeles Times*, October 1, 1908.

12. *Los Angeles Herald*, October 1, 1908.

13. *Los Angeles Herald*, July 30, 1908. See also the *Los Angeles Times* for the local commission's attempt to form a "purely amateur water polo league" (December 6, 1908).

14. *Los Angeles Herald*, October 16, 1908.

15. *Los Angeles Times*, November 5, 1908.

16. See the *Santa Monica Outlook* (July 28, 1908) for Holborow as a Venice lifeguard.

17. *Los Angeles Herald*, October 16, 1908.

18. Ibid.

19. *Santa Monica Outlook*, December 7, 1908.

20. See New York's *Evening World* (November 17, 1914) and *New York Times* (November 22, 1914) for women's admission into the AAU. European women competed in Olympic swimming events beginning in 1912.

21. For historical examples of Hawaiian women surfers, see Moser, *Pacific Passages*, 19–48, 55–59, 80, 108–111.

22. *Honolulu Advertiser*, July 20, 1908.

23. *Los Angeles Herald*, September 6, 1908.

24. *Los Angeles Times*, September 8, 1908. The article misspells Freeth's name as "Freith."

25. Newkirk won the 50-yard freestyle at the Southern California Swimming Championships in Naples the previous month, with Gordon coming in second (*Los Angeles Times*, August 17, 1908). For Freeth competing against Ludy Langer, see the *Redondo Reflex*, July 7, 1910; for Freeth competing against Duke, see the *Redondo Reflex*, October 4, 1912.

26. *Santa Monica Outlook*, December 7, 1908.

27. Joining the national organization: *Los Angeles Herald*, July 26, 1908; profile: *Los Angeles Herald*, October 18, 1908.

28. Noble, *That Others May Live*, 152–53. The organization eventually combined with another agency, the U.S. Revenue Cutter Service, to form the U.S. Coast Guard in 1915. An article in the *Los Angeles Herald* for August 9, 1908, offers a good overview of a contemporaneous lifesaving station at Long Branch, New Jersey.

29. United States National Archives and Records Administration.

30. My description is generally based on the first account, which appeared in the *Santa Monica Outlook* the day of the rescue; on the *Los Angeles Herald* report, which names the two Russians; and on the official affidavits submitted to the U.S. Treasury. Area newspapers follow the general description in the *Outlook*, though with differences in the order of the rescued boats: *Los Angeles Times*, *Los Angeles Herald*, *Los Angeles Examiner*, *Los Angeles Express*, and *San Francisco Call*.

31. Matsuma's name is mentioned in the *Los Angeles Examiner*.

32. *Los Angeles Herald*, December 17, 1908.

33. United States National Archives and Records Administration.

34. The official affidavits for the medal mention only three boats and seven Japanese fishermen.

35. John A. Downing, "Hypothermia: Understanding and Prevention," Minnesota Sea Grant, University of Minneosta Duluth, http://www.seagrant.umn.edu/coastal_communities/hypothermia.

36. *Los Angeles Examiner*, December 17, 1908.

37. *Pacific Commercial Advertiser*, September 29, 1910.

38. *Los Angeles Herald*, December 17, 1908.

39. *Los Angeles Examiner*, December 17, 1908.

40. *Los Angeles Herald*, December 17, 1908.

41. *Pacific Commercial Advertiser*, December 29, 1908.

42. *Los Angeles Times*, July 22, 1930.

43. American Red Cross, *Lifeguarding Today*, 3.

Chapter 5. Amateur Troubles

1. *Los Angeles Herald*, December 18, 1908; *Santa Monica Outlook*, December 17, 1908.

2. Ibid.

3. Alexander, *Abbot Kinney's Venice-Of-America*, 215–16.

4. Ibid.

5. *Los Angeles Times*, December 17, 1908; *Los Angeles Herald*, December 18, 1908.

6. *Los Angeles Herald*, December 18, 1908.

7. Not all newspapers are represented in the count. Some that would have reported the rescues—the *Venice Vanguard*, for example—are no long extant from those early years.

8. A couple of articles mention Freeth's ineligibility for the medal as a professional lifeguard: *Los Angeles Herald*, December 20, 1908, and February 17, 1909. For the Carnegie award criteria, see "Mission of the Carnegie Hero Fund Commission," https://www.carnegiehero.org/about-the-fund/process/, and Chambers, *Century of Heroes*, 12.

9. *Los Angeles Times*, December 17, 1908.

10. *Los Angeles Herald*, December 20, 25, 27, and 30, 1908; *Los Angeles Times*, December 21, 1908.

11. *Los Angeles Times*, December 21, 1908; *Los Angeles Herald*, December 22, 1908.

12. *Los Angeles Herald*, January 8, 1909. The *Los Angeles Times* reported that the group won second place in this category, which came with twenty dollars and a red banner (January 2, 1909).

13. *Redondo Reflex*, August 4, 1910.

14. *Santa Monica Outlook*, December 22, 1908.

15. *Santa Monica Outlook*, March 2, 1909.

16. *Los Angeles Herald*, February 25, 1909.

17. Charles Kenn Collection, MS Group 361, box 18, folder 7. The early years of the *Venice Vanguard* are thought to be lost.

18. *Los Angeles Herald*, January 14, 1909.

19. *Redondo Reflex*, April 1, 1909; *Los Angeles Times*, April 3, 1909. It doesn't appear that the event ever took place at the world's fair.

20. *Los Angeles Herald*, February 17, 1909.

21. Ibid.

22. *Los Angeles Herald*, March 19, 1909.

23. *Los Angeles Herald*, April 3, 1909.

24. *Los Angeles Herald*, April 8, 1909.

25. *Official Handbook*, 129.

26. *Los Angeles Herald*, April 11, 1909.

27. *Los Angeles Times*, April 18, 1909.

28. *Los Angeles Times*, May 14, 1909.

29. *Los Angeles Herald*, May 6, 1909.

30. *Los Angeles Times*, February 4, 1909.

31. *Los Angeles Times*, February 6 and March 4, 1909.

32. *Cincinnati Enquirer*, November 16, 1909.

33. *Los Angeles Times*, May 9, 1909.

34. *Honolulu Advertiser*, February 16, 1909. The article reports that Marjorie Freeth got married, but it was her younger sister, Dorothy Muriel, who did.

35. For a notable connection between the Campbells and the Freeths (the princess was the daughter of industrialist James A. Campbell), see the article where George Freeth Sr. is in San Francisco and helps James Campbell after his kidnapping misadventure (*San Francisco Call*, August 6, 1896).

36. *Los Angeles Herald*, May 9, 1909; *Hawaiian Gazette*, May 14, 1909.

37. *Honolulu Advertiser*, December 28, 1908, and May 8, 1909. Marjorie had been attending the College of Notre Dame in April 1906 during the San Francisco earthquake (*Honolulu Advertiser*, April 26, 1906).

38. *Los Angeles Herald*, May 9, 1909.

39. *Los Angeles Times*, May 13, 1909.

40. *Los Angeles Herald*, May 13, 1909.

41. *Los Angeles Herald*, May 2, 1909.

42. *Los Angeles Times*, April 18, 1909.

43. *Los Angeles Times*, April 30, 1909.

44. *Los Angeles Times*, April 25, 1909.

45. *Los Angeles Times*, May 5, 1909.

46. *Los Angeles Times*, May 9, 1909.

47. *Los Angeles Herald*, May 6, 1909.

48. *Los Angeles Herald*, May 20, 1909.

49. It doesn't appear that those championships were ever held. See the *Los Angeles Herald*, August 24, 1909.

50. *Los Angeles Times*, May 9, 1909.

51. *Los Angeles Times*, May 20, 1909.

52. *Los Angeles Herald*, June 24, 1910.

53. *Los Angeles Times*, August 7, 1910.

54. Moser, *Pacific Passages*, 74. The description of "almost amphibious" comes from the journal of Lieutenant James King. See also in *Pacific Passages* the journals of Charles Clerke (67) and William Ellis (69).

55. Hinch, "Man Who 'Walked on Water,'" 22.

56. *Los Angeles Herald*, May 13, 1909.

Chapter 6. A Gold Life-Saving Medal

1. *Redondo Reflex*, July 1, 1909. Information on the bathhouse is also taken from the *Los Angeles Times*, July 2, 1909, and the *Los Angeles Herald*, July 4, 1909.

2. *Los Angeles Herald*, October 3, 1909.

3. *Los Angeles Times*, April 6, 1910.

4. Krintz, "Pleasure Piers & Promenades," 40.

5. *Los Angeles Herald*, April 8, 1909.

6. *Los Angeles Herald*, August 13, 1909.

7. *Los Angeles Herald*, July 2, 1909. This article mentions that Huntington's bathhouse cost $250,000. The *Los Angeles Times* reported the water polo score as two to one (July 2, 1909).

8. *Los Angeles Times*, July 18, 1909.

9. *Los Angeles Times*, August 1, 1909; *Los Angeles Herald*, August 4, 1909.

10. *Los Angeles Herald*, August 7, 1909.

11. *Los Angeles Herald*, September 5, 1909; *Los Angeles Times*, September 5, 1909.

12. *Los Angeles Herald*, September 5, 1909.

13. *Los Angeles Herald*, July 23, 1910. The *Herald* article from the day before reported that the two men had never been matched before, but they had raced in the 50-yard freestyle in 1908 (as amateurs) at the opening of the Venice bathhouse (*Los Angeles Times*, June 22, 1908). Holborow won that contest as well.

14. *Los Angeles Herald*, December 12, 1909.

15. *Los Angeles Times*, May 18, 1910.

16. *Los Angeles Herald*, September 10, 1909.

17. *Redondo Reflex*, November 4, 1909.

18. *Los Angeles Times*, October 20, 1909; *Los Angeles Herald*, October 21, 1909; *Los Angeles Times*, October 24, 1909.

19. *Los Angeles Times*, October 24 and December 12, 1909.

20. *Los Angeles Herald*, March 25, 1909.

21. *Los Angeles Herald*, October 10, 1909.

22. *Redondo Reflex*, October 7, 1909.

23. *Redondo Reflex*, October 21, 1909.

24. *Hawaiian Star*, March 12, 1908.

25. *Honolulu Advertiser*, June 23, 1907.

26. *Los Angeles Herald*, March 26, 1910. The *Herald* mistakenly reported that the offer was for Coney Island rather than Atlantic City.

27. *Hawaiian Star*, March 11, 1910.

28. *Hawaiian Gazette*, June 3, 1910; *Hawaiian Star*, June 7, 1910. The exhibit opened at Atlantic City on May 21, 1910.

29. *New-York Tribune*, June 26, 1910.

30. *Buffalo Sunday Morning News*, August 7, 1910.

31. *Evening Star* (Washington, D.C.), August 28, 1910. See also the article reprinted in the *Honolulu Advertiser* (August 29, 1910) where Keech notes the board weighed about seventy pounds.

32. For the musicians riding "boards or skidders" at Asbury Park in July 1910, see Davis, *Waterman*, 68. Vinnie Dicks has found compelling evidence that the earliest surfing on the East Coast occurred in July 1888 at Asbury Park by Emma Spreckels, the seventeen-year-old daughter of sugar magnate Claus Spreckels (personal correspondence, December 16, 2019). See "Sounds from the Sea," *Pittsburg Press*, July 31, 1888.

33. *Los Angeles Herald*, July 5, 1910; *Redondo Reflex*, July 7, 1910.

34. *Los Angeles Times*, June 24, 1910; *San Francisco Call*, August 13, 1910.

35. *Los Angeles Herald*, March 18, 1909.

36. *Los Angeles Times*, July 2, 1909.

37. Hinch, "Man Who 'Walked on Water,'" 22.

38. United States National Archives and Records Administration.

39. *Los Angeles Herald*, July 20, 1910; *Santa Ana Register*, July 16, 1910; *Los Angeles Herald*, August 4, 1910; *Redondo Reflex*, July 21, 1910.

40. The official criteria for receiving the medal are as follows: "The Gold Life-Saving Medals may be awarded to those persons who endanger their lives by extreme and heroic daring in saving, or endeavoring to save, life from perils of the sea, from shipwreck or from drowning, in waters over which the United States has jurisdiction, or upon any American vessel." Kennedy, *Code of Federal Regulations*, 43. For Freeth's award description, see *Annual Report of the United States Life-Saving Service*, 47–48; p. 43 lists the number of medals awarded.

41. *Redondo Breeze*, August 6, 1910.

42. The six affidavits are part of Freeth's folder at the U.S. National Archives and Records Administration: Emil C. Hopp (proprietor of a confectionary store in Venice), F. K. McCarver (advertising manager of the Abbot Kinney Company and president of the Venice Chamber of Commerce), Fred Y. Burns (cashier of the Abbot Kinney Company), Ward E. McFadden (one of the proprietors of the Ship Hotel restaurant), H. W. Eichbaum (city electrician), and C. M. Young (resident of Venice).

43. *Redondo Reflex*, August 4, 1910. See also Kennedy, *Code of Federal Regulations*, 43–45.

44. *Redondo Reflex*, December 7, 1911; *Redondo Breeze*, December 9, 1911.

45. *Redondo Reflex*, July 21, 1910.

46. *Honolulu Advertiser* (December 6, 1908) reported forty-eight; the *Los Angeles Times* (December 17, 1908) reported "approximately 50 lives" within the past two years, a number that was picked up in an editorial the next day in the *Los Angeles Herald* (December 17, 1908); the *Redondo Reflex* (August 4, 1910) reported that he'd rescued "nearly 50 lives" before saving the Japanese fishermen; the *Honolulu Advertiser* (September 29, 1910) credited him with saving seventy-eight lives.

47. The list includes Carl Balmer (*Redondo Reflex*, February 27, 1908); Fred Ravilla (*Santa Monica Outlook*, June 15, 1908); an anonymous swimmer at the opening of the Venice bathhouse (*Los Angeles Times*, June 22, 1908); B. Nolle (*Los Angeles Herald*, July 27, 1908); the seven Japanese fishermen on December 16, 1908; Jo Bisbee and Ralph Redeker (*Redondo Reflex*, October 21, 1909); the father and son and E. C. Butterfield, at the Redondo plunge (*Redondo Reflex*, July 21, 1910); and an anonymous swimmer in Redondo (*Evening Vanguard*, May 10, 1912). The count is undoubtedly short since early issues from newspapers like the *Venice Vanguard* are no longer extant; other area papers like the *Redondo Breeze* have not yet been digitized.

48. This was the case, for example, when Freeth and Frank Holborow rescued a swimmer who nearly drowned in the plunge on the opening day of Kinney's bathhouse (*Los Angeles Times*, June 22, 1908). On May 9, 1912, Freeth pulled a man out of a riptide in Redondo: "As soon as he was revived the stranger, who did not give his name took the car returning to Los Angeles" (*Los Angeles Times*, May 10, 1912).

49. *Los Angeles Times*, May 4, 1912; New York, *Documents of the Assembly of the State of New York*, vol. 31, 16: "Silver medals are awarded only in cases where there has been actual risk of life in making the rescue" (14). Earlier editions of the *Documents of the Assembly of the State of New York* list Freeth's name as having saved seven lives, so it's not clear why the newspaper listed nine lives. (See the 1910 edition, for example: vol. 17, nos. 29–32, p. 21)

50. *Los Angeles Times*, August 14, 1910. See also the *Los Angeles Herald*, August 14, 1910.

51. *Hawaiian Gazette*, August 1, 1911. The *Evening Bulletin* in Honolulu reported that Freeth had received "word through the mail yesterday" that the town had been named after him (July 29, 1911).

52. *Los Angeles Times*, August 24, 1910.

53. *Redondo Reflex*, September 1, 1910; *Los Angeles Herald*, August 29, 1910.

54. *Redondo Reflex*, September 1, 1910.

55. *Los Angeles Times*, January 8, 1911.

56. *Los Angeles Times*, June 20, 1911.

57. For hula circuits on the mainland in the 1890s, see Imada, *Aloha America*, 59–102.

Chapter 7. Return to the Islands

1. *Hawaiian Star*, September 27, 1910; *Honolulu Advertiser*, September 27 and 29, 1910.

2. *Honolulu Advertiser*, September 29, 1910.

3. *Redondo Reflex*, November 3, 1910; *Pacific Commercial Advertiser*, September 12, 1907.

4. *Evening Bulletin*, September 29, 1910. See also the *Honolulu Advertiser* for the same date.

5. *Honolulu Advertiser*, September 29, 1910; *Evening Bulletin*, September 29, 1910.

6. For Robertson as captain, see *Honolulu Advertiser*, February 12, 1910. Cottrell is listed as a player in the *Honolulu Advertiser* recap of the game (October 2, 1910), but a picture of the team in the same paper (November 6, 1910) shows an image of L. A. Quinn instead. The final player listed is Jack Watlington.

7. *Honolulu Advertiser*, September 29, 1910.

8. Ford listed May 19, 1908—the date the lease was signed—as the official beginning of the Outrigger Canoe Club (*Honolulu Advertiser*, May 15, 1910).

9. *Honolulu Advertiser*, July 20 and October 19, 1908; *Evening Bulletin*, December 7, 1908, and June 13, 1910. The winner of this latter contest "came in on his board from the big waves far out at sea almost to the beach, standing perfectly erect on his board." An additional contest had been planned for November 7, 1908, but the swell died. There were no surfing contests held in 1909 due to leadership problems at the Outrigger Club.

10. Yost, *Outrigger*, 50; *Honolulu Advertiser*, May 15, 1910. For the development of Waikīkī as an elite social community, see Ejiri, *Development of Waikiki*, 175.

11. *Honolulu Advertiser*, August 14, 1911.

12. Alexander Hume Ford wrote in the the *Advertiser* for May 15, 1910, "The strong stand taken at the last annual meeting [1909] for surfing by club members as a purely amateur sport has caused some friction, but it has almost wiped semi-professionalism out of the club."

13. Ford, "Out-Door Allurement," *Hawaiian Almanac and Annual*, 1911, 146; *Honolulu Advertiser*, August 14, 1911.

14. *Evening Bulletin*, June 13, 1910.

15. Ibid.

16. *Honolulu Advertiser*, September 29, 1910.

17. *Honolulu Advertiser*, November 6, 1910: "Freeth and a part of his [water polo] team are at present engaged in business at Pearl Harbor." The report probably indicates that Louis Hammel and possibly L. A. Quinn were also hired as divers. Freeth's letter to the Department of the Treasury (dated December 17, 1910) acknowledging receipt of the medal back in August was written from Watertown.

18. *Souvenir of the Trip of the Congressional Party to Hawaii in 1907*, ed. Lorrin A. Thurston (Honolulu: Hawaiian Gazette Co., [1907?]), 55–58.

19. Congress first appropriated funds to dredge Pearl Harbor in 1901, but this only consisted of removing sand. Because the coral heads remained, only small ships could enter the base. U.S. Department of the Interior, "Historic American Engineer Record: U.S. Naval Base, Pearl Harbor, Dry Dock No. 1," https://cdn.loc.gov/master/pnp/habshaer/hi/hi0700/hi0747/data/hi0747data.pdf.

20. *Hawaiian Star*, April 26, 1910.

21. *Honolulu Advertiser*, October 13, 1911; *Hawaiian Star*, October 24, 1911.

22. *Honolulu Advertiser*, December 18, 1910.

23. A report in the *Reflex* (January 19, 1911) indicates that Louis Hammel returned to Redondo Beach by January 14, 1911. Freeth was working at Pearl Harbor "but expects to return to Redondo Beach in the near future."

24. For the story of the shark god Ka'ahupahau and Pearl Harbor, see U.S. Department of the Interior, "Historic American Engineering Record," https://cdn.loc.gov/master/pnp/habshaer/hi/hi0700/hi0747/data/hi0747data.pdf.

25. Peter T. Young, "Watertown," Images of Old Hawai'i, May 13, 2014, http://imagesofoldhawaii.com/watertown/; *Evening Bulletin*, November 13, 1909.

26. *Hawaiian Star*, February 3, 1909. For period labor practices, see Center for Labor Education & Research, University of Hawai'i–West O'ahu, "The *Maka'āinana*, Ancient Hawai'i to 1850," History of Labor in Hawai'i, https://www.hawaii.edu/uhwo/clear/home/HawaiiLaborHistory.html.

27. *Evening Bulletin*, February 11, 1911.

28. *Honolulu Advertiser*, January 9, 1910. Peixotto had founded the club for the "betterment of working men's sons" with the motto of "clean living, clean thinking and clean sport." The fifty young men were on a world tour performing songs, athletics, and vaudeville acts. See also the *Evening Bulletin*, January 6, 1910.

29. *Honolulu Advertiser*, March 1, 1910.

30. *Evening Bulletin*, March 21, 1910.

31. *Honolulu Advertiser*, March 1, 1910.

32. Ibid.

33. During the nineteenth century, the Big Island garnered much attention for surfing because of the writings of such travelers as Mark Twain, Charles Nordhoff, and Isabella Bird. See Moser, *Pacific Passages*, 108–122.

34. *Evening Bulletin*, June 28, 1901.

35. *Garden Island*, August 15, 1911.

36. *Hawaiian Star*, August 9, 1911.

37. *Hawaiian Star*, August 10, 1911.

38. *Official Handbook*, 65. Reinstatement also required the matter to be voted on.

39. For a list of the dives and regulations, see the *Official Handbook*, 89–90.

40. *Honolulu Advertiser*, August 14, 1911.

41. *Maui News*, August 19, 1911.

42. William C. Kea Sr., "Oral Histories: Eight Old Time Members," July 8, 1968, Outrigger Canoe Club, https://www.outriggercanoeclubsports.com/occ-archives/oral-histories/eight-old-time-members/. The official site of Hui Nalu lists 1908 as the founding year (https://huinalu.org).

43. *Los Angeles Times*, December 19, 1911.

Chapter 8. From Competitor to Mentor

1. *Los Angeles Times*, May 9, 1909.

2. *Honolulu Advertiser*, December 27, 1911.

3. *Hawaiian Star*, January 4, 1912.

4. Rawlins had also acted as referee for Lizzie's bankruptcy in December 1905 (*Hawaiian Star*, December 29, 1905).

5. *Hawaiian Star*, January 5, 1912.

6. *Honolulu Advertiser*, August 25, 1910.

7. For Duke's own career-long struggles with professionalism, see Davis, *Waterman*, 78.

8. *Los Angeles Times*, March 14, 1912.

9. *Hawaiian Star*, March 9, 1912.

10. *Redondo Breeze*, March 23, 1912.

11. *Los Angeles Times*, March 17, 1912.

12. *Redondo Breeze*, March 23 and 30, 1912.

13. *Honolulu Star-Bulletin*, October 1, 1912.

14. *Los Angeles Times*, March 16, 1912; *Redondo Breeze*, April 13, 1912.

15. *Los Angeles Times*, August 26, 1912.

16. *San Francisco Call*, September 28, 1912.

17. *Redondo Breeze*, May 17, 1913. For Dolly Mings's marriage, see *Redondo Reflex*, January 3, 1913.

18. *Los Angeles Times*, July 5, 1913; *San Francisco Call*, July 6, 1913; *Mercury*, May 1913.

19. *Redondo Reflex*, August 8, 1913.

20. *Redondo Reflex*, September 13, 1912.

21. *Redondo Breeze*, August 16, 1913. The *Los Angeles Times* called it the "McLean Cup" (August 12, 1913).

22. *Los Angeles Times*, August 12, 1913; *Redondo Reflex*, August 15, 1913.

23. *Redondo Reflex*, November 8, 1912.

24. London, "Riding the South Seas Surf."

25. *Redondo Reflex*, January 25, 1912.

26. *Los Angeles Times*, May 3, 1912.

27. *Los Angeles Times*, May 24, 1913.

28. *Los Angeles Times*, June 2, 1912.

29. *Los Angeles Times*, July 14, 1912.

30. Starr, *Americans and the California Dream*, 418.

31. I am indebted to Marianna Torgovnick's *Gone Primitive* for the idea of imagining "alternative stories" (247–48) in terms of what could have happened with women and surfing/lifeguarding in California.

32. *Los Angeles Times*, July 28, 1912.

33. *Los Angeles Times*, November 7, 1912.

34. See Chris Brewster's "Letter to the Editor" in the *International Journal of Aquatic Research and Education* ([August 2007]: 195–97) for a description of this device. Brewster offers a broader history of beach lifeguarding in Tipton and Wooler, *Science of Beach Lifeguarding*. Brewster also notes in both works that the "rescue can" or "rescue cylinder" that Freeth introduced was first devised by Captain Henry Sheffield in 1897 while visiting Durban, South Africa.

35. *Los Angeles Times*, June 17, 1912. See "For Safety of Bathers" in the *Redondo Reflex* (February 22, 1912) for an early description of the device before it was built.

36. *Los Angeles Times*, June 26, 1912.

37. *Redondo Reflex*, November 22, 1912. For the ukulele: *Honolulu Advertiser*, November 11, 1912.

38. *Long Beach Telegram*, November 23, 1912.

39. *Los Angeles Times*, February 18, 1913.

40. *Redondo Breeze*, February 15, 1913.

41. *Redondo Reflex*, March 7, 1913. Freeth had lifeguarded in California less than five years altogether rather than eight.

42. *Los Angeles Times*, May 28, 1913; Redondo Beach City Council Minutes, July 14, 1913. In this era, lifeguards fell under the jurisdiction of the police department.

43. *Redondo Reflex*, March 7, 1913; *Redondo Breeze*, March 8, 1913.

44. *Los Angeles Times*, March 8, 1913.

45. *San Pedro Daily News*, June 23, 1913; Edholm, "Mile-a-Minute Life Guards." See also the *Redondo Reflex* (June 27, 1913) for a picture of Freeth and Langer on the front page riding the motorcycle.

46. *Redondo Breeze*, June 28, 1913.

47. *Los Angeles Herald*, August 12, 1912. Douglas Thompson mentions that the article confuses Hermosa Beach and Manhattan Beach, with the latter being the site of the rescue (personal correspondence, September 11, 2020).

48. *Los Angeles Times*, August 29, 1913.

49. B. Walker, *Mack Sennett's Fun Factory*, 281. The film can be viewed on YouTube.

50. *Los Angeles Times*, September 18, 1912; *Redondo Breeze*, September 21, 1912.

51. *Los Angeles Times*, July 10, 1913.

52. Davis, *Waterman*, 80; *Los Angeles Times*, July 12, 1913.

53. *Los Angeles Times*, September 12 and 24, 1913; *Redondo Reflex*, September 12, 1916; *Redondo Breeze*, September 20, 1913.

54. Redondo Beach City Council Minutes, September 22, 1913.

55. *Redondo Breeze*, November 1, 1913.

Chapter 9. Coaching Duke

1. See the *Mercury* (May 1912) for a detailed overview of the twelve floors of the LAAC.

2. *Mercury*, January 1913, 44.

3. *Mercury*, December 1913, 123–26.

4. *Los Angeles Times*, October 15, 1913; Davis, *Waterman*, 77–78.

5. *Los Angeles Times*, October 15, 1913.

6. Davis, *Waterman*, 86–87.

7. *Los Angeles Times*, July 14, 1914.

8. *Los Angeles Times*, July 24, 1914; *Ogden Standard*, August 15, 1914.

9. *Los Angeles Times*, August 17, 1914.

10. For readings of race issues behind Duke's title, see Westwick and Neushul, *World in the Curl*, 52, and Dina Gilio-Whitaker, "Appropriating Surfing and the Politics of Indigenous Authenticity," in Zavalza Hough-Snee and Eastman, *Critical Surf Studies Reader*, 223–28.

11. *Santa Ana Register*, September 14, 1914; *Los Angeles Times*, September 15, 1914. The *Los Angeles Times* reported in 1916 that "Felix Modjeska, one of the few real surfboard riders on the Pacific Coast," had a board that weighed seventy-two pounds and rode the breakers "in the real Hawaiian style" (August 9, 1916). Felix used the masculine form of his surname "Modjeski."

12. *Long Beach Telegram* and *Long Beach Press*, June 11, 1914; Zambrano, *Surfing in Huntington*, 9.

13. *Los Angeles Times*, July 1 and 5, 1914.

14. *Los Angeles Times*, July 26, 1914.

15. *Los Angeles Times*, August 17, 1914.

16. *Los Angeles Times*, August 25, 1914.

17. *Los Angeles Times*, September 23, 1914.

18. *Redondo Reflex*, May 22, 1974; *Los Angeles Times*, August 18, 1974. See also *Los Angeles Times* (August 23, 1973) for an article on Kai Nowell, the first female lifeguard hired by the Los Angeles City lifeguard service.

19. *Los Angeles Times*, May 25, 1938.

20. *Los Angeles Times*, November 3, 1914; *San Francisco Examiner*, January 26, 1915.

21. *Los Angeles Times*, January 20, 1915.

22. *Mercury*, January 19 and 25, 1915.

23. *Los Angeles Times*, March 28, 1914 and January 10, 1909. See also Westwick and Neushul, *World in the Curl*, 49–50.

24. *San Francisco Examiner*, January 26, 1915.

25. *Venice Daily Vanguard*, February 19, 1915; *Los Angeles Times*, February 21, 1915.

26. *San Francisco Chronicle*, March 2, 1915. The paper misspelled his name as "Frieth."

27. *Honolulu Star-Bulletin*, March 22, 1915.

28. G. Alexander, *America Goes Hawaiian*, 64–65, 83.

29. *San Francisco Chronicle*, March 2, 1915.

30. *Los Angeles Evening Express*, March 1, 1915.

31. For a detailed history of Duke's influence on Australian surfing, see Phil Jarratt, *That Summer at Boomerang*.

32. Redondo Beach City Council Minutes, June 14, 1915; *Riverside Daily Press*, June 17, 1915; *Los Angeles Times*, June 17, 1915.

33. *Redondo Reflex*, June 18, 1915; Redondo Beach City Council Minutes, May 22, 1916.

34. Redondo Beach City Council Minutes, June 28, 1915.

35. *Los Angeles Times*, June 9, 1915; *Redondo Reflex*, June 11, 1915.

36. *Los Angeles Times*, May 18, 1914; *Redondo Reflex*, May 22 and 29, 1914; *Redondo*

Breeze, May 23, 1914; Van Court, "He Sure Can Swim," 85–86; *Daily Breeze* (Torrance, CA), February 24, 1974.

37. *Redondo Breeze*, June 29, 1915; "History Room," Trinidad Colorado, https://www.trinidad.co.gov/history-room.

38. *Redondo Breeze*, July 27, 1915.

39. *Los Angeles Times*, July 26, 1915.

40. *Los Angeles Times*, August 4, 1915.

41. Redondo Beach City Council Minutes, August 2 and September 13, 1915.

42. *Los Angeles Times*, August 4, 1915.

43. "UK: Incoming Passenger Lists, 1878–1960. Aboard the *New York* from New York to South Hampton, arriving December 20, 1913"; "England & Wales, National Probate Calendar (Index of Wills and Administrations), 1858–1995 for George Douglas Freeth." Both from Ancestry.com.

44. *Honolulu Star-Bulletin*, February 5, 1913.

45. *Honolulu Star-Bulletin*, July 15 and 22, 1916.

46. Wills of James Holt Freeth and George D. Freeth Senior obtained from gov.uk: "Search probate records for documents and wills (England and Wales)."

47. *Redondo Reflex*, February 4, 1916.

48. *Los Angeles Herald*, March 28, 1916.

49. *Redondo Reflex*, March 31, 1916.

50. *Los Angeles Times*, June 11, 1916.

51. *Los Angeles Times*, July 18, 1916.

52. *Redondo Reflex*, July 7, 1916.

Chapter 10. A New Beginning in San Diego

1. The club's original name was the Excelsior Rowing Club; it changed its name to the San Diego Rowing Club in 1891. Schaelchilin, *Little Clubhouse*, 1; San Diego Rowing Club Minutes, July 13, 1916; *San Diego Union*, July 9, 1916.

2. *San Diego Sun*, July 8, 1916. Most of the *San Diego Sun* articles were found either on microfilm or in "Scrap books" at the San Diego History Center (San Diego Rowing Club Records, MS 8).

3. *San Diego Union*, July 9, 1916.

4. *San Diego Union*, July 13, 1916.

5. *Evening Tribune*, July 13, 1916.

6. *San Diego Sun*, July 15, 1916.

7. *San Diego Union*, July 13, 1916.

8. *San Diego Sun*, July 15, 1916.

9. *San Diego Sun*, July 20, 1916.

10. See Moser, *Pacific Passages*. Cook's official journal dubs surfing "a favourite diversion" (75) and Twain calls it "the national pastime" (117).

11. *San Diego Union*, July 24, 1916.

12. Gamble, *First Coastal Californians*, 31–35.

13. "Our History," The Yurok Tribe, https://www.yuroktribe.org/our-history.

14. *Evening Tribune*, July 11 1907.

15. *Evening Tribune*, September 15, 1915; *San Diego Union*, September 19, 1915.

16. *San Diego Union*, June 25, 1916.

17. *Evening Tribune*, July 3, 1922. The article mentions that Tent City had been trying for two years to convince Duke to come. See *San Diego Union*, June 30, 1920. For reference to early San Diego surfer Ralph Noisat, see John C. Elwell, Jane Schmauss, and the California Surf Museum, *Surfing in San Diego*, 11.

18. San Diego Rowing Club Minutes, August 4, 1916.

19. *San Diego Union*, August 7, 1916.

20. *San Diego Union*, August 7, 1916.

21. *San Diego Sun*, August 14, 1916.

22. *San Diego Sun*, August 14 and 18, 1916.

23. *San Diego Sun*, February 14, 1917.

24. Davis, *Waterman*, 155–56.

25. *San Diego Union*, July 26, 1916; *Evening Tribune*, July 28, 1916.

26. Stieglitz, "Swimming the Crawl," 164–65.

27. *San Diego Union*, July 29 and 31, 1916.

28. *San Diego Union*, August 20, 1916.

29. *Los Angeles Times*, August 21, 1916.

30. *San Diego Union*, September 5, 1916.

31. *San Diego Union*, September 7, 1916.

32. San Diego Rowing Club Minutes, September 14, 1916.

33. *San Diego Sun*, October 9, 1916.

34. *San Diego Union*, November 22 and 26, 1916; *Evening Tribune*, November 22, 1916.

35. *San Diego Union*, November 24, 1916.

36. Charmian London, *Our Hawaii*, 291–95.

37. L. P. Thurston, "Surf-Board Riding in Hawaii," 321.

38. As quoted in Timmons, *Waikiki Beachboy*, 30.

39. *San Diego Sun*, February 2 and March 2, 1917.

40. *San Diego Sun*, February 26 and March 15 1917.

41. *San Diego Union*, January 2, 8, and 14, 1917; *San Diego Sun*, January 22, 1917.

42. *San Diego Sun*, February 26, 1917.

43. *San Diego Union*, April 3, 1917.

44. *San Diego Union*, March 6, 1917.

45. *San Diego City and County Directory, 1917*.

46. The city directories of Redondo Beach for 1912–1914 list Freeth living at 203 Emerald with six other renters in the house. *Directory of Redondo Beach and Hermosa Beach California*.

47. *Evening Tribune*, March 29, 1917.

48. *Chamber of the Common Council of the City of San Diego*, June 6, 1917, https://www.sandiego.gov/sites/default/files/legacy/digitalarchives/pdf/historicalocd/minutes/RecordofCommonCouncil43.pdf; *San Diego Union*, June 7, 1917.

49. *San Diego Union*, April 21, 1917; San Diego Rowing Club Minutes, May 24, 1917. Freeth was paid twenty-five dollars a week.

50. *Los Angeles Times*, May 18, 1917.

Chapter 11. Chief Lifeguard

1. *San Diego Union*, June 4, 1917.

2. Robertson, *Camp Pendleton*, 17–18; "Historic California Posts, Camps, Stations and Airfields: Camp Kearny (San Diego County)," Military Museum.org, updated July 2, 2017, http://www.militarymuseum.org/cpKearney2.html.

3. *Hotel Del Coronado History*, 32, 136.

4. *San Diego Sun*, April 21 and June 2, 1917.

5. *San Diego Union*, May 13, 1917; *Evening Tribune*, May 25, 1917.

6. *San Diego Union*, June 5 and July 17, 1917.

7. *San Diego Union*, June 17 and 18, 1917.

8. *Los Angeles Times*, July 5, 1917.

9. *San Diego Union*, July 21, 1917.

10. *San Diego Union*, August 22 and 24, 1917.

11. *Evening Tribune*, July 31, 1917.

12. *San Diego Union*, September 3 and 5, 1917.

13. *Redondo Reflex*, October 26, 1917; *Los Angeles Times*, October 28, 1917.

14. *San Diego Sun*, November 2, 1917.

15. *San Diego Union*, October 26, 1917.

16. *San Diego Union*, December 18, 1917.

17. San Diego Rowing Club Minutes, November 8 and December 27, 1917.

18. *San Diego Sun*, February 22 and 17, 1917.

19. *Los Angeles Evening Express*, March 14, 1918.

20. San Diego Directory Co., *San Diego City and County Directory*, 1918, Internet Archive, https://archive.org/details/sandiegocityco1800unkn.

21. Chauvaud's name appears with various spellings in newspaper accounts and city documents (Chauvaud, Chauvaund); "Chauvaud" is taken from San Diego Directory Co., *San Diego City and County Directory*, 1916 (https://archive.org/details/sandiegocityco1600unkn) and *San Diego City and County Directory*, 1917 (https://archive.org/details/sandiegocityco1700unkn).

22. "Report of Investigation of the Death of Several Persons by Drowning, at Ocean Beach, San Diego, California, and Recommendations of Action to be Taken to Prevent a Repetition of the Same," San Diego City Clerk Archives, May 6, 1918, pp. 1–2.

23. Ibid., p. 8.

24. *Evening Tribune*, May 8, 1918.

25. *San Diego Union*, May 19, 1918; *Evening Tribune*, May 20, 1918.

26. "Ocean Beach Community Plan and Local Coastal Program, Appendix C: Historic Context Statement," 2015, https://www.sandiego.gov/sites/default/files/ocean_beach_2015.pdf.

27. *San Diego Union*, May 30 and June 2, 1918.

28. *San Diego Union*, June 1, 1918.

29. Martino, *Lifeguards of San Diego County*, 9.

30. California, Voter Registrations, 1900–1968, San Diego County, 1918, *Index to Great Register of San Diego County*, Precinct No. 75, https://www.ancestry.com/search/collections/61066.

31. *San Diego Union*, July 4, 1917.

32. *San Diego Sun*, September 27, 1918.

33. *Evening Tribune*, June 14, 1918.

34. *Evening Tribune*, June 29, 1918; *San Diego Union*, July 11, 1918.

35. *San Diego Union*, July 15, 1918.

36. *San Diego Union*, July 28 and 30, 1918.

37. *Evening Tribune*, August 12, 1918.

38. *Evening Tribune* and *San Diego Union*, August 14, 1918.

39. *Evening Tribune*, October 4, 1918.

40. *San Diego Union*, July 11, 1918.

41. *San Diego Union*, August 30, 1918.

42. Byerly, "U.S. Military and the Influenza Pandemic," fig. 3; Opdycke, *Flu Epidemic*, xiii–xiv.

43. Byerly, "U.S. Military and the Influenza Pandemic."

44. *Minutes of the Common Council*, San Diego City Clerk's Office, December 4, 9, and 11, 1918.

45. *San Diego Union*, December 18, 1918.

Chapter 12. Last Breath

1. Information on Freeth's time in the hospital and his eulogy taken from the Freeth folder in the Charles Kenn Collection, MS Group 361, Box 18, folder 7.

2. Byerly, "U.S. Military and the Influenza Pandemic," https://www.ncbi.nlm.nih.gov/pmc/articles/PMC2862337/; see also Opdycke, *Flu Epidemic*, 1, 6, 50.

3. *Evening Tribune*, March 20, 1919; *San Diego Union*, March 20, 1919.

4. Davis, *Waterman*, 118–20.

5. *San Diego Union*, March 23, 1919.

6. *Honolulu Star-Bulletin*, March 18, 1919; *San Francisco Call*, April 1, 1919; *Los Angeles Times*, April 9, 1919.

7. Hinch, "Man Who 'Walked on Water,'" 23; see also Haynes, "Wave of the Future," 31.

8. *San Diego Sun*, April 8, 1919.

9. Davis, *Waterman*, 120.

10. *San Diego Sun*, April 9, 1919; *San Diego Union*, April 10, 1919.

11. *Honolulu Advertiser*, May 4, 1919.

12. *San Diego Sun*, April 11, 1919.

13. *San Diego Union*, April 9, 1919.

14. *Coronado Eagle and Journal* (aka *The Strand*), April 19, 1919; *San Diego Union*, April 10, 1919.

15. Charles Kenn Collection, Bishop Museum, box 18, folder 7, pp. 1–7. All quotations for Freeth's eulogy are from this source.

16. *New-York Tribune*, April 22, 1919.

17. Van Court and Merritt, "He Sure Can Swim," 85; Moser, *Pacific Passages*, 153; *Evening Tribune*, March 29, 1917.

18. *Los Angeles Herald*, January 10, 1909.

19. Sheffield and Sheffield, *Swimming Simplified*, 143.

20. *Long Beach Telegram*, June 17 and 18, 1919.

21. "Surf-Board Riding Is Some Sport," *Los Angeles Times*, July 13, 1919.

22. *Los Angeles Times*, July 4, 1919; *Heartsease*, dir. Harry Beaumont, Goldwyn Pictures Corporation, 1919.

23. *San Diego Union*, March 5, 1923.

24. Westwick and Neushul, *World in the Curl*, 74.

25. For extensive treatment of this process, see Westwick and Neushul, *World in the Curl*, 64–80.

26. Verge, *Los Angeles County Lifeguards*, 7; *Los Angeles Times*, July 19, 1926. See also Olmsted Brothers, *Parks, Playgrounds, and Beaches*.

Bibliography

Newspapers

The availability of digitized newspapers has helped fill in significant gaps in Freeth's life, and I have depended on them for much information about his movements. More details about Freeth will certainly become available as the archive of digitized media grows. Although newspapers provide a gold mine of new material about Freeth and the early history of surfing and beach culture in general, they also print incomplete, inaccurate, biased, or contradictory details. I have tried to rely only on information that I felt could be verified by cross-checking multiple newspapers or by consulting additional published and archival sources. Any discrepencies are mentioned in the notes. Open access sites that I used include the Library of Congress's *Chronicling America*, the California Digital Newspaper Collection, and *Imagine Santa Monica* for the *Santa Monica Outlook*. Paid sites included the comprehensive newspapers .com and newslibrary.com (for San Diego newspapers). In citing these sources, I have recorded the name of the newspaper, the date of the article, and where necessary the state designation of the newspaper and a keyword search item. Occasionally a newspaper will misspell Freeth's name, and I have given the misspelling to more easily locate the reference. A couple of key newspaper sources—the *Redondo Breeze* and the *San Diego Sun*—have not yet been digitized. One can nevertheless find them on microfilm: the *Redondo Breeze* material is located at the Hawthorne Public Library, and the *San Diego Sun* articles can be found at the San Diego History Center (on microfilm and in the San Diego Rowing Club "Scrapbooks").

Archival Sources

Admiralty's Officers' Service Records for the Royal Naval Reserve, National Archives, Kew, Richmond, United Kingdom

Adolph Sutro Collection, San Francisco History Center, San Francisco, California

British Army Soldiers up to 1913, National Archives, Kew, Richmond, United Kingdom

Charles Kenn Collection, Bishop Museum, Honolulu, Hawai'i

District Court (O'ahu First Circuit), Kapolei, Hawai'i

General Register Office for England and Wales, Southport, Merseyside, United Kingdom

Jack London Papers, Huntington Library, San Marino, California

Minutes of the Common Council, Office of City Clerk, San Diego, California

Pacific Chemical and Fertilizer Company, 1890–1956, Hawai'i State Archives, Honolulu, Hawai'i

Records of the U.S. Coast Guard, United States National Archives and Record Administration, Washington, D.C.

Redondo Beach City Council Minutes. Redondo Beach City Clerks Department. http://laserweb.redondo.org/WebLink/Browse.aspx?startid=10.

Registrar of Bureau of Conveyances, Deed Records, 1846–1900. Hawai'i Bureau of Conveyances, Honolulu, Hawai'i

San Diego Rowing Club Records, San Diego History Center Document Archives, San Diego, California

Ships Passenger Manifests, Hawai'i State Archives, Honolulu, Hawai'i

United States National Archives and Records Administration, Washington, DC: Record Group 26, U.S. Coast Guard, Entry 235, Correspondence Concerning Lifesaving Medals, File for George Freeth, Jr. (Location 14E4 14/8/3 box 7)

Other Sources

Alexander, Carolyn Elayne. *Abbot Kinney's Venice-of-America, Volume One: The Golden Years: 1905–1920*. Venice, CA: Venice Historical Society, 1991.

——. *Venice, California*. Charleston, SC: Arcadia, 1999.

Alexander, Geoff. *America Goes Hawaiian: The Influence of Pacific Island Culture on the Mainland*. Jefferson, NC: McFarland, 2019.

American Red Cross. *Lifeguarding Today*. St. Louis, MO: Mosby Lifeline, 1995.

Annual Report of the United States Life-Saving Service. Washington, DC: U.S. Government Printing Office, 1911.

Atoll Research Bulletin Nos. 432–434. Washington, DC: Smithsonian Institution, February 1996.

Ball, John H. *California Surfriders: 1946*. Reprinted as *Early California Surfriders*. Ventura, CA: Pacific Publishings, 1995.

Brewster, Chris. "Letter to the Editor." *International Journal of Aquatic Research and Education* (August 2007): 195–97.

Byerly, Carol R. "The U.S. Military and the Influenza Pandemic of 1918–1919." *Public Health Reports*, v. 125 (Suppl 3) (2010): 82–91.

Chambers, Douglas R., ed. *A Century of Heroes*. Pittsburgh: Carnegie Hero Fund Commission, 2004.

Clark, John R. K. *Hawaiian Surfing: Traditions from the Past*. Honolulu: University of Hawai'i Press, 2011.

Cleghorn, Thomas Alexander Kaulakahi. The Watamull Foundation Oral History Project, 1979. University of Hawai'i at Mānoa. https://evols.library.manoa.hawaii .edu/handle/10524/48595?mode=full.

Cooley, Timothy J. *Surfing about Music*. Berkeley: University of California Press, 2014.

Culver, Lawrence. *The Frontier of Leisure: Southern California and the Shaping of Modern America*. Oxford: Oxford University Press, 2010.

Davis, David. *Waterman: The Life and Times of Duke Kahanamoku*. Lincoln: University of Nebraska Press, 2015.

Delgado, James P., et al. "The History and Significance of the Adolph Sutro Historic District: Excerpts from the National Register of Historic Places Nomination Form Prepared in 2000." https://www.nps.gov/goga/learn/historyculture/upload/ sutro_history.pdf.

Desmond, Jane C. *Staging Tourism: Bodies on Display from Waikiki to Sea World*. Chicago: University of Chicago Press, 1999.

Directory of Redondo Beach and Hermosa Beach California. Alhambra, CA: Southern California Directory Co., 1913.

Durand, Charles James, et al. *Elizabeth College Register, 1824–1873: With a Record of Some Earlier Students*. Guernsey: Frederick Clarke, 1898.

Edholm, C. L. "Mile-A-Minute Life Guards." *Technical World Magazine*, August 1914, 822–24.

Ejiri, Masakazu. "The Development of Waikiki, 1900–1949: The Formative Period of an American Resort Paradise." PhD thesis, University of Hawai'i, May 1996.

Elwell, John C., Jane Schmauss, and the California Surf Museum. *Surfing in San Diego*. Charleston, SC: Arcadia Publishing, 2007.

Ely, Charles A. and Roger B. Clapp. *Atoll Research Bulletin No. 171: The Natural History of Laysan Island, Northwestern Hawaiian Islands*. Washington, D.C.: Smithsonian Institution, 1973.

Finney, Ben. "Hawaiian Surfing: A Study of Cultural Change." Master's thesis, University of Hawai'i, 1959.

Finney, Ben, and James D. Houston. *Surfing: The Sport of Hawaiian Kings*. Rutland, VT: Charles E. Tuttle, 1966. Reprinted as *Surfing: A History of the Ancient Hawaiian Sport*. San Francisco: Pomegranate Artbooks, 1996.

Flamming, Douglas. *Bound for Freedom: Black Los Angeles in Jim Crow America*. Berkeley: University of California Press, 2005.

Ford, Alexander Hume. "Our Japanese Territory." *Collier's Outdoor America*, July 24, 1909, 12–13.

———. "Out-Door Allurement." *Hawaiian Almanac and Annual for 1911*, 142–46.

———. "Surf Riding for the Motion Picture Man." *The Mid-Pacific*, September 1912, 276–81.

Friedricks, William B. *Henry E. Huntington and the Creation of Southern California*. Columbus: Ohio State University Press, 1992.

Gamble, Lynn H., ed. *First Coastal Californians*. Santa Fe, NM: School for Advanced Research Press, 2015.

Gault-Williams, Malcolm. *Legendary Surfers*. Vol. 1: *2500 B. C. to 1910 A. D.* Cafepress.com, 2005.

Gilio-Whitaker, Dina. "Appropriating Surfing and the Politics of Indigenous Authenticity." In *The Critical Surf Studies Reader*, edited by Dexter Zavalza Hough-Snee and Alexander Sotelo Eastman, 223–28. Durham, NC: Duke University Press, 2017.

Haynes, F. S. "Wave of the Future." *Westways*, 1976, 27–31.

Hinch, Charles. "The Man Who 'Walked on Water': America's First Surfer in Redondo Beach." *South Bay Magazine*, July 1980, 22–23.

Hotel Del Coronado History. Coronado, CA: Hotel del Coronado Heritage Department, 2013.

Husted's Directory of Honolulu and Territory of Hawaii 1905–6. Honolulu: Hawaiian Gazette Co., 1905.

Imada, Adria L. *Aloha America: Hula Circuits through the U.S. Empire*. Durham, NC: Duke University Press, 2012.

Jarratt, Phil. *That Summer at Boomerang: From the Waves of Waikiki to the Sand Dunes of Freshwater, the True Story of Duke Kahanamoku in Australia*. Richmond, Victoria: Hardie Grant Books, 2014.

Jefferson, Alison Rose. *Living the California Dream: African American Leisure Sites during the Jim Crow Era*. Lincoln: University of Nebraska Press, 2020.

Kennedy, Bernard R., ed. *Code of Federal Regulations: 1949 Edition*. Washington, D.C.: U.S. Government Printing Office, 1949.

Korsgaard, Robert. *A History of the Amateur Athletic Union of the United States*. PhD thesis, Teachers College, Columbia University, 1952.

Krintz, Jennifer Lynn. "Pleasure Piers & Promenades: The Architecture of Southern California's Early Twentieth-Century Beach Resorts." Master's thesis, University of Georgia, 2009.

Laderman, Scott. *Empire in Waves: A Political History of Surfing*. Berkeley: University of California Press, 2014.

Lane, J. C., ed. *Directory and Hand Book of the Kingdom of Hawaii*. San Francisco: McKenney Directory Co., 1888.

———. *Directory and Hand Book of the Kingdom of Hawaii*. Oakland: Pacific Press Publishing Co., 1888.

Langley, Henry G. *The San Franciso Directory*. San Francisco, CA: Henry G. Langley, 1876.

Lawler, Kristen. *The American Surfer: Radical Culture and Capitalism*. New York: Routledge, 2011.

Lencek, Lena, and Gideon Bosker. *The Beach: The History of Paradise on Earth*. New York: Viking, 1998.

London, Charmian K. *Our Hawaii*. Honolulu: Patten Co., 1917.

London, Jack. "Aloha Oe." *Lady's Realm*, December, 1908.

———. "The Joys of the Surf Rider." *Pall Mall Magazine*, July–December, 1908, 326–31.

———. "My Hawaiian Aloha." *Cosmopolitan*, September 1916.

———. "Riding the South Seas Surf." *Woman's Home Companion*, October 1907, 9–10.

Mak, James. "Creating 'Paradise of the Pacific': How Tourism Began in Hawaii." Working Papers 2015-1, University of Hawai'i at Mānoa, Department of Economics. https://uhero.hawaii.edu/RePEc/hae/wpaper/WP_2015-1.pdf.

Martino, Michael T. *Lifeguards of San Diego County*. Charleston, SC: Arcadia Publishing, 2007.

México Secretaría de Relaciones Exteriores. *Isla de la Pasion: Llamada de Clipperton*. México: Imp. de A. García Cubas Sucesores Hermanos, 1909.

Moser, Patrick. "The Endurance of Hawaiian Surfing." *Journal of the Polynesian Society* 125 (December 2016): 411–32.

———. "The Hawaii Promotion Committee and the Appropriation of Surfing." *Pacific Historical Review* 89 (Fall 2020): 500–527.

Moser, Patrick, ed. *Pacific Passages: An Anthology of Surf Writing*. Honolulu: University of Hawai'i Press, 2008.

New York State Legislature. *Documents of the Assembly of the State of New York, One Hundred and Thirty-Third Session, 1910*. Vol. 17, nos. 29–32. Albany, New York.

———. *Documents of the Assembly of the State of New York, One Hundred and Thirty-Fifth Session, 1912*. Vol. 31, nos. 52–58. Albany, New York.

Noble, Dennis L. *That Others Might Live: The U.S. Life-Saving Service, 1878–1915*. Annapolis, MD: U.S. Naval Institute Press, 1994.

Nordyke, Eleanor C., and Y. Scott Matsumoto. "The Japanese in Hawaii: A Historical and Demographic Perspective." https://evols.library.manoa.hawaii.edu/bitstream/10524/528/2/JL11174.pdf.

Official Handbook of the Amateur Athletic Union of the United States. New York: American Sports Publishing Company, 1907.

Olmsted Brothers and Bartholomew and Associates. *Parks, Playgrounds, and Beaches for the Los Angeles Region*. Los Angeles, CA: 1930.

Opdycke, Sandra. *The Flu Epidemic of 1918: America's Experience in the Global Health Crisis*. New York: Routledge, 2014.

Pelletreau, William S. *A History of Long Island from Its Earliest Settlement to the Present Time*. Vol. 2. New York: Lewis Publishing Company, 1905.

Pyle, Peter. "Nomenclature of the Laysan Honeycreeper *Himatione [sanguinea] fraithii*. *Bulletin of the British Ornithologists' Club* 131, no. 2 (2011): 116–17.

Robertson, Breane. *Camp Pendleton: The Historic Rancho Santa Margarita y Las Flores and the U.S. Marine Corps in Southern California*. Quantico, VA: Marine Corps History Division, 2017.

Rothschild, Walter. *The Avifauna of Laysan and the Neighboring Islands*. London: R. H. Porter, 1893–1900. https://www.biodiversitylibrary.org/page/44039276#page/7/mode/1up.

San Diego City and County Directory, 1917. San Diego: San Diego Directory Co., 1917.

Schaelchilin, Patricia A. *The Little Clubhouse on Steamship Wharf: San Diego Rowing Club 1883–1983*. Leucadia, CA: Rand Editions, 1984.

Sheffield, Lyba M., and Nita C. Sheffield. *Swimming Simplified*. San Francisco: Hicks-Judd Company, 1920.

Smith, Joel T. "Reinventing the Sport: Part III—George Freeth." *Surfer's Journal* 12, no. 3 (2003): 90–95.

Starr, Kevin. *Americans and the California Dream: 1850–1915*. Oxford: Oxford University Press, 1973.

Stewart, Robert, Jr., and Mary Frances Stewart. *Adolph Sutro: A Biography*. Berkeley, CA: Howell North, 1962.

Stieglitz, Olaf. "Swimming the Crawl to Educate the Modern Body: Visual Material and the Expanding Market for Participatory Sports in the USA, 1890s-1930s." In *Body, Capital, and Screens: Visual Media and the Healthy Self in the 20th Century*, edited by C. Bonah and A. Laukötter, 159–79. Amsterdam: Amsterdam University Press, 2020.

Surdam, David George. *Century of the Leisured Masses: Entertainment and the Transformation of Twentieth-Century America*. London: Oxford University Press, 2015.

Thorpe, James. *Henry Edwards Huntington: A Biography*. Berkeley: University of California Press, 1994.

Thurston, Lorrin A. *Memoirs of the Hawaiian Revolution*. Honolulu: Advertiser Publishing, 1936.

Thurston, Lorrin A., ed. *A Souvenir of the Trip of the Congressional Party to Hawaii in 1907*. Honolulu: Hawaiian Gazette Co., [1907?].

Thurston, Lorrin P. "Surf-Board Riding in Hawaii." *Mid-Pacific Magazine*, April 1915, 317–25.

Timmons, Grady. *Waikiki Beachboy*. Honolulu: Editions Limited, 1989.

Tipton, Mike, and Adam Wooler, eds. *The Science of Beach Lifeguarding*. Boca Raton, FL: CRC Press, 2016.

Titcomb, Margaret. *Native Use of Fish in Hawaii*. Honolulu: University of Hawai'i Press, 1972.

Torgovnick, Marianna. *Gone Primitive: Savage Intellects, Modern Lives*. Chicago: University of Chicago Press, 1990.

Trask, Haunani-Kay. *From a Native Daughter: Colonialism and Sovereignty in Hawai'i*. Honolulu: University of Hawai'i Press, 1993.

Van Court, Carroll, and M. C. Merritt. "He Sure Can Swim." *Recreation*, August 1915, 85–86.

Verge, Arthur C. "George Freeth: King of the Surfers and California's Forgotten Hero." *California History* (Summer/Fall 2001): 82–105.

———. *Los Angeles County Lifeguards*. Charleston, SC: Arcadia Publishing, 2005.

Walker, Brent E. *Mack Sennett's Fun Factory: A History and Filmography of His Studio and His Keystone and Mack Sennett Comedies, with Biographies of Players and Personnel*. Jefferson, NC: McFarland, 2010.

Walker, F. D. *Log of the Kaalokai*. Honolulu: Hawaiian Gazette Co., 1909.

Walker, Isaiah Helekunihi. *Waves of Resistance: Surfing and History in Twentieth-Century Hawai'i*. Honolulu: University of Hawai'i Press, 2011.

Warshaw, Matt. *A History of Surfing*. San Francisco: Chronicle Books, 2010.

Westwick, Peter, and Peter Neushul. *The World in the Curl: An Unconventional History of Surfing*. New York: Crown, 2013.

Wood, Houston. *Displacing Natives: The Rhetorical Production of Hawai'i*. Lanham, MD: Rowman and Littlefield, 1999.

Yost, Harold H. *The Outrigger: A History of the Outrigger Canoe Club, 1908–1971*. Honolulu: Outrigger Canoe Club, 1971.

Zambrano, Mark. *Surfing in Huntington Beach*. Charleston, SC: Arcadia Publishing, 2019.

Index

PATRICK MOSER is a professor of writing at Drury University and editor of *Pacific Passages: An Anthology of Surf Writing.*

Sport and Society

The University of Illinois Press
is a founding member of the
Association of University Presses.

———————————————————

University of Illinois Press
1325 South Oak Street
Champaign, IL 61820-6903
www.press.uillinois.edu